THE TREASURY OF
Chess Lore

Edited by

FRED REINFELD

DOVER PUBLICATIONS, INC.
NEW YORK • NEW YORK

Published in Canada by General Publishing Company, Ltd., 30 Lesmill Road, Don Mills, Toronto, Ontario.
Published in the United Kingdom by Constable and Company, Ltd., 10 Orange Street, London WC 2.

This Dover edition, first published in 1959, is an unabridged and unaltered republication of the work originally published by David McKay Company in 1951.

Standard Book Number: 486-20458-8

Library of Congress Catalog Card Number: 59-9674

Manufactured in the United States of America
Dover Publications, Inc.
180 Varick Street
New York, N.Y. 10014 ·

ACKNOWLEDGMENTS

The Editor wishes to express his thanks to editors, authors and publishers for their permission to use the following material:

Australasian Chess Review: "The Dream of the Tactful Chess Reporter" from [*Among These Mates*] by "Chielamangus."

Birmingham Post: "Trickery, Ancient and Modern" and "Poe's Fallacy" by B. H. Wood.

British Chess Magazine: "A Classification of Chessplayers" by T. E. W. Widdows; "Counsel's Opinion" by R. F. Walton; "The Martyrdom of the Problemist" and "Stalemate!!" by G. Legentil; "A Game of Chess" by Basil G. Wood; "Chess in an R.A.F. Prisoner of War Camp" by F. A. O'Malley; "Labourdonnais Plays McDonnell" by G. H. Diggle; "Morphy's Estimate of Staunton"; "Evans Gambit Declined and Accepted"; "Simpson's Divan" by Charles Tomlinson; "Modern Simpson's" by A. G.; "Purssell's"; "Hastings, 1950" by Lord Dunsany; "Chess of the Future" by Siegbert Tarrasch; "The Stalemate Fallacy" by T. H. Tylor; "Sir Walter Scott on Chess" by H. R. H.; "John Ruskin and Chess" by B. Goulding Brown; "Buckle as a Chessplayer" by Charles Tomlinson.

Check!: "Thirteen Centuries of Chess" by C. J. S. Purdy.

Chess: "A Chess Caprice"; "Black to Move" by E. W. Chandler; "Check!" by T. H. Chetwynd; "Sidelights on Alekhine" by Thomas Olsen; "These Fuelish Things" by Desperdan; "Mrs. Carlyle Plays at Chess" by Jane Welsh Carlyle.

Chess Review: "Advice to Beginners" by Hector Rosenfeld, copyright, 1938; "The Gentle Art of Annoying" by Donald MacMurray, copyright, 1933; "Does the Cap Fit?" by "Roamer," copyright, 1940; "Tales of a Woodpusher: Never Give Up until You're Mated" by Fred M. Wren, copyright, 1947; "Vacation in London" by Fred M. Wren, copyright, 1936; "The Female of the Species" by H. D. Sheldon; "Tales of a Woodpusher: Woodpusher's Woodpile" by Fred M. Wren; "Chess in a Knightclub" by Bruce Hayden; "The First International Chess Tournament" by Paul Hugo Little;

"Ah, the Good Old Days" by Fred Reinfeld, copyright, 1940; "Paul Morphy, King of Chess" by John C. Rather; "Unconventional Surrender" by Hans Kmoch and Fred Reinfeld; "Pronunciation" by Nat Halper; "The Mind Is Quicker than the Eye!" by Fred Reinfeld; "The Triumph of Unreason" by Hans Kmoch and Fred Reinfeld; "A Masterly Example of My System" by Hans Kmoch; "Mannerisms of the Masters" by Paul Hugo Little, copyright, 1937; "What Is a Brilliancy?" by I. A. Horowitz; "The Myth of the Brilliancy Prize" by Dr. Savielly Tartakover; "Time without End" by Edward Krisch, copyright, 1946; "The Time Machine" by Fred Reinfeld, copyright, 1946; "Recollection of Alekhine" by H. Golombek; "An American Champion" by Fred Reinfeld, copyright, 1946; "A Day with Dr. Euwe" by T. Liket, copyright, 1938; "1937: Champion and Challenger" by Paul Hugo Little, copyright, 1937; "The Score Doesn't Tell" by Hans Kmoch; "Interviewing a Child Prodigy" by Thomas Sweeney, copyright, 1941; "Ballad of Chess" by Paul Hugo Little, copyright, 1933; "On Changing the Rules of the Game" by Barnie F. Winkelman, copyright, 1937; "This Made Chess History" by Kenneth Harkness and John Straley Battell, copyright, 1947; "Santayana Looks at Chess," by George Santayana, copyright, 1937.

Chess World: "*Punch* on Postal Chess"; "Last Round" by Kester Svendsen (and by special permission of the author).

Illustrated London News: "Alekhine Pays a Debt," "Chess: To Be or Not to Be," and "Books about Chess" by B. H. Wood.

London Times: "World Championship: A Layman's View."

DAVID MCKAY COMPANY: "The Feminine Viewpoint" [from *Chess for Fun and Chess for Blood* by Edward Lasker, copyright, 1942, 1950] by Leonore Gallet; "Emanuel Lasker: Philosopher," "Premature Celebration," and "Sammy, the Chess Wonder Child" [from Chess *Secrets*] by Edward Lasker, copyright, 1951; "An Old Question" from [*Modern Ideas in Chess*] by Richard Reti.

New York World-Telegram and Sun: "The Chess Bug" by Alton Cook.

G. P. PUTNAM'S SONS: "Chess Generalship" [from *The Field Book of Chess Generalship*] by Franklin K. Young, copyright, 1923.

All the illustrations appear by permission of CHESS REVIEW. The Editor wishes to acknowledge the kindness of John F. Harbeson and the Metropolitan Museum of Art in permitting the use of Illustrations 2, 3, 5 and 6.

Contents

THE WOODPUSHERS

THE GOLDEN AGE

THE MODERN MASTERS

CHESS LORE

CHESS CELEBRITIES

OF CHESS AND CHESSPLAYERS

THE TREASURY OF
Chess Lore

Chess is the art of human reason.—GUSTAVUS SELENUS

Chess, like love, like music, has the power to make men happy.—TARRASCH

The game of chess is the touchstone of the intellect.—GOETHE

Chess yields us, when we need them most, Companions for our loneliness.—MU'TAZZ

What chess has in common with science and fine art is its utter uselessness.—CASSIRER

Surely chess is a sad waste of brains.—SCOTT

Chess is as much a mystery as women.—PURDY

It will be cheering to know that many people are skillful chessplayers, though in many instances their brains, in a general way, compare unfavorably with the cogitative faculties of a rabbit.—MORTIMER

The Woodpushers

A CHESS CAPRICE
(*Adapted from the Italian*)

Oh, to express
With worthy stress
And real success
The heartiness
With which I bless
The manliness
And charm of chess.

For who can guess
What broad excess
Of steadiness
And thoughtfulness
One must possess
So that success
May crown one's chess?

And I confess
That no duress
Or dire distress
Could e'er repress
The eagerness
With which I press
To play at chess.

1

No pitiless
Fair sorceress
By soft caress
Or looks or dress
Could dispossess
Me of my—yes!
My *love* for chess.

Chess, 1936

THE CHESS BUG

By Alton Cook

An avid postal player, the film critic of the New York World-Telegram *and* Sun *knows whereof he writes when he describes the chess bug.*

If the hobbyist takes up bridge, he plays bridge and that is an end of it. The same can be said about such games as golf or tennis. Conceivably the addict can quit, too.

But if that old chess bug ever bites, the victim is enthralled for keeps. The really enthusiastic chessplayer sometimes may die but he never quits. Sometimes they try. Soon they are haunting the chess clubs again.

Playing the game itself is only one phase of devotion to chess. There are the problem composers and solvers, collectors of books and fancy sets of chessmen, club organizers and workers, volunteer chess journalists, the post-card players and, lowliest of all, the inveterate kibitzers. Contrary to a popular notion, topflight chess is distinctly a young man's game.

This country had a crop of strong young master players who blossomed all in one group some 20 years ago, headed by Samuel Reshevsky, Reuben Fine, Arnold Denker, Al Horowitz, I. Kashdan and a few others. They are now referred to as the "Old Guard" because some of them are beginning to hit their forties.

For some reason, America seems to produce master chessplayers only in 20-year cycles. The present "Old Guard" went unchallenged until the past couple of years when a new young guard began to emerge and take a share of chess titles. Some of these, no longer promising but full fledged tournament masters, are Arthur Bisguier, Larry Evans, George Kramer, Robert and Donald Byrne and Walter Shipman. They are all of high school and college age.

One of the instruments used by chessplayers to rob their pastime of any semblance of relaxed ease is the chess clock. This is really two clocks, only one of which runs at a time. While one player is studying the board, his clock runs. When he makes a move, he punches a button that stops his clock and starts the opponent's.

The usual rate of play in American tournaments is 20 moves an hour. Leisurely as that may sound to the outsider, any chessplayer will testify that chess clocks are the fastest running timepieces under the sun. It is common to find both players in a game forced to make a dozen moves in a few seconds as their time runs out.

The only relaxed chess is "skittles," informal games with any opponent who happens along. These are the joy of the kibitzers because, since nothing is at stake, they feel free to comment and suggest moves.

A player who has developed no skill at "skittles" is referred to as a "patzer" or "pfuscher." Much of chess parlance comes from German. A slow player has "sitzfleisch," a term which also describes dogged courage. "Blitz" is a game in which both players must move without a moment's hesitation. There is a German book of advice to kibitzers, in which all pages are blank except the first, which reads, "Keep quiet!"

Another relaxed but very intent group are the correspondence players, who send moves on postal cards. An average game will last about a year.

Jack Straley Battell, who conducts the postal chess department of *Chess Review,* has about 3000 active players on his list.

Many a correspondence player is an ailing or crippled shut-in. Some are in jail. But the great majority are sheer enthusiasts looking for more ways to fill their leisure with chess.

Jack Battell tells of one player, Robert Wyler, Glendale, Calif., who had 1000 games going at one time. So far as Mr. Battell knows, that is the high record.

A player who lived in a boarding house found his games were unaccountably snarled. Later he discovered that prankish fellow boarders were changing the moves on his cards before he got them.

Some postal players cheat by getting advice from masters. Frank Marshall, late American champion, once advised a member at the Marshall Chess Club and a few days later was astonished by a request for advice from the other player in that same game. For several months he played both sides of the game, holding things absolutely even. Both players felt the opponent must be some sort of superman to hold the great Marshall to level terms.

Collecting chessmen is another phase of the hypnosis worked by the game. These range from fantastically elaborate carvings in ivory to sets inspired by current events. The materials run through just about anything that can be molded or carved. This is decidedly a luxury hobby because prices go well up into four figures for some of the sets. The market right now is full of Oriental sets brought back by men who saw service in India and China during the last war.

Chess books are another collector's item. The literature of chess, going back to the fifteenth century, dwarfs the writing devoted to any other game. Probably no one could or would want to collect all the books written for players of various classes. So the collectors become specialists.

One of the specialties is tournament books, which are published with game scores and other details after most master tournaments. They are some 600 of these and Albert S. Pinkus has come within about 40 of owning all of them. Imagine what those stacks of books do to a home.

Chessplayers do sometimes try to quit but they seldom succeed. A good case is Reuben Fine, one of the half dozen strongest players in the world. He had devoted his entire life to playing chess and writing books and magazine pieces about it until a few years ago he decided he wanted his life shaped toward some more substantial end.

He took a degree as a psychologist but his awareness of all the latest technical developments in the game is a good tipoff on how he spends spare time, resolutions or not.

Albert Simonson, another New Yorker, gave up chess to salvage a business career right after he had narrowly missed winning the national championship. For a half dozen years he seemed to be the one who would disprove the axiom that chessplayers never quit.

A year ago, he quietly returned to the Marshall Chess Club and resumed his old place on the team. The lure of the little playthings on the chessboard can be resisted just so long.

New York *World-Telegram and Sun*, 1951.

ADVICE TO BEGINNERS
By Hector Rosenfeld

These cynical maxims are the fruit of a lifetime of skittles playing. The author may not have been an authority on chess, but he was certainly an authority on what has come to be called "gamesmanship." This might be defined as the art of playing the opponent, rather than the board.

1. Always impress your adversary with the belief that you have beaten recognized players. It will fill him with a wholesome awe, which is a great advantage.

2. Lead off with P-K4 with the careless swing of assurance. It will set your opponent thinking, and it is a move that has won a great many games.

3. Always attack your adversary's queen when you can. You may waste a move, but it will worry him, which is always advisable.

4. On the other hand, when your queen is attacked, regard the move with contempt, and reply instantly with an unexpected and entirely irrelevant move. This will give color to the suspicion that

you are planning a Morphian combination beyond the discernment of your antagonist, who will accordingly refuse to take the queen.

5. When through an oversight you have lost a piece, any hesitation in making your next move will be fatal. Therefore, answer quickly, keeping up the impression in your adversary's mind, suggested in No. 4.

6. Never resign until you are mated, and even then, you may induce your antagonist to let you take back the last three or four moves, and still win.

7. When your opponent's game is hopeless, let him try ALL the moves at his command; this can do you no harm, and will give you a reputation for liberality.

8. Finally—check whenever you can. It may be mate.

Chess Review, 1938.

THE GENTLE ART OF ANNOYING
By Donald MacMurray

The author of this delightful essay was a brilliant master whose shockingly early death blasted what promised to be a notable career. Let every reader ask himself: "How many of these faults do I have?!" The results of this soul-searching should be interesting!

As everyone knows, the worst thing that can happen to a chessplayer is to lose a game. Because this is so, it is evident that what the chess public needs is a method of winning easily without first mastering the difficult and unnecessary technique of making good moves.

To begin with, you must realize clearly that your principal object is to disturb your opponent as much as possible in order to distract his attention from the game. Of the numerous ways of accomplishing this, the easiest and most common is talking.

Talking to annoy may be done in several ways. You may, for example, talk *to your opponent,* either pointing out bad moves to him, or making any other misleading remark about the position. If your opponent so much as comes near to touching a piece it is always disconcerting to say sternly, "Touch-move." If this involves you in an argument with him, so much the better for your chances of upsetting his train of thought.

An example from actual experience will serve to demonstrate the practicability of this piece of advice. Several years ago, in the interscholastic championship tournament in New York, there arose an endgame position where White, who was on the defensive, had only one way of saving the game, to wit, by pushing a certain pawn. He permitted his hand to hover over the pawn, without touching it, whereupon Black cried gleefully, "You touched it!" White denied the charge vigorously, and, when the referee finally decided the fight in his favor, triumphantly proceeded to move another piece, thus losing the game.

You may also talk to the kibitzers, preferably discussing the previous game with them so heatedly that you draw your opponent into the argument, and so take his mind completely off whatever he was considering.

If you like, you may talk *to yourself*. Every chess club boasts at least one genius of the talk-to-yourself school. Curiously enough, the favorite method of these experts is the recitation of nonsense rhymes. The eminent champion of the West has great success in declaiming passages from Lewis Carroll's *Hunting of the Snark*, while one of the most prominent American professionals has confided to me that about half of his yearly income is derived from the recitation, at critical points in his games, of *Mary Had a Little Lamb*.

Another ready means of annoying which you have at your disposal is music. There are several different ways of employing music for this purpose. If you are a timid player, you may try humming, which is the most unobtrusive of the lot, and the least likely to call forth rebuke, but which, when raised to high pitch and accompanied by the gestures of a conductor, will throw your opponent entirely off his game.

As your courage waxes, you will find a shrill, piercing whistle more effective than even the most artistic humming. The tune must be one far too difficult to be whistled correctly, so that it will sound at best like an undecided peanut roaster.

Finally, being carried away by the beauty of your noises, you may break into full song, accompanying yourself as before, with appropriate gestures, or else by tapping in time with your feet.

If you do not happen to be musically inclined, you will still find a big field open to you in drumming and tapping, either with hands or feet. This is one of the best ways known to induce your opponent to make a hasty move, and is favored by nearly all the masters who have no confidence in their singing voices.

Other great resources which you possess are coughing, sneezing, and blowing your nose during the progress of the game. These are to be used freely, both as a general distraction and to instill in your adversary the fear of germs.

Similarly, when your opponent does not move quickly enough to suit you (and if you are a right-minded chessplayer, this should be nearly all the time), you should first heave a sigh, then yawn and look at your watch, and finally groan mournfully.

A large class of nuisances not yet touched upon comprises those which aim at distracting the visual attention of the enemy. Of these, the one most highly sanctioned for your adoption is the system of blowing smoke rings across the board. This is useful, not only because it obscures the position, but also because it will surely get into your opponent's eyes or choke him, and thus put him completely at your mercy.

Another annoyance of this type is adjusting pieces which you would like your opponent to take, or else pieces which are on the other side of the board from where your threat is.

If you habitually rest your head on your hand, be certain to keep your elbow constantly on the edge of the board, shifting its position from time to time so as to be always concealing under it at least two or three important squares.

As the evening wears on, you may resort to stretching, in doing which you should take care to fling at least one arm all the way across the board.

Whenever you have what you think is a fairly good position, rock your chair back and forth on its hind legs, assuming meanwhile a complacent attitude, with your thumbs in your vest pockets, as much as to say, "Why do you not resign, you duffer?"

There is only one more kind of disturbance worth mentioning. Although it is infrequent of occurrence, and, when it does happen, it is entirely accidental, it is as upsetting as anything else. It is making a strong move.

Chess Review, 1933.

DOES THE CAP FIT?

By "Roamer"

The more the behavior of chessplayers changes, the more it remains the same!

I watched a game of chess in a Belfast club the other night and was interested in, and somewhat amused by, the behavior of the players. Their opening moves were accompanied by bantering remarks, but soon, as the issue was joined, their faces became set and grim, and stolid silence was maintained to the end. One player initiated a sharp attack which promised well. The reaction of his opponent to this, as he made the answering moves which he hoped would ward off looming disaster, was to shuffle about in his chair as if in acute discomfort. His hands made strange gestures. Well-groomed hair became rather disheveled. A pipe from a pocket was hastily returned there after a brief but dazed inspection. Instead a handkerchief was brought forth to mop a fevered brow. Legs were crossed and uncrossed, and occasionally a tentative finger was nervously thrust between collar and throat as though strangulation was imminent.

Meanwhile, the attacking player's behavior took the milder form of gently patting the back of his head with the palm of one hand and tapping the table with the fingertips of the other. When his attack seemed assured of success he sat back in his chair, looking like a crusader in a just cause. His opponent, faced with mate on the move, looked at the board in utter dejection. He had apparently reached the nadir of despair, and it would almost have been fitting if a black cap or a coffin had made a magical appearance. At last he reluctantly resigned, then remarked that he thought he should have won! The winner, with feigned magnanimity, and with a trace of pity in his voice, said that he himself had had all the luck!

Chess Review, 1940.

EXCUSES FOR LOSING
By B. H. Wood

Excuse, thy name is legion! Without trying, Wood lists eighteen excuses. What chessplayer could not compile a list of at least fifty from his own experience!

Chess is a more complex game than bridge. If you lose at bridge it is through (a) a bad partner or—if he or she has enough personality to deter you from saying this—(b) bad cards. Loss at chess, on the other hand, may be due to interference by spectators, the noise of traffic, toothache, headache, backache, the foulness of your opponent's pipe, his constant humming or finger-drumming on the table, bad light, blinding light, defective chessmen, a board too large, a board too small, hypnotism, an atomic explosion in Siberia, the Government, the Inland Revenue, or a bluebottle blundering across the fairway.

How tawdry these face-saving formulas sound when they fall from the lips of others! For have we chessplayers not encountered every conceivable excuse in our careers? Of course, we have never employed such excuses ourselves, though we have occasionally actually lost games through interference by spectators, the noise of traffic, etc.

It was old Burn, veteran British master of the '90s, who was heard to remark plaintively towards the end of his long life that he had never had the satisfaction of beating a perfectly healthy opponent. When the inner meaning of his remark dawned on his assembled friends, they nodded sagely.

Illustrated London News, 1949.

TALES OF A WOODPUSHER: NEVER GIVE UP UNTIL YOU'RE MATED

By Fred M. Wren

Chary as I am of superlatives, I have no hesitation in saying that nobody has written more entertainingly or more charmingly of the joys and tribulations of "the unknown chessplayer." Those who have read all the articles of his famous series must treasure the issues of Chess Review *in which they were published. Reading Wren on chess, you feel that "there but for the grace of God go I"; for Wren has summed up the fun, the heartache, the triumph, the misery, the amiable cocksureness, and the quest for improvement that all make the woodpusher what he is.*

To everyone who has played chess over a period of several years, without ever having attained the heights of city or even club championship, it must be apparent, as it is to me, that the masters, and even the Class A players, dream dreams, think thoughts, devise strategies, and execute tactics which are absolutely incomprehensible to the less accomplished player.

Even when the score of a game played between masters is published in a magazine or book, and when the fine and subtle variations of masterplay are annotated either by one of the players or by some other master, the ordinary, average Class B player doesn't understand it. He can follow the chain of exclamation points and question marks which have been distributed by the annotator, and from a certain diagramed position he can carry through the exquisite combination which means glory to one of the players and curtains to the other. But as to *how* that particular diagramed position happened to be reached, or *why* most of the moves leading up to the tragedy were made—that is a closed book to him, as it is to me.

In 1931, while the Capablanca-Euwe match was being played, I happened to be living in Holland. Through mutual friends I was presented to Capablanca, and we became good friends. After one of his two victories over Euwe I asked him why Euwe resigned when he did, as it seemed to me there were a lot of pieces on the board, and a lot of play left.

He looked at me as I would look at a four-year-old child who had just asked me a foolish question, and said, "Why, he was a pawn down."

Just like that! I knew that Euwe had lost a pawn, but I still didn't know why he resigned. Then I got my first glimpse of the truth that is still hidden from thousands, maybe millions, who play chess: that the masters are not as we are; that their games are played on a different plane than ours; that when one of them loses a pawn he resigns!

After returning from Europe I was in Buffalo, New York, for a few years, and I became a member of the strong club which maintained permanent quarters in the Lafayette Hotel. I played in all the club tournaments (in Class B, of course), and had the privilege of playing skittles games with all the Class A players, some of whom were either in or on the thin edge of the master class. I took boards in simultaneous exhibitions given by Marshall, Kashdan, and Alekhine. Marshall let me strangle myself in a close game in which my queen bishop and queen rook were never moved. Kashdan let me set the pace—so I thought—for about twenty moves. Then he looked at his watch, saw that it was getting late, and let me have both barrels in the form of a five-move combination to win a piece.

Against Alekhine I not only did not do well—I didn't even have a good time. Every time the Champion came around he would glare at me as much as to say, "For Pete's sake! Haven't you gone home yet?" and when I would make my faltering move he would make his reply without either looking at the board or even breaking his steady pace around the table. I found out later that this attitude towards his opponents was a pose adopted for use in simultaneous play, the purpose being to soften up his adversaries. They would get so mad that they would make some foolish mistake and quit in disgust. He achieved his purpose with me, for after losing a bishop I resigned.

Having nothing to do for the rest of the evening I stood behind the chair of Dr. Frucella, one of Buffalo's strongest players, to watch the mincemeat the World Champion was bound to make of him. I learned a lot while standing there that night. I noticed that Alekhine didn't pass Frucella's board without stopping. I saw that the champ's scowl was just as ferocious as it had been before my board, but there was one tremendous difference—it didn't bother Frucella at all because he never looked at Alekhine. He just sat there and played a game of chess, watching the board all the time, and seeing no more of his famous opponent than an occasional hand moving a piece.

And the moves they made! I couldn't see the reason or the plan behind any of them. Then, all of a sudden, with the board still full of pieces, Alekhine resigned, his only loss of the evening. As they shook hands, I think Frucella got his first glimpse of the defeated World Champion.

Later I asked Frucella why Alekhine had resigned. The position looked perfectly innocuous to me. Again the pitying glance from a master chessplayer, and again the simple but meaningless explanation: "Why I had him all tied up, and no matter what he did I was bound to win something."

This was worse than Capablanca's explanation. He, at least, had won a pawn, and Euwe had resigned. But Frucella hadn't won anything—he was just *going to win something,*—but the champion of the world had seen the inevitable, and had resigned. I still couldn't understand it.

The next day, as I entered the club, Dr. Frucella called to me, and I joined him at a chess table. He had the pieces set up in the final position of the night before. Then, slowly, and with infinite patience, he went through about six different variations to prove the truth of what he had said the night before—that no matter what Alekhine might do, Frucella would win material. At last I could see what they had been talking about the night before. Sure, anyone could see that —but could they? I asked Roy Black, one of the kibitzers, if he had seen the possibilities before Frucella's exposition.

"Sure," he said. "Any chessplayer could see that."

I resented that. "Oh yeah?" I retorted. "I didn't see it, and I'll bet that half the members of this club wouldn't have seen it either."

"The statement still stands," grinned Black. "Any chessplayer could see it. Maybe some of you woodpushers couldn't see it, although it's as plain as the nose on your face."

So much for ratings and classifications. I had at last found my level. Not Class A. Not Class B. Not even a chessplayer. Just a woodpusher!

I found that I was not alone in this class. I even learned that at least two-thirds of the people who play chess never become chessplayers according to the standard set by Bro. Black. They were, are now, and always will be woodpushers. That doesn't mean that they do not have a lot of fun. It doesn't even mean that they will not knock off a duly qualified "chessplayer" in a skittles game, or even in a tournament game, now and then. It simply means that there is a class of chessplay so far above their modest plane that many of them live a full and satisfying life without ever knowing of its existence.

What a blessing to maintain this blissful ignorance, neither knowing nor caring what Lasker hit Capablanca with in 1914 at St. Petersburg! To be able to make a move without thinking, "Is this what Fine played against Botvinnik at Nottingham?" To be able to play the Fegatello just for fun, and not worrying about whether or not your opponent had read Pinkus' analysis of that variation. Yes sir, the woodpushers may not make much money by playing or writing about chess, but they do have all the fun.

This fun was denied me. I had played just enough chess to like the game. I had had revealed to me visions of the land beyond the woodpushers' territory—the rich and green realm of the true "chessplayer." The land where five-move combinations were the rule rather than the exception; where masters resigned when they lost a pawn; where world champions resigned when they saw that they were going to lose material; where simultaneous exhibitions paid the visiting master at least $100 for a few hours' play. Brother, that was for me. How long had this been going on?

I subscribed to *Chess Review*. I bought books. I studied them all. The strongest players of the Buffalo Chess Club were very considerate of the struggling dub. They played with me, analyzed my games, pointed out my mistakes, praised my triumphs. There was no doubt about it. I was improving, and on the way to become a real "chess-player."

Someone said, "A little knowledge is a dangerous thing." It certainly is dangerous to one's peace of mind if he suddenly gets a yen to master the strategy and tactics of chess. It is something like being out on a dark night and seeing three or four stars. You get a sudden desire to know something about the science of astronomy. You buy a book on that subject, and you identify the stars you saw the night before. But the next night you go out and you see the sky filled with thousands of stars, and your book tells you that there are thousands of others which you can't see without a telescope, and that there are others which you can read about but can never see in your lifetime, even with a telescope, since they are visible only once in nine thousand years. Then you begin to realize that you have not learned a damned thing, except for the fact that no one man can ever hope to more than touch the fringe of the curtain covering a full knowledge of astronomy.

It's just the same with chess. The more you study and learn, the keener becomes the realization that life just isn't long enough to master chess the hard way—the way any woodpusher has to do it. Of course, if you are one of those fortunate mortals who doesn't have to do it the hard way—one of those guys who just knows by instinct, when he begins to play the game, all the things that we dubs have to study over and have explained to us—if you are one of those chaps, walk right in and take a master's chair. You can start in at a higher level than most of us will ever reach.

Anyway, I learned a little about chess, and graduated to the Class A group in the Buffalo Club. Then I was transferred, spent a few years in various small towns along the Maine border, and finally landed in Halifax, Nova Scotia. Here I found a club in operation, holding weekly meetings in a small hotel.

I learned something the first night I played in that club. I had as my first opponent an elderly clergyman who played a keen game of chess. After playing about a half an hour I lost a bishop, through a stupid oversight on my part. I immediately resigned, and suggested another game.

"Aren't you going to play this one out?" said the old gentleman, looking at me over his glasses.

"There isn't much use in playing you a piece down," I replied.

"We always play them out here," said the clergyman. "No one here gives up until he's mated."

So we played it out, and a few moves later he made a mistake which allowed me to win.

"There," said my opponent, nodding with satisfaction, "that shows you that I was right. You never want to quit a chess game until you are mated."

From Capablanca and Frucella I had learned that a "chessplayer" resigned when he lost, or saw that he must lose, material of any value. From the good padre in Halifax I learned the slogan of the "wood-pusher"—"Never give up until you are mated."

That slogan has stood me in good stead for the past ten years, and has accounted for many of my wins. Of course, if you are playing against an opponent of master strength you are not only wasting his time and yours to continue the game after you have lost material—you are also insulting his intelligence. But, on the other hand, we do not meet many masters in this section of the world, and when wood-pushers get together the precepts of the masters are forgotten. We play for fun and glory under the unwritten law that it's not enough to establish a winning position—we have to demonstrate the win.

Chess Review, 1947.

TRICKERY ANCIENT AND MODERN
By B. H. Wood

A book could be written about the art of "gamesmanship" as applied to chess. Where to draw the line between the legitimate and the unethical often becomes a problem of serious proportions. Of course, if the task becomes too onerous, one can always resort to making moves on the board.

"I suppose you know all the questionable tricks at chess," remarked a friend to me recently. This slanderous compliment was prompted by a magazine article in which I had recommended a new resource against an unpleasant surprise move—to offer your opponent a cup of coffee! If you can secure a brief adjournment of the game to break the tension, you probably will be able to appraise the situation much more collectedly on return.

Unfortunately, my remark has received so much publicity that I may have to drop this particular tactical resource from my own repertoire for a while!

As a guest at Stockport Chess Club's centenary dinner recently, I was wondering what to talk about when the Mayor of Stockport suddenly provided a perfect cue. "One thing about chess," he was saying. "You can't cheat...."

There is more scope for trickery at chess than I could possibly expound in one article. In 1561 that famous Spanish bishop, Ruy Lopez, wrote: "Arrange the board so that it reflects the light into your opponent's eyes."

In a casual game, your opponent holds out two clenched fists, to decide color. You tap one—it is found to hold a black pawn. If you insist on checking up on the other, you may find that he has accidentally picked up a black pawn with that one, too.

Are you coughing, your eyes streaming, almost before the game starts? It may be no pure accident—on the contrary very impure design—that your opponent's pipe is so foul. Some of Lasker's most brilliant wins, I have heard seriously argued, were founded on his awful cigars. Nimzovich did almost as well through getting tournament organizers to compel habitual smokers to abstain.

One coffee-house professional is said to have habitually, in castling, brought his rook deftly to his king's or queen's square in the one operation. When some poor rabbit protested, "You can't castle like that," he responded, "Why not?" "This is how I castled; the proper way"—demonstrating. "Well, this is the way I castle," the professional would roar. "You can castle your way if you like, I'll castle mine."

In one crowded club, a player whose game was going badly had developed his king's rook, after P-KR4, via KR3 to the middle of the board, and lost it. Suddenly he had an inspiration. Taking advantage of a burst of conversation, he castled on the same side of the board, utilizing for the purpose the queen's rook from the next table. The maneuver being unobserved, the only remaining problem was to win the game with the aid of this extra material before the neighbor to his right discovered the loss; and I understand he just managed this.

Napoleon, whose prowess at chess was far from negligible, is said to have hated losing so intensely that, whenever the game began to go against him, he would start making illegal moves. A bishop, crossing the board, would profitably wander on to the next diagonal, and so on. Whether this trait was only a reflection of his tactics in war, only an historian could confirm.

The most involved trick I ever heard of concerns a known "rabbit" who wrote two professionals offering to play each at correspondence chess. He only stipulated that he be allowed several days to consider each of his moves and that, in the matter of stakes, he should receive odds of two to one. Knowing well how very badly he played, both his prospective opponents agreed. All he did was to pair one against the other, by the simple expedient of sending off each move as he received it from one as his own move to the other, and vice versa. He was on a sure winner, as long as they did not meet and compare notes.

Of course, nothing like this ever happens in Birmingham chess. But it's extraordinary how often, when a team turns up a man short, it's the fellow who would have played at board one, so that it's the other team's strongest player who has to kick his heels all the evening and win his game by default.

Birmingham *Post*, 1949.

BLACK TO MOVE
By E. W. Chandler

The classic chess story dealing with the supernatural is generally considered to be Moxon's Master *by Ambrose Bierce, in which an automaton presumably kills its human adversary. But the story is set forth in a stilted, fuddy-duddy prose which is more likely to tickle the modern reader's funny bone than to make his flesh creep. Chandler's story, it seems to me, is a much more impressive achievement.*

> "Cliff Edge,"
> Hathercombe,
> August 11th

Dear John,

I wonder if you'd like to come down here and stay with me for a few days? I do wish you would; as perhaps you have heard, Eric fell over the cliff here last week and was killed, and I feel a need for companionship. Send me a wire to say when you're coming.

> Yours sincerely,
> Arthur Hargreaves.

The note was characteristic: almost brutally direct. I had heard about his cousin's death; the newspapers had contained a report of the inquest a couple of days before, though it had consisted of little more than the bare facts conveyed by Hargreaves' letter and the verdict—accidental death.

Neither did Hargreaves volunteer any more details as we walked from the station. He apparently considered that he had told me the essentials and that there was nothing more to add. As usual, he was silent and reserved, though he had seemed glad to see me in his undemonstrative way. I doubt if anyone could claim any real intimacy with him. Although I had been acquainted with him for a number of years, I knew little more about him than a stranger could have learnt in a day: he was unmarried, an architect by profession, and a brilliant chessplayer.

Only in this last respect had he resembled his friend and co-dweller, loquacious Eric Ankerton. It seemed curious to think that Ankerton was dead—the bungalow still contained his belongings everywhere.

Hargreaves had designed the building, and it bore the impress of his blunt personality. Perched on the very edge of the cliff, half a mile from the village or any other dwelling, its steel windows commanded a magnificent view of the sea and rugged coast. On the opposite side of the one large room were a showerbath, a tiny kitchen, and a recess containing two bunks.

"You take the lower one, old chap," he begged. "I hope I shan't disturb you; I haven't been sleeping too well."

But he did disturb me—considerably. All night he tossed and turned and muttered in his sleep. I caught odd words: "knight" and "bishop" and "threat." In the morning I taxed him with it.

"You seemed to be playing chess all night," I remarked.

He stared at me. "How do you know?" he demanded curtly. "Oh, I suppose I talked in my sleep. Did I say anything else?"

"No."

"Sorry, John." He hesitated. "Well, I might as well tell you. I've been dreaming about a game Eric and I left unfinished the night before he was killed."

"You mean you play it over again?"

"Not exactly. It...well, it keeps on. We play a few more moves each night."

"Pretty silly ones, I expect."

"By no means. As a matter of fact, I don't think I've ever played better. Look." With accustomed fingers he set up the chessmen. "I was White. He defended with a Sicilian."

He shifted the pieces rapidly, with a few words of laconic explanation. I was forced to agree that I could not have bettered any move. It was a close, keenly-contested struggle.

"Well, that's where we are now. What do you think of it?"

" 'Um...Black looks like getting a nasty queen's side attack."

Suddenly the strangeness of the situation struck me. Black was getting a nasty attack—and Black's shattered body lay in the village churchyard. But Hargreaves was apparently unconscious of anything incongruous.

"Yes, that's what I thought." He drummed nervously on the table—for him, an unusual sign of perturbation. "Come on, let's go and have a bathe."

So three days passed. We rambled over the downs and bathed and did bachelor housework. In the evenings, Hargreaves pored over his chessboard. And at night he played his adjourned game with his dead cousin. I warned him that it was becoming an obsession.

"Yes, I know," he said. "It's silly, but I can't help it. I somehow feel that this is the most important game I've ever played. I *must* win it."

"But you're playing both sides," I pointed out. "You decide on Black's moves as well as White's."

"But he...but Black makes moves I haven't thought of."

"They must occur to you subconsciously. You know how it is when you're solving a chess problem; the key sometimes comes when you're not thinking about it. So now you saturate your mind with the position during the day, and your dreams at night are the result."

He looked at me meditatively. "Yes, maybe, maybe...Now, if I play knight to bishop four..."

The next day we had an unexpected visitor. Hargreaves answered a knock on the door, and I heard him exclaim: "Oh, it's you again, Rogers. What do you want this time?"

A slow country voice answered: "Just a question or two, if you don't mind, sir," and a stout police sergeant came into the room. He seated himself firmly in the most uncomfortable chair.

"Now, I wonder if you could give us any more details about how Mr. Ankerton fell over the cliff?"

"Damn it, I told you all I knew at the inquest. I was walking in front, heard a cry, and turned round just in time to see him disappear."

"Well, sir, we've found some marks on the grass that we can't quite explain. You're sure you can't tell us any more?"

"No, I cannot," snapped Hargreaves. "Is that all?"

The policeman's moronic calm was undisturbed. He asked suddenly: "You had a quarrel with the deceased on the morning of his death, didn't you?"

"Eh? Oh, that. A little disagreement. It was nothing."

"What was the disagreement about, Mr. Hargreaves?"

"What the hell has that got to do with you?"

"We have to investigate all the facts that may be relevant...and any reactions that may be relevant too." The sergeant rose heavily. "Let me know if you remember anything else, won't you? It may save a lot of trouble. Good night, Mr. Hargreaves. Good night, Mr. Nolan."

Hargreaves moved to the side window and scowled at the policeman's clumsy form lumbering down the path to the village. "Great blundering bucolic lout," he growled. "He couldn't detect a cow in a field."

I wasn't so sure. "What was he trying to detect, anyway?" I asked.

He swung round and faced me: "How the devil should I know?" he shouted. Then he turned immediately to his eternal chessmen.

His face was drawn and haggard. When playing chess, that most nerve-racking of games, he had been notable for his imperturbability. Now his hand hovered indecisively over the board, and his mouth twitched nervously. I looked at the position over his shoulder. Certainly White was in a bad way. His pieces were scattered ineffectually, while the Black queen and rooks had broken through on the queen's side.

"I think you might as well resign," I remarked.

"Resign?" His gaze wandered out over the sea. "Resign? No, I'll never resign."

"Come to bed and forget about it," I said, rather irritably. "You'll have a nervous breakdown if you keep on like this."

He left the chessmen reluctantly. "I'll come to bed, anyway," he promised with a wry grimace, and began to undress.

When I awoke, the moonlight streaming through the windows told me that several hours had passed. I could hear Hargreaves breathing heavily and moving restlessly in his bunk. I wondered if I should wake him from his nightmare, and dragged myself reluctantly out of bed.

I was shocked at his appearance. His features were distorted and ghastly pale in the wan light, and great beads of glistening sweat stood on his forehead. Low, indistinguishable words and phrases were forced between his clenched teeth. His hands fluttered incessantly over the bedclothes, clenched and unclenched. His eyes opened wide, and glared unseeing into space. For a moment there was utter silence.

Suddenly his face twisted in an agony of terror and rage, and he spoke distinctly: "Queen to bishop eight, mate." A convulsive shudder shook his frame, and he groaned violently. Then he lay still...quite still.

Filled with fear, I peeped into his relaxed features. I shook his shoulder; his body moved limply under my hand. I felt his heart; there was no beat.

"Wake up!" I cried. But he was dead.

Dazed and horrified, I turned away. My eye fell upon the chessboard. The position had changed since I last saw it: the black queen, supported by a rook, was at KB8, leaving the white king on Kt2 without defense or retreat. White was doomed.

I suppose he *could* have got up while I was asleep and moved the pieces....

Chess, 1950.

A CLASSIFICATION OF CHESSPLAYERS
By T. E. W. Widdows

This is a valuable contribution to chess sociology. Although I have combed chess literature for descriptions of gentlemanly opponents, I have yet to find the like of du Mont's tribute: "The average Britisher may not take his chess as seriously as his continental rival. But I feel sure that nowhere is the game of chess played in a more pleasant and sporting spirit than in this land of ours. I shall never forget Edward Lasker, when he won the championship of the City of London Chess Club after beating Sir George Thomas in a game which did credit to both sides, saying with awe and admiration in his voice:

'I have never known anyone to lose an important game with such dignity. You are a nation of gentlemen.'"

The only surviving member of the commission appointed by the Worcester City Chess Club to attempt the classification of chessplayers having reached a place beyond the law of libel, it is now thought safe to publish its findings.

The following types of player have definitely been classified:

1. Drawist
2. Rattler
3. Chair Manipulator
4. Pencil Thrower
5. Hand Clasper
6. Non-smoker
7. Body Swayer
8. Spectacles Cleaner
9. Hand Hoverer
10. Hair Disarranger
11. Table Tapper
12. Low Whistler
13. Ejaculator
14. Foot Shuffler
15. Post-mortem **Maniac**
16. Nose Tweaker
17. Kneecap Kneader
18. Necktie Tugger
19. Sniffer
20. Elbow Waggler
21. Shoulder Twitcher
22. Mock Annoyance Gesticulator

The nomenclature used for Nos. 5, 8, 10, 11, 12, 14, 15, 16, 17, 18, 19, 20, and 21 is thought to be self-explanatory. The commission has issued a supplement to the report, giving explanations of the terms used, some extracts being given below:

1. *Drawist.* Always wants a draw, preferably after 1 P-K4, P-K4. His ingratiating smile is proportional in width to the material down, and he wears a look of pained astonishment when his offer is refused.

2. *Rattler.* Has just taken a week-end course in psychology and specializes in irregular openings. His opening move is made by banging the piece hard down on the board, then affixing his opponent with a hypnotic glare. The victim is undecided whether to resign on the spot or attempt to hold out for ten moves as a token effort.

3. *Chair Manipulator.* Goes through a cycle of operations consisting of rising, twiddling his chair, resting his foot on it, balancing the chair on one leg, etc.

4. *Pencil Thrower.* Writes down his move; if his pencil is thrown nonchalantly upon the table, he is embarking on a reckless plan; if it is laid down carefully he has some subtle scheme afoot.

6. *Non-smoker.* Little is known of this type as he is practically non-existent, and therefore his inclusion is purely nominal.

7. *Body Swayer.* One of the most dangerous types. The body is oscillated with metronomic precision, but when the safe angle of twenty degrees is exceeded, the resulting crash may wreak havoc on adjacent boards. The temper of the players on these boards may become ugly. And then what?

9. *Hand Hoverer.* He cannot make up his mind; out pops his hand, he will, he won't, he scratches his ear, yes, no, etc.

13. *Ejaculator.* Emits a long low oh! ah! or eh! in varying tones indicative of surprise, shock, or horror, depending upon the exact type of mess in which the player has landed his game.

22. *Mock Annoyance Gesticulator.* Very cunning; preys on the weakness of human nature. He puts one of his pieces *en prise,* then makes a gesture of annoyance. His opponent snaps up the piece, then realizes he has fallen for it, hook, line and sinker.

British Chess Magazine, 1945.

COUNSEL'S OPINION
By R. F. Walton

The English are expert at turning out this sort of thing: sly humor, operating by understatement, portrays a pompous bully as seen through the eyes of a half-intimidated, half-exasperated milquetoast narrator.

I had been inveigled into playing a game with old Woolhead, much against my better judgment, for it is common knowledge and a fact accepted by all in the club that though old Woolhead may have been at one time a competent barrister he never was and never could be a chessplayer He had slowly and carefully played himself into the usual inextricable jam and for some time had remained in a state of moody inactivity, blowing gently through his large walrus mustache as each possible or impossible move was considered, weighed, found wanting, and reluctantly rejected.

I had been chatting the while with Feathergay, the club secretary, and was fairly well advanced in the exposition of my latest theory concerning night trout fishing—my latest idea, quite unique, being a luminous fly—when I was, I think I may say, rudely, interrupted by a loud and excited cry of "Mate!" from old Woolhead. I turned in irritable surprise to the board; old Woolhead lifted a bishop from its square, banged it down again noisily and repeated defiantly, "Check, sir, I say, and mate!"

I took in the position at a glance. Old Woolhead had brought his White bishop from KN2 to QB6 to check my king on K1, overlooking that his bishop was securely pinned in front of his king by my rook at KN3. Oddly enough, my rook was pinned, too, by his queen at KR5. There was no vacant square for my king to move to and nothing to interpose, a smothered mate in fact, if his move had been playable. Just the sort of idiotic position that old Woolhead loves to get a game into.

"My dear sir," I said, kindly, but firmly, "you cannot move your bishop."

"And why not, sir?" he demanded somewhat truculently.

"Because, sir," I said, "you expose your king to check from my rook."

"Balderdash, my dear sir!" came the unexpected answer in a voice quite unwarrantably calm and confident. I noticed out of the corner of my eye that that aimless fool Feathergay had slunk away during the altercation and I realized that the chance of explaining the advantages of my luminous fly was irrevocably lost for that night.

My temper was badly frayed, and I said a trifle loudly, "Don't you know the rules of the game?"

"Certainly I do, sir, but it appears that you are not fully seized of the import of the alleged rule which you pretend to quote." Old Woolhead cleared his throat judicially, fumbled in the capacious pocket of his old tweed jacket and drew forth a much worn and bethumbed *Modern Chess Primer* (Edition 1899).

He waved the book at me. "You recognize this book, sir?"

"Certainly I do" (I was brought up on Cunnington).

"You recognize the Reverend E. E. Cunnington, Master of Arts, as an accepted authority upon the laws of chess?"

"Most certainly," I said, somewhat bewildered and wondering what on earth the old fox was driving at.

"Then allow me to refer you to page 33, sub-heading 'Exposed': you said, did you not, sir, that I exposed my king by moving my bishop?"

"You most certainly did, I mean I did say that."

"Very well, sir, let us consider the legal interpretation of the word *Exposed* as given by the Reverend Cunnington." The old fellow produced a pair of battered pince-nez, perched them at a rakish angle on the end of his nose, cleared his throat even more solemnly than before, and read from the book: " 'Exposed: A man is "exposed" when it is liable to be captured by a man of the other side.' That, sir, is what the Reverend Cunnington says, and I would draw me lud's—tut-tut—your attention to the operative words 'liable to be captured.' " He fixed upon me a challenging glance and rapped out suddenly, "Can you or can you not move your rook?"

"Of course I can't," I said.

"Then, sir, is it not obvious to the meanest intelligence that if, as you say, you cannot move your rook, my king is not liable to be captured, and therefore he cannot be claimed to be exposed as laid down in paragraph 4, page 33 of the *Modern Chess Primer,* which authority we both admit and accept? It follows, then, that my move is legal, sir, and that you have lost the game."

With this he hastily brushed the pieces aside, shambled over to his favorite armchair, and settled down to the *Times* leader as if there was no more to be said. I haven't played him since. You never know where you are with these lawyer fellows.

British Chess Magazine, 1946.

VACATION IN LONDON
By Fred M. Wren

Read all about the greatest chess jag in history! When this item first appeared in Chess Review, *it was modestly signed by "The Black Knight." But the Wren touch is inimitable—and unmistakable!*

While on the Continent in 1933, I received a telegram from my chief requesting me to come at once to London for a conference. At any season of the year London holds a great fascination for me, but at this particular time, after a cold, foggy Dutch winter that telegram seemed a passport to the promised land. London, with its theatres, its great stores, its hot night spots! Oh, boy!

As I entered the train in The Hague I found that I had to share a compartment with a young Hollander who gave me the usual *"Dag, mijnheer"* and subsided into the protection of his morning paper. I produced one of my own and prepared to spend a silent three hours before reaching Flushing where I was to get the boat for England. The International Team Tournament in Folkestone had just been won by the American chess team, and my paper contained the game played between Kashdan and Flohr. I was trying to follow the game through in my head when my companion broke all traditions and spoke.

"Do you, perhaps, play chess?"

"Yes, a little."

"Have you a pocket set?"

"No. I came away in such a hurry that I forgot to put it in my bag."

"Can you, perhaps, play without seeing the board?"

"Not very well, but we'll try it if you like."

"All right. I'll start. E2-e4."

Wow! I knew enough about the Dutch nomenclature of the pieces and their system of notation to follow a game printed in the paper, but to carry on a mental game in this style was more than I had bargained for. I did the best I could, but after about 15 moves I got mixed up with my d's and e's and resigned.

Then it was my turn to play White. I decided that my only chance was to spring something which would either win or lose in a hurry, so I chose a Muzio. The opening seemed to bother him, and I hoped I had found something which was new to him. When he pushed the pawn to KN5, I played N-B3 instead of castling. "So," said he, "the McDonnell variation of the Muzio! Do they still play that in America?" What could I do with a bird like that? By the time we reached Flushing where we got on the boat he had won five or six games, and I had lost interest in mental chess, but I was just aching to get at him over the board. We squared ourselves away at a table in the smoke-room of the ship, gave the steward orders to produce a chess set and board, and went at it.

From Flushing to Harwich we played steadily and finished 21 games. From Harwich to London in the train we accounted for nine more. (I forgot to say that we bought the set from the steward on the ship, paying him the equivalent of $4.00 for the outfit. I suppose he pocketed this sum, and reported that some crazy Dutchman had stolen the set, but that was his lookout.) I had engaged a room in the Victoria Hotel in London. My opponent had engaged one in another hotel, but he never went near it and came to the Victoria with me. We played most of that night in the hotel. The next morning I went to my conference, and two hours later was back in the hotel playing chess. We played until after midnight that night.

The following morning we played on the boat train again, and all the way across the Channel, and again on the train from Flushing to

The Hague where I disembarked. When we parted, never to meet again, I had won the board and set by a score of 46 wins against his 42. The dozen or so draws which we played were not counted.

I have often wondered what he thought about that trip in his more lucid moments. I wonder what he went to London for anyway? Whatever it was, he must have taken care of it in the two hours that I spent in my chief's office, for when I returned to the hotel he was there waiting for me, and he was not out of my sight at any other time during the waking hours of our trip. I didn't even know his name, and I'm sure he didn't know mine. He did volunteer the information that he came from Groningen, in Holland, and that he had once been city chess champion there, but that's all I know about him. All, except for the following facts:

1. That he had a double fianchetto attack which I never weathered.

2. That he was a sucker when defending a Ruy Lopez.

3. That he was a chess fiend whose enthusiasm for the game equaled my own.

And my vacation in London! Not a show did I see; not a night club did I visit. I didn't even buy the usual trip present for the wife. One day and two nights in London, and I was out of the hotel just two hours! To misquote the words of a song popular a few years ago, "You call it Love, but I call it Goofy"—to the nth degree.

Chess Review, 1936.

CHESS GENERALSHIP
By Franklin K. Young

Players of an earlier generation will recall Young's efforts to establish chess teaching on a military basis. Although he failed in his attempt, he left us some good stories. The first relates to the famous "Normal Position" in the Evans Gambit—after 1 P-K4, P-K4; 2 N-KB3, N-QB3; 3 B-B4, B-B4; 4 P-QN4, BxP; 5 P-B3, B-R4; 6 P-Q4, PxP; 7 O-O, P-Q3; 8 PxP, B-N3. For decades controversy raged about the question of White's best ninth move, some partisans favoring Morphy's 9 N-B3, with others backing Anderssen's 9 P-Q5. Incidentally, the story, as unfolded here, was later attributed to Reuben Fine!

Father Stone and the Ghost

In ye olden time in Boston chess circles, Hon. Henry N. Stone, familiarly known as "Father Stone," a chief rival and intimate crony of the famous George Hammond, king of New England chessplayers, became mightily interested in the subject of spiritualism.

After attending a number of not altogether satisfying seances under the auspices of mediums of more or less dubious character, Father Stone within his inner consciousness devised a test which to himself at least would forever settle the veracity of spirit communication.

Hence, on a certain evening the Hon. Mr. Stone, in his long-tailed black frock coat, high silk hat, and immaculate white choker, appeared at the appointed rendezvous and quietly inserted his two hundred-odd pounds of six feet four into the midst of the mystic circle.

In due time his turn came and in response to an invitation to hold converse with some dear departed he announced:

"I want to talk with George Hammond."

After some slight delay, necessary to establish connection with the spirit world, Father Stone was notified that George Hammond was on the wire and the following colloquy ensued:

"Good evening, Mr. Hammond," began Father Stone with the formal courtesy peculiar to those days. "I trust you are in good health and happily situated, sir."

"Good evening, Mr. Stone," came the reply. "I am well and happy. My regards to yourself and to all inquiring friends, sir."

"Yes. Ahem!" continued Father Stone. "Is it permissible to inquire as to your present whereabouts, Mr. Hammond?"

"Certainly, Mr. Stone. I am in Heaven, sir."

"Really! Ahem!—er—quite extraordinary!—er—how astonished— pardon me—er—I mean how distrait you must be, Mr. Hammond!"

"Not at all, Mr. Stone—not at all, sir! I am entirely *en rapport* with my surroundings, sir!"

"Yes! Quite so. Ahem! By the way, Mr. Hammond, do you play chess up there?"

"Frequently, Mr. Stone—frequently, sir!"

"Yes! Ahem! Not better, of course. That would not be possible. But with a broader and more comprehensive understanding of the game, I presume, sir?"

"Entirely true, Mr. Stone—entirely true, sir. I now know what when on Earth I merely was absolutely certain of, sir."

"Yes! Ahem! You know everything about chess, whereas in the flesh you merely were thoroughly convinced that you knew all about it?"

"Well put, Mr. Stone—well put, sir. Quite so, I assure you—quite so, sir."

"Yes! Ahem! Now that you know all about chess, may I ask you kindly to relieve my mind of a harassing uncertainty?"

"Certainly, Mr. Stone, I will answer you with the greatest pleasure, sir."

"Well, George, old boy! Who was right—you or me?—What IS White's best ninth move in the Evans Gambit?"

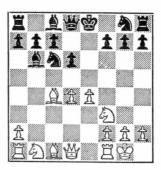

White to play

Tableau! Great uproar occasioned by the rapid departure of the ghost of the great Hammond, pursued by the vociferate demands of Father Stone for the promised information.

Grand finale! Exit Father Stone escorted by two policemen and proclaiming to the wide world that bare-faced fakerism which tried to palm off as the spirit of George Hammond a thing so ignorant of chess play as never to have heard of the famous New Englander's well-known dictum:

White 9 N-B3.

The Major Tells a Story

Among the chess magnates of former times, you probably well remember Major Otto E. Michaelis, the recognized chess champion of the United States Army. Polished and well-read, and something of a martinet, the Major when in the mood was delightfully companionable and a past master in the art of story-telling. Here is one of them:

"During the Civil War, the Major, then a subaltern, was orderly on the staff of one of the Federal Corps commanders, who, at the northerly advance of the Confederate Army under General Lee in 1863, was summoned to a council of war by General Meade.

"Among the more vociferous at this council was an officer who for every contingency presented a plan which he advocated with insistency and persistency, complacently offering as a *dernier* resort in all events of possible miscarriage:

"'Why, in that case, I retire into the interior of Pennsylvania!'

"In all post-mortems by a defeated opponent, when assailed by the query: 'I go there, Major. What would you do now?' Michaelis would reply coldly: "'Oh! I retire into the interior of Pennsylvania,' and leave his mystified interrogator to think it out."

Major Michaelis' skill at chess play, which was great, was equaled by his moderation. Seldom did he finish a game on the day it was begun. On one occasion, the Major having deliberated more than an hour, his opponent ventured to inquire: "What are you going to do, Major?" Michaelis regarded the speaker blankly for a moment and unseeing. Then, recovering himself with a start, he answered: "What, me? Do? I'm going to think," and proceeded with his reflections.

Field Book of Chess Generalship.

MR. BROWN DONE BROWN

By Jacob Elson

Every chess club is burdened with at least one savage-tempered tyrant and monumental boor on the order of Mr. Brown. To see him get his comeuppance makes singularly sweet reading.

Mr. Brown was the presiding elder of the Hoganville Chess Club, the recognized champion, the whole thing. That he was a man of more than ordinary talent can be gleaned from the fact that he would bully his adversaries out of such games that he could not win by superior play.

Like all men of genius he had certain peculiarities. A contempt for all chess books and chess openings was one of them, and a sweeping and uncompromising contempt for chess problems was another.

None of his satellites or slaves would dare to show him any new wrinkle in the openings or place any "White to play and mate" before him. It was enough for him to tolerate such things now and then in the other players. Things were at this stage when the proprietor of the drug store at the corner changed hands and a young man from a neighboring city took the place of his departing clerk. Pincus was the name of the new young man. He was tall, slim, with mild blue eyes, and a plentiful shock of light hair. His manners apparently were as mild as his eyes. Mr. Pincus was a devotee of Caissa, and would stroll now and then to the chess club, when not engaged in the building of "Pink Pills for Pale People" or the concoction of an infallible panacea for that "tired feeling" that chessplayers and even some other people are subject to at times.

It was a daring thing to do, but Mr. Pincus, after about the fourth stroll to the club, having so far only looked on, asked Mr. Brown to play a game with him.

Mr. Brown had it on his tongue to say "Play some of the others first," but there being a strong attendance at the club that evening, he thought he would show them how a drug clerk should be laid out, and consented.

Things did not seem to come Mr. Brown's way, however. After about twenty-five moves, it dawned on him that his queen was lost.

Mr. Brown now had recourse to other tactics.

"Oh, of course," he bellowed, upsetting the pieces, "I can't play with a man who takes fifteen minutes to every move. You can't outmaneuver me, but you can outsit me, that's plain enough."

"Why, Mr. Brown," mildly observed Mr. Pincus, "the whole game has not lasted much longer than half an hour, and we made over twenty moves each; how is it possible that I could have taken fifteen minutes to each move?"

"Oh, I know all about it," growled Mr. Brown, rising from the table, sitting down some distance off and picking up a newspaper.

Mr. Pincus wanted to propitiate him, but did not know what dangerous ground he was treading on. "Let me show you the latest variation in the Ruy Lopez, Mr. Brown," he said, setting up the pieces.

"I don't want to see any variation in the Lopez or lobster opening either," snarled Mr. Brown; "my own analyses are good enough for me."

"Mr. Brown appears to be of a frugal turn of mind," innocently observed Mr. Pincus to one of the bystanders. That individual, however, having been cowed into abject submission to the Brown supremacy long ago, moved away with a scared look without making a reply.

"Well," said Mr. Pincus, "maybe you are interested in problems. Here is a little beauty in two moves by Mackenzie."

"Problems!" sneered Mr. Brown, without stirring from his seat. "I can about tell you the solution of it. First move, queen turns around and stands on her head. Second move, pawn to king's eight becoming a mule, mate."

This observation was not quite original with Mr. Brown. He had once heard someone else use it. But like many other persons that could be named he was indebted to his memory for his wit and to his imagination for his facts.

"I would not solve a problem if I could and I could not solve one if I would," added Mr. Brown.

"You could not solve it if you would!" cried Mr. Pincus. "You underrate yourself; you surely could."

"No," repeated Mr. Brown, deliberately, "I could not if I would."

A man of the caliber of Mr. Brown having made a deliberate statement once could not recede from it. Great men cannot do that, or else the country is done for.

"I will bet you ten dollars for a supper for the club tomorrow night," said Mr. Pincus, dropping his extreme mildness of manner, "that I can show you a two-move problem with three different lines of play which you would have to solve whether you wanted to or not."

"Here is a chance to get even with him for that game," thought Mr. Brown. "No matter how simple the position I won't make the right moves."

"Done," said Mr. Brown, and both he and Mr. Pincus deposited a ten-dollar bill into the hands of a third party.

Mr. Pincus quickly put on the board the following position:

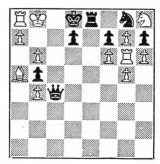

White to play and mate in two moves

Mr. Brown approached the board with the air of a conqueror.

"I'll play NxPch. Then Black queen must take knight, and now I can make any old move," he said.

"Well, please make any old move," quietly said Mr. Pincus.

"No, that won't do," said Mr. Brown. "I'll play P-N7"—discovering check for the first move—"no, I won't, either; I'll play K-N7," discovering check. And he fumed and fretted around the board for fully ten minutes, and finally changed color just about ten dollars' worth.

"It's a humbug," he said at last; "a confounded silly swindling humbug, but I am beat."

"A great position it is truly," he added with an attempt at a sneer; "look at both White rooks imprisoned by their own pieces."

"As for that matter," replied Mr. Pincus, "history has shown us many instances where some of the best people who ever lived have been imprisoned by their own friends, as mark 'the Man in the Iron Mask,' and others. In fact," he added, with a tremor in his voice, "in my own family, I had a dear cousin once—"

"Oh, hang you and your cousin," roared Mr. Brown. "I will not be here tomorrow night, and I guess you can have supper without me."

Perceiving that he did not cut much of a figure that evening, Mr. Brown put on his hat and walked off, slamming the door after him.

But he did come to that supper. He concluded in his giant mind that it would not do to let the others eat it all, particularly since he was paying for it, and he could be seen that night with the naked eye, with a sandwich in each hand, taking alternate bites out of each, and drinking beer out of a big bottle, without the preliminary of pouring it first into a glass.

As Mr. Brown, however, was a man of very direct ways, this little irregularity did not create any comment. Mr. Brown's bullying did not appear to have any effect on Mr. Pincus in their future doings at the club. His superiority as a player was quickly recognized by the other club members, who threw off their yoke, and much to Mr. Brown's chagrin, he was compelled to play second fiddle.

Lasker's Chess Magazine, 1905.

THE MARTYRDOM OF THE PROBLEMIST

By G. Legentil

M. Legentil has the droll knack, variously ascribed to Frenchmen, mathematicians, or certain types of lunatics, of taking a plausible idea and pursuing it with remorseless consistency to such lengths that

*the consequences become unforeseeably weird. This playful trait is
nicely illustrated in his fantasy about what might happen to a problemist who insists on transferring his hobby to the realm of over-the-
board play.*

The game was of the greatest importance for me; should I succeed
in winning I became the champion of my club. Unfortunately, I was
Black. And I play badly with Black. My opponent sat down and with
an amiable nod he beckoned me to take my seat opposite him. At that
moment I took a heroic decision and challenging all accepted custom,
I sat down quietly on his left.

"But, sir," said my rival to the coveted title, "you are Black."

"I know, sir, but I don't believe that there is any law which compels
both players to sit opposite one another. What is not forbidden is
permissible. With your permission I shall play the Black pieces while
sitting on the White side."

"You will admit that this is contrary to common usage and nothing
can justify a decision so extraordinary, so uncalled for to say the least."

Clearly my adversary was getting heated and I tried to calm him
down.

"You must not believe, sir, that I am trying to be funny, but you
will understand my reasons and will appreciate their justice when I
tell you that I am a problemist."

"I don't see ..."

"I use a pocket chessboard when composing problems; you well
know that you can't turn around such a chessboard as you can an
ordinary board; the pieces would be upside down and they would be
very awkward to fit in the slots. Therefore, I always have the White in
front of me. In this position there are four pieces to the left of the
Black king. If I sit down opposite you as is usual, there would be only
three Black pieces to the left of my king, everything would be inverted,
out of line. I have in the course of years, made such a habit of playing
in this manner that I feel certain that I should lose with the Black
pieces next to me. I might castle with my queen and give unexpected
checks with my own king. I am sure you would not like to win

under such conditions. Ah! if we were both blindfold players the problem would be solved...."

"That's all very well, my dear sir, but we should both be perfectly ridiculous and I am not anxious to become the butt of the gallery. We would look as if we were playing a piano duet!"

Some guffaws—a little too pointed for my taste—followed this repartee.

The gallery were enjoying themselves.... Already two camps were being formed. The problemists and the solvers were on my side. I must admit that the majority were loud in support of my opponent.

This was a memorable evening in the annals of the club, but it did much harm to the reputation for calm and discretion which up to then the chessplayers enjoyed.

The customers in the café were amused, but looked with amazement at these maniacs, ordinarily so motionless and silent. Already, Émile, the waiter, was putting the chairs on the marble tops to clear up.

And the decisive game for the championship was not played that night and that's how matters stand at present.

I appeal to all chessplayers: on what authority can a player be compelled to sit opposite his opponent?

And I maintain, if necessary against the whole world, that as long as F.I.D.E. has not given a definite ruling in this controversy, freedom and self-determination must prevail.

British Chess Magazine, 1946.

PUNCH ON POSTAL CHESS

What we gain by being more systematic we lose by forfeiting some of our spontaneity. Trust Punch *to extract some chuckles from even this portentous trend.*

"I had always considered chess a game of pronounced taciturnity with about as much conversation involved as when Yorkshire play Lancashire at cricket"—writes a contributor to Punch, *extracts from whose article follow.*

I have been enlightened by a study of *Grieg's Code Book for Correspondence Players*. This contains two hundred and twelve numbered remarks to offer your opponent during the course of a postal game and is a happy cross between the Naval Code and a Continental phrase book. Apparently you append to your move the number of the remark you want to make, thus transforming the match into a spirited yet economical conversation piece. For, to quote the Introduction, "This code makes it possible for friendly messages to be sent by each player to the other without the risk of being surcharged postage." (I am not sure, however, that the essence of true friendliness is to be found in Message 195——"You forget to stamp your letter.")

The first section is headed "On Beginning a Game." If you are of a formal disposition you will probably select the first phrase: "Greetings! I hope we may have an enjoyable game." To which your courteous opponent will doubtless briefly respond "2" ("Thank you: I am glad you have a 'Code' Book!").

More frivolous players, into whose souls the true sanctity of chess has not yet entered, might prefer an exchange consisting of "1a" and "2a" ("Hi de hi!" and "Ho de ho!" respectively). I imagine it would be something of a solecism to answer "1" with "2a," and might even lead to an abrupt abandoning of the match on the plea of incompatibility.

In "Discussing Last Move," a note of irrelevance has crept in when the literary vanity of the correspondent impels him to inquire "21" ("What do you think of my reply?"). A cross-reference gives you the choice of three answers to this one, of which the least approving is "138" ("Search me!").

Self-esteem comes up again in "145," where the correspondent interrupts the game perfectly gratuitously to brag, "I am playing for the county." There is no prescribed answer, though the ready Coder might remark rather fawningly, "202" ("I am beginning to realize that you are a very great player").

Skimming rapidly through "Re Late Answer" ("Have you not again exceeded your time?"—a nasty one, that), "Various Questions" and "Various Answers," we come to a short stern piece on "Illegal Moves," culminating with the rather weak admonition, "You can't do that there 'ere." Here again one fails to sense the lofty solemnity of chess as we knew it at the White Rock Pavilion at Hastings.

The final sections are "On Termination," "Suspending Play," and "Oversight," the concluding phrase of the book being the rather pathetic one, "I know I shall lose but would like to play on. It is so interesting."

The only drawback to the "Code" book that I can see is that the conversation may grow slightly monotonous when the game is sliding along into the sixth or eighth month and all the phrases have been used up. I doubt if the most merry-hearted player could raise a smile when repetition set in and his opponent wittily remarked for the fifth time, "35" ("A poor move but 'mine own'").

Chess World, 1947.

THE FEMALE OF THE SPECIES
By H. D. Sheldon

Mrs. Sheldon's interesting comment on women as chessplayers was called forth by this passage from The Fireside Book of Chess:

"Every radio comedian and night-club wit has several entries in his card-index file about the possibility of a woman's becoming President of the United States. The idea that a woman might become our chess champion seems equally 'comical.'

"Yet both of these possibilities are less remote than they were in, say, 1930.... The chief obstacle to further popularization of chess among women is, paradoxically enough, the nature of the male ego. There cannot be many men who are capable of losing a game to a woman without turning purple with rage. We venture to predict that as soon as men learn to accept defeat more gracefully, more women will play chess and play it better. But when are men likely to start accepting defeat more gracefully?"

In regard to the "Women in Chess" piece in the December issue, I have often been puzzled by my own sex—and even by myself (I used to play at the Marshall Chess Club in the late '30s)—in relation to chess.

Sometimes I just decided that I was a temperamental, decadent weakling, and that those ten thousand women chessplayers one heard about in Russia were the real stuff. Since then I have aged a little, and, although I don't know any more than I did about the ten thousand lady Botvinniks, I have concluded that we are probably not so different. Counting myself as one of the more fluctuating temperaments, still I believe that I have observed a much greater tendency to a fluctuation in aggressiveness among women than among men. By aggressiveness, I don't mean just bad temper but that sustained tenacity of purpose that makes a person plan and dream and study, day in and day out, for the overthrow of an opponent's plans within a given sphere. Plus the sustained combative energy that is needed in tournaments.

Women have the mental agility, the interest in puzzles, the scientific spirit, the pleasure in intellectual beauty, and they have the energy to sustainedly move mountains, shovelful by shovelful, in making a garden or refining pitchblende—but they do not, I believe, have that sustained combativeness. Only at times, say, half the time, did I ever feel the compelling, hunting spirit that drives one to work doggedly in preparation for a tournament. The rest of the time, I simply enjoyed myself. You get men players like that, too, of course, but they do not chalk up great scores. And I think many women are like that.

Thus, while I appreciate the writer's kind words, I think that top women chessplayers will always be drawn from a small minority of women with a constant metabolic level characterized by—in a layman's concept—a high adrenaline output. Personally, I should imagine that this is a more hopeful situation for the future of civilization than if we were all Botvinniks. ... But you certainly are right about the men —I have seen 'em throw over table, board and all after losing.

Chess Review, 1951.

THE FEMININE VIEWPOINT
By Leonore Gallet

In response to an inquiry from Edward Lasker, a woman gifted out of the ordinary gives her views on chess. Her reply suggests the "eternal feminine": always the same, and always interesting!

Until I received your letter I had never considered why I liked chess. I just enjoyed playing it; perhaps because in chess at least, as distinguished from life, the queen is given greater freedom and power than the king.

Speaking seriously, the appeal probably stems from the fact that chess lets one enter a realm of fantasy in which one can carry out the things she dreams about without being hampered by the limitations imposed upon women in most fields of endeavor.

I don't consider it possible for any woman, though, to become a chessmaster. She won't be able to keep her mind on the game long enough without letting her thoughts wander. When she thinks of a beautiful move she is liable to think also about how beautiful she looks in making it. Then there is that sale she saw advertised! Oh, and so many other things!

You always say chess trains one to concentrate. I don't believe a word of it!

Chess for Fun and Chess for Blood.

TALES OF A WOODPUSHER: WOODPUSHER'S WOODPILE
By Fred M. Wren

Wren has written so many delightful pieces that it is difficult to find one's favorite; but I believe that the stories evoked by his chess sets are perhaps the most appealing of all his writings. Wren's genial indignation at Reshevsky's lack of a chess set reminds me of a story of du Mont's about a visit to Capablanca, with the great man bringing out a weird conglomeration of 32 tatterdemalion orphans. The only two pieces that matched were the White rooks—both lumps of sugar! In the good old days Reuben Fine had a worn pocket set with pieces so well-fingered as to be indistinguishable from each other. In disgust I christened them "Fine's monkeys," but he never went wrong when using the set.

Several years ago, just after the smoke had rolled away from the finale of a United States championship tournament, *Chess Review* published on its cover a photograph of the winner—Grandmaster Reshevsky. The photograph, posed in the champion's home, was scanned by thousands of other chess fans, I suppose, with the same intense scrutiny to which I subjected it. Chessplayers and fans are only human after all—press reports, cartoonists, and long-suffering wives to the contrary notwithstanding. We are interested in the minor details of where and how our chess idols live, even though the public relations branch of chessdom seems to have failed sadly in the dissemination of this kind of information. Hence the enthusiasm with which the chess world turned its collective bifocals upon this excellent study of the champion of the United States.

I suppose some fans were interested in the synthetic game which was set up on the board before him. One probably tried to figure out what and how many moves had been made to reach the pictured position. Another probably went over all Sammy's games in that tournament to see if he could identify any position in one of them with the one in the picture. Probably the ladies, after a casual glance at the board and pieces, looked more carefully at the background of the photograph to see if they could discern any evidence which might indicate that Mrs. Reshevsky was other than a perfect housekeeper. None of that stuff for me. I was interested in the set of pieces lined up on the board, and a brief examination of the picture caused me to give a mental cheer for our champion. No cumbersome imported set with a nine-inch king; no intricately carved ivory pieces; no fabulously expensive set with the White pieces of sterling silver and the Black of solid gold for Sammy! Just a common plastic set—exactly like one which I was using at that time—which retailed for about $6.50 f.o.b. New York. My heart warmed toward the new champ as I turned to the text of the magazine to find out what it was all about.

Then came the shock. After the conventional documentary report on the tournament results had been digested, I came to an item of information about the photograph on the cover. It told me, among other things, that the set in the picture was a prop, furnished by *Chess Review's* staff photographer, due to the fact that Reshevsky, the chess champion of the United States, and probably one of the three or four strongest players in the world, did not own a chess set. At first, I was stunned. I couldn't understand it. Gene Autry without a guitar? Could be. Roy Rogers without a horse? Possible. But Reshevsky without a chess set? Incredible. As well think of Humphrey Bogart without an automatic, or Betty Grable without—well, you see what I mean.

After the first shock, however, I accepted the irrefutable evidence, and I began to pity the guy. That's a laugh, of course, for a wood-pusher like me to be pitying a grandmaster. But I did, and I still do—even if he has acquired a set in the meantime. I'll explain what I mean.

As I write, there are ten chess sets within twenty feet of me. One of them belongs to my son. The other nine are mine, and I love every one of them—each one for a different reason. Let me tell you the stories of some of them.

For several years, I worked in the American Consulate in Rotterdam. One morning, the consul came in my office and asked if I would pay a cheer-up visit to an American veteran of World War I who was living in The Hague, and who was seriously sick. I found the veteran living with his sister and brother-in-law. He was receiving total disability compensation from the United States Veterans Administration. He had been gassed, not by the enemy, but through negligence in one of our training camps in the United States. His heart was seriously affected, and it was no secret to him, or to anyone familiar with his case, that he might die at any minute. The doctor had given him six months as a maximum—he couldn't hope for more than that.

He was born in Holland. He had emigrated to the United States in

1912, had become a naturalized citizen in 1917 and had enlisted in the Army in the same year. He had lived in Denver and, after being hospitalized out of the Army, he had returned to that city. He was a member of the American Legion Post there, which he claimed (I never bothered to confirm this) was the largest in the world. After a year or two of failing health in Denver, he decided to go back to Holland where his pension would serve the double purpose of supporting him better than it could in the United States and of being of substantial assistance to his sister's family budget. When I first met him in 1930, he had been in Holland for eight or nine years and was longing for a chance to speak and hear the English language.

On my first visit, he asked if I could play chess. When I said that I could, a volley of Dutch splattered off the four walls of the room; and, almost instantly, the sister appeared with a board and a set of pieces. We played a couple of games that day and, on each of my subsequent visits, we knocked off two or three games. We were just about equal in playing strength; so it was really fun. It was also encouraging to see that chess relaxed his grim tense attitude of waiting—so painfully apparent at other times. He began to get stronger; and, although the doctor did not revise his former estimate, the patient started taking little walks outside the house to which he had been confined for so long.

Shortly afterward, perhaps three months after I first met him, a message came to me in my office in Rotterdam that someone in a taxi on the street in front of the office would like very much to see me, and would I please go down, as he could not leave the car. I went down, and there was my chess-playing veteran. He was all dressed up, and there was some baggage on the rack of the taxi.

"Where the hell are you going?" I blurted.

He grinned. "The doctor tells me I'm going to die before I get to New York, but I know better. I'm sailing on the *Nieuw Amsterdam* tonight, and I'm going to Denver."

I started to argue with him, but he laughed at me. "Cut it out. I know what I'm doing. If I die on the boat—so what? If I die on the train between New York and Denver—so what? I've only got a month or two left anyway. *But,* if I can stick it out, so I can see Denver again—then I'll really die happy. My sister will get the insurance, and the Legion will bury me, and she won't have to fuss with that. So it's best all around. Don't you think so?"

What could I say? While I was saying it—silently and a bit mistily —he went on. "I called to say so long to you. You've been swell coming to see me, and I've enjoyed our chess games. Will you accept this gift to remember me by?"

And he held out the little varnished box which held, and still holds, the chess set with which we played so many hot games. When the *Nieuw Amsterdam* came back from that trip, I learned that he made it as far as New York all right, and that he had started the rail trip to Denver, confident that he would make that too. I hope he did, for he wanted to so desperately; but I never heard from him again. Nor have I forgotten him. Every few weeks I set up the pieces of the modest wooden set which he gave me and go over a game or two with them. As I do this, I am always able to visualize him clearly; sometimes as he used to look when lying in his sickbed, craning his neck to see the pieces on the board beside him; but usually—and preferably—as he looked in the taxi that afternoon in Rotterdam as he gave me the set, bade me farewell and set his course confidently for Denver. That's the story of one of my sets.

Chess Review of March, 1936, carried a story under the title, "Vacation in London,"* explaining the circumstances under which I acquired another of the sets which I prize so highly.

So there's another of my sets. Just a cheap wooden affair, with the varnish pretty well worn off most of the pieces. The White king's cross has vanished somewhere in the shuffle of the years; and, when you plunk a Black knight down in an enthusiastic fork of White's queen and rook, the horse's head and the base of the piece are very likely to part company. Yet the set represents my first incursion into international play, and it will always be treasured as a trophy of the screwiest and longest match of my career, and perhaps of all time.

* See p. 28—F. R.

After all, the Labourdonnais-McDonnell match went to only 85 games, counting 13 useless draws.

Most parents are willing to admit that, although they know they should not show favoritism among their children, there are nevertheless moments in which one of their offspring stands a bit higher in their emotional evaluation than another. I have to confess the same feeling toward one of my chess sets. Since the others, being inanimate and inarticulate, are supposedly without the power to harbor resentment or to protest against my partiality, it is probably in order to admit and to explain my preference.

Allow me to use the movies' flashback technique to set the scene for you.

In 1849, one Nathaniel Cook registered with the appropriate authorities in England a design for a set of chessmen, substantially the same as what is now known as the Staunton design. This registration, valid for only three years, was never renewed. On August 11, 1852, the English master, Howard Staunton, made a deal with Nathaniel Cook, authorizing the latter to use a facsimile of Staunton's signature as a trademark to attach to the boxes in which his sets were sold. In 1900, the firm established by Nathaniel Cook was absorbed by John Jaques and Son, Ltd., of London, who continued to turn out excellent and expensive wooden chess sets in boxes each of which was stamped with the Staunton signature trademark.

In September, 1937, *Chess,* the leading chess magazine in England, carried an advertisement reading in part as follows: "Genuine Staunton chessmen. We are prepared to stake our reputation on the statement that these sets are identical with those offered by the best dealers in the trade at prices 20-50 per cent higher."

In November, 1937, Messrs. Jaques issued a legal writ claiming the following: 1. An injunction to restrain *Chess* from passing off sets of chessmen not of Jaques' manufacture as chessmen of Jaques' manufacture by advertising such as "Genuine Staunton Chessmen" or "Staunton Chessmen"; 2. Delivery up of all labels, leaflets, and other advertising matter, the use of which would be a breach of the injunction prayed for; 3. Damages; 4. Further or other relief; 5. Costs.

The fight was on, and was to rage through the English courts for three years. Jaques' case was based on the claim that the name, "Genuine Staunton" or "Staunton," indicated chessmen of their manufacture exclusively. The defense put up by *Chess* was that the names quoted indicated chessmen of a certain pattern or design and nothing more. Most of the witnesses for Jaques were dealers and retailers of chess sets who testified that their experience had led them to understand that "Staunton" or "Genuine Staunton" chessmen were those manufactured by Jaques. An imposing array of defense witnesses, including Sir George Thomas, Dr. Max Euwe, L. Prins and other leading players and chess authorities, testified that to them the quoted words indicated merely a standard design and that, in responding to *Chess's* advertisement, they would not expect to receive a set manufactured by Jaques.

A decision for Jaques in May, 1939, was appealed to a higher court, and in March, 1940, findings of the lower court were reversed by the Appellate Branch. It was held that the evidence had clearly demonstrated that the words, "Genuine Staunton" or "Staunton," signified nothing of the origin of chessmen so designated but referred only to a general pattern or design, as claimed by *Chess*.

In May, 1942, *Chess* carried a different advertisement which interested me. They invited inquiries about used sets, saying they had them in all materials and in all styles and designs. I had seen and admired a set which came from Denmark and was anxious to get one something like it. I wrote describing the set that I wanted as Staunton in piece design, but with the bases larger and the pieces shorter than the conventional proportions generally associated with Staunton sets. I think I described the pieces as squat and dumpy, as if they had been subjected to pressure from above while in their formative stage, with the result that each piece had been forced down into itself.

Back came a letter from *Chess,* from which I now quote: "I have a 'stubby' little set in nut ivory which answers fairly well to your description. The only trouble is, it has great sentimental value to me being a set produced in evidence in my great lawsuit with Jaques. It bears on the box the official imprint of the courts showing this. The great collector and authority, Alexander Hammond swore on oath in the trial that this set was at least 150 years old, thus pre-dating the foundation of Jaques, his predecessor, Nathaniel Cook, who first registered the design, in 1849, and Howard Staunton, himself—although the set is recognizably of what is now known as the Staunton design. It may safely be said that this set played a great part in winning the famous legal battle, and I am not anxious to part with it. You may, however, *if you are frightfully keen,* have it for—"

The underlining was his, the price was steep, but the set is now mine, and the editor of *Chess* need not worry about his little set falling into unappreciative hands. It is my favorite set, from a practical as well as a sentimental standpoint. In spite of its history and basic material, it is not a set to be placed on a shelf at home or in a club just to be looked at and admired. It is a real *playing* set, the one I like to have available at all times for use in going over published games or for banging off six or eight hot games whenever a friend drops in for an evening of chess. It is unimpressive to look at, with its $1\frac{3}{4}$-inch kings, its $1\frac{1}{2}$-inch queens, and its pawns just slightly shorter than the $1\frac{1}{4}$-inch rooks. The maroon staining of the Black pieces has worn through in places, and the White pieces have attained the mellowed, yellowish patina of frequently-handled old ivory.

But it is a friendly set and one which I like to believe is surrounded by an aura to which each of the thousands of good games, in which it must have participated before coming to me, has contributed its share. An aura composed of everything which is good about chess and the people who play it and which has become so saturated with these qualities throughout the years that it cannot absorb any more without shedding a few of the old ones to make room for the new. How else can I explain the inspired strategy and tactics at my command when I am using this set? One of my chess-opponent friends has a less romantic explanation. He was ever a scoffer, however, and so no credence should be given to his claim that the set was carved from the teeth of a sacred crocodile by some dusky devotee of voodooism and that its inherent malevolence has in no way been sweetened by a recent and liberal application of the well-known Wren luck. What can he expect, when he is playing me with a set which can call upon its old friends—Philidor, Labourdonnais, McDonnell, Staunton, among others—for inspiration and guidance of its new and appreciative owner?

I have other sets, some of which I bought because of their looks, and others which have been given to me. There is a large club-size wooden set which came to me about six months ago as a legacy from a dear friend who learned his chess while attending college in Boston in the days when Pillsbury, Barry, and Franklin K. Young were reaching the heights of chess maturity. He knew all three well and was present when Barry announced the famous mate in 13 against Pillsbury.

Another set was given to me during the war by the chief steward on a small ship which called regularly at Halifax. Every time he came in, he would visit the club for a few games if he could get away from the ship. Sometimes he would give me a call, and I would go on board for a few games and a drink (or a few drinks and a game), or perhaps he would come to my home for a few of each. On one visit, he showed me this set which a passenger had given to him.

He said, "I couldn't refuse it, but I don't need it. Why don't you take it? If you ever have a crowd in and need an extra set you can use this."

As he had just remarked, I couldn't refuse it, and I couldn't tell him that I didn't need it any more than he did. So I took it, thinking that I would pass it on to some welfare organization. A few days later, a top-secret rumor told us that his ship had been torpedoed off Iceland. Weeks later, it was confirmed officially that the ship had been lost with only one survivor. He was not the chief. So the boxed set has reposed on my desk ever since, as a memento of a genial woodpusher who never hesitated to grab a proffered pawn.

I have a little leather pocket set, with flat celluloid pieces, which was a Christmas gift to me about ten years ago and which is one of my most prized possessions. I can almost hear you say, "So what?" Well, I don't pretend to know the theological implications which have caused some of my friends to call me a liar when I told them where I got the set. I don't even care about them. All I know is that a good friend, and one of my bitterest chess club rivals, came to my door on Christmas Day and gave me this set. How do I know why a Jewish rabbi would do a thing like that? The point is that he did and that I am proud of the gift and the spirit of friendship which prompted it.

Now you see why the news that Reshevsky didn't have a chess set of his own shocked me. I hope that the foregoing has also explained my feeling of pity for him. I have told you the stories of a few of my sets. I have tried to show you that each of them really meant something to me—that each one possesses a sentimental value far in excess of its possible market value. Call it what you may: pride of possession, miserly instincts, unhealthy sentimentality; for one reason or another I love every one of my sets and feel that, through their possession and through my appreciation of the sentimental ties which bind them to me, my life has been greatly enriched.

If these nine sets, which probably would not bring $100 at any auction, have done so much for me, just think of the collection which Sammy could have amassed since he first toured the United States as a prodigy of nine. How prosaic and limited and unromantic have been my travels as compared with his. How great a gap between the planes on which our respective chess experiences have taken place. My games have been with other woodpushers—his with the greatest players in the world. My greatest claim to fame is a fluky draw with Yanofsky, whereas he has battled on even terms or better with world champions, and he has been knocking off masters and grandmasters for nearly twenty years. Wouldn't you think that when he took a pal home he would like to be able to point out his sets? He could say, "Here's the set I used to beat Euwe in the AVRO Tournament," or "This is the one the Maharajah gave me, after winning the tournament at Magidoor," or "Here's a little thing I picked up in a shop on Cornhill." But, no. If he wants to play a game with a friend, or to check up on Fine's latest analysis in *Chess Review,* he has to run over to the Y, or to the City Club, and borrow a set. Poor guy!

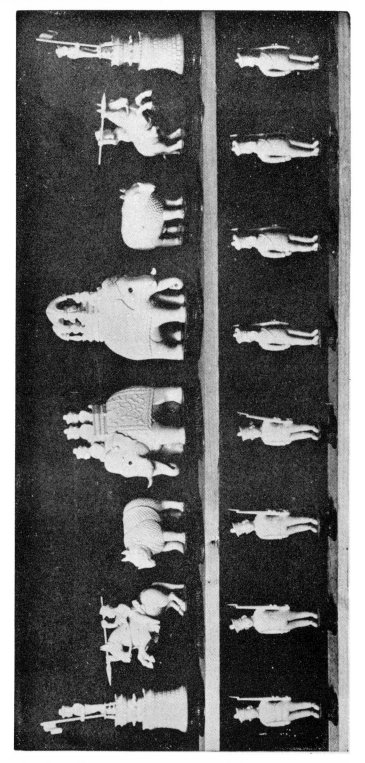

Delhi Chess Set (see 1, page 303).

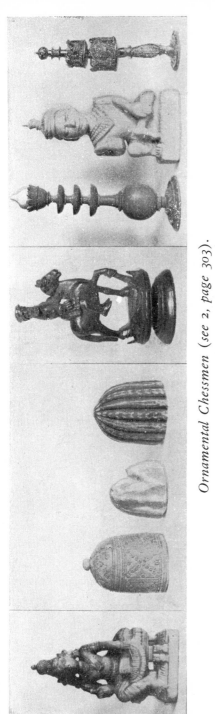

Ornamental Chessmen (see 2, page 303).

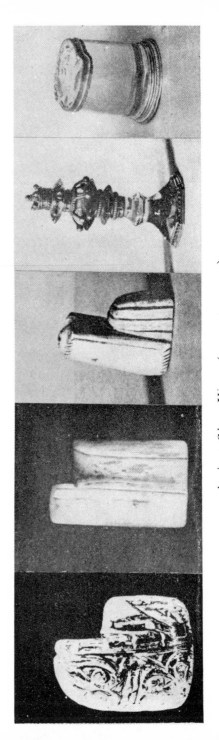

Ancient Chess Kings (see 3, page 303).

CHESS IN A KNIGHTCLUB

By Bruce Hayden

The idea of playing chess in a nightclub is all the more timely as Billy Rose is considered a connoisseur of chess as well as chest.. Our swankiest nightspots may soon be featuring chessboards with diamond-encrusted squares, chess pieces made of precious metals and dressed in ermine and mink, and the kings and queens wearing priceless jewels in their crowns.

Pass under the winking lights of London's Piccadilly Circus, turn left up Shaftesbury Avenue, then left again up Wardour Street past the offices of the big movie corporations, and you're in Soho. This is one of the bohemian quarters of the world's biggest city where every race, color, and creed foregathers to work together and play together. Where money rubs shoulders with poverty. Where a Hungarian shoe shop is neighbors with a Chinese laundry or an Italian wine bar. Where the cabs wheel and stop and the doors of the foreign eating-houses blink open and shut and music leaks out from a hundred hidden corners.

Meard Street is where we shall find Harold Lommer's club. It's a wide, dim passageway, and we come to a door with a brass plate, engraved "Mandrake Club." We enter and descend a winding, carpeted stairway. A uniformed attendant swings open more doors, and we are inside. All is noise and movement. *This can't be a chess club!* At the far side of the room, guitarists strum while one sings *O Ungrateful Heart* in Italian. Food is being carried to tables. In the rooms beyond, drinks are being passed over bars. Pretty girls are sitting with their escorts. At one table, a newspaperman is telling of his experiences in Korea. At another, a group of serious businessmen talk earnestly. *But where is the chess?*

"Chess?" says a blond, youthful-looking man, "Through here." And, as he leads us through to another room, we hear voices intoning the traditional chant of the skittles players with a clocked bell timing rapid-transit at the further end.

Yea, verily, brother, there's certainly chess here all right!

The room is filled with masters, enthusiastic amateurs, and, of course, the patzers. W. Winter plays here. So do I. Konig, E. Klein, and Gabriel Wood (who currently is in the running for the finals of the World Correspondence Chess Championship). Even Herman Steiner from faraway Los Angeles is a member and has played his favorite Schliemann Defense to the Ruy with these black pieces. It was in this room, too, that Grandmaster Ossip Bernstein won the Club's international masters tourney in 1949.

How comes it that a nightspot finances and stages events for drinkers of cups of cold coffee—when they remember?

Q. E. D. Our youthful-looking friend is Harold Lommer. Throughout the chess world, Harold is known as a chess poet—a composer of beautiful endgames. His book, *1234 Modern Endgame Studies,* is a world-famous classic. Harold, in fact, is just another guy who can't get chess out of his system.

In 1947, Harold went into partnership with one Boris Watson, a fellow addict. Boris, a gentle, scholarly man of precise speech, is a tall, majestic figure of 20 stone who suffers from wood-thumpingitis of the right arm—he's an enthusiastic wood-thumper and likes nothing better than to moor himself solidly against a chess table and play quick skittles. Harold gives Boris the odds of 10 stone and a knight, and it wasn't long before a board and men appeared among the club's tables, near the orchestra. More players as mysteriously appeared and, in less than four beats to the bar, boards, men, and clocks were collected, a chess room set aside and a chess team formed.

The boy and gal art students who use the club walls to exhibit their paintings quickly took to the game. It was noted that hypermodern schools soon adopted Alekhine's Defense while the classicists favored the Giuoco Piano and considered even castling queen-side slightly flashy—perhaps actually in bad taste. Currently, the Picasso school is experimenting with the double fianchetto of the rooks.

Last year, the club entered the British National Chess Club Championship and reached the semi-finals. (Cambridge University was the victor.) This year, the team has entered again, and the members hold firm to the belief that Chess Through Joy—plus a few masters at the top boards—will overcome those from the Halls of Learning.

When the Mandrake Club announced that its international tourney would be held on its premises and that Grandmaster Bernstein, Winter, Golombek, and other masters would compete, eyebrows were lifted. "A chess tourney amidst all that noise, talk and music? Impossible!" But an oasis of silence was sealed off in the chess room, and the tourney was duly played.

Bernstein, who flew in from Paris, won as expected: his only loss being to Winter. It was during the critical stage of that game that another crisis took place.

A gentleman, flushed with the good things at the bar, appeared in the room and unsteadily made his way over to the board. When there, he intently eyed the players and the position. The room suddenly became electric, and the silence, brittle. The irreverence for the hallowed game by many of the children of Bacchus is well-known, and an urgent S. O. S. brought two breathless, uniformed attendants on the run. As they appeared at the door, the alcoholic one swayed around. His lips moved to speak. He raised his hand. The silence was about to be broken.

"Ssh!" he said.

Then he swayed around again and continued to goggle solemnly at the game. Eventually, when Bernstein turned over his king, he unsteadily made his way from the room with a look of infinite despair on his face—to recuperate at the bar.

The Swiss have contributed much to chess, and Harold, who was born in England of Swiss stock, tells how, after learning the moves as a boy, he was fascinated by the beautiful combination of the great Zukertort in his famous game with Blackburne in 1883.

Zukertort became his hero. So, when Harold learned that it was in London he died—he was carried from Simpson's Divan to Charing Cross Hospital nearby—Harold searched the big city for his grave.

He found it, neglected and overgrown with weeds, in a cemetery in Kensington, a genteel quarter. Shocked, he spent two afternoons in clearing and trimming the plot, and since then a fine afternoon is likely to make Harold feel restive. Before long, he is on his way to Kensington with his gardening outfit to keep the grave of the great man in shape. His task done, Harold will sit around in the sun for a while with his pocket set, and some of his best conceptions have come during these moments.

He is also a strong player, but this he denies sadly, though he admits that much practice in his youth with Emanuel Lasker taught him a lot. As a youngster, back in the 1920's he was in the habit of showing his compositions to the chessists who gathered at the Vienna Café near Leicester Square.

One day he set up a rook study for one of them and, after a time, said, "Don't waste your energy trying to solve it," and volunteered to show the solution. "Solve it!" was the astonished reply. "I solved it minutes ago. I'm trying to cook it!" The speaker was the great Emanuel Lasker himself, and that was how they met. Lasker played rarely in those days, but he would watch the games of others, especially those of Harold. One day, after the youngster had brought off a brilliant sacrificial finish, he remarked: "Lommer, you will always be a born tactician." At the time, this was considered high praise, but Harold thinks otherwise. Whenever he brings off a good finish—and he is likely to beat anyone—he'll say sadly that it wouldn't have worked against correct, positional play. "Lasker once said to me," he'll add, " 'Lommer, you will always be ... ' "

A few years on from his first meeting with Lasker, back in 1925, the 21-year-old composer was picked to face Alekhine in one of his exhibition games at Geneva.

He shook that great master and the onlookers with a variation which left him with a won game. He shook the onlookers much more later by letting His Greatness get away with a draw.

Ask him about it, and he'll say: "A positional player would have rammed home the win. Lasker once said to me ... "

But he can't get chess out of his system or resist a nice sacrifice.

Nightly he plays a skittle or two or sits down to coach a group of keen youngsters.

To the patzers, he concedes rook odds, and the games are weird and wonderful to watch. Unlike most odds-givers, Harold is always prepared to steer for the ending and for his king to venture out front and run the risk of a hail of threatened mates, to pick up the wood and win.

Meanwhile the pretty gals pass by, the plates rattle, the Italian crooner implores the customers to *Return to Sorrento* and a voice from the chess room cries: Check!

Chess Review, 1951.

STALEMATE!!
By G. Legentil

It would be a pity if the reader, misled by M. Legentil's delightful foolery, were to get the idea that there are really two sides to the argument. The fact that Black has overstepped the time limit transcends all further argument. Or—on second thought—does it?! The man makes one's head spin!

My game was lost—impossible to stop the advance of my opponent's three connected passed pawns! The most reasonable as well as most sporting course was for me to resign. This was the position—

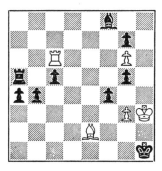

White to play

I was in despair. This hopeless game meant for me the loss of the club championship.

I examined the position yet once more and it suddenly dawned on me that there was an outside chance of bringing about a stalemate. My opponent was very short of time and possibly, with a little luck, he might fall into the trap. True, it would save half a point but not my championship, alas. For that I needed a whole point.

Accordingly, I played

   1 B-R5   ....

My opponent seemed surprised and instantly played ...

   1 ....   P-R6

My second move ..

   2 R-Q6   ....

played without a moment's hesitation brought the automatic reply ...

   2 ....   BxR

I heaved a sigh of relief and played ...

   3 P-N4   ....

Black had made a big blunder in playing 2 ... BxR; but how can you avoid making mistakes with only one minute left for three moves?

My opponent, with his head between his hands, carefully if belatedly scrutinized the position.

I was watching the clock. The flag rose and fell while my opponent was still seeking the right reply. I was saved. I was scoring a whole point and was still the champion!

After three or four minutes my rival said: "Sir, I congratulate you. You have managed to engineer a very pretty stalemate position. I thoughtlessly fell into the trap, but I was so hardpressed for time! And so the game is drawn. You are stalemated."

"I beg your pardon," I objected, "the game is not drawn! I claim a win, for you have largely exceeded the time limit!"

"But, my dear sir, whether I have exceeded the time limit or not is of no importance in the circumstances. I have no move to circumvent the stalemate. Whether I play the rook, king, bishop or pawn, you are and remain stalemated. The game is a draw whether I make a move or not, there is no alternative. You surely would not claim a win when the game is and can only be a draw!"

"Your argument would be unanswerable, my dear sir, if you had in good time made one of the numerous moves at your disposal. Did you refrain from playing because you had seen the unavoidable stalemate or because you took too long to realize that the position was drawn? How could I know? I must rest my claim on existing regulations which quite clearly secure me the win."

As could be expected, the gallery took a hand. Older players took my part, a rule is a rule and made to be applied in all cases. But the younger ones took the opposite view: the position is quite exceptional and regulations have not provided for it. In respecting the rule you respect the letter but not the spirit of the law. It is absurd to claim a win for White in a drawn position and equally absurd to say that Black has lost when he cannot possibly lose whatever move he plays. Common sense points to a draw.

There was a fine hullabaloo, but after interminable arguments no finality was reached.

And here is another knotty point for the F. I. D. E. to decide.

In the meantime I am claiming the game!

British Chess Magazine, 1948.

A GAME OF CHESS
By Basil G. Wood

No longer, alas, is it correct to say that the charm of chess lies in its utter uselessness. In a war-ridden world even chess has its useful aspects. In this and the next sketch we see some of the wartime uses for chess.

Two men are playing chess—serious, concentrated. What a psychologist would call their "focus of consciousness" is confined within the four sides of a flat plane marked out in squares, and occupied by wooden figures of varying shape. It is a minute two-dimensional world, for the third dimension, height, disappears when viewed from above and the clock on the mantelpiece indicating the passage of time, the fourth dimension, ticks away the minutes unnoticed by them.

Such is their concentration that the greater and realer world around them is but on the fringe of their conscious minds—the comfortably furnished room with its thick carpet; the fire burning cosily in the hearth; the thick curtains covering the windows, against which rain and wind drive furiously—and a door communicating with an inner room, where matters of great moment are in dangerous progress.

They are hardly aware of these things; at least one of them is not, and it is the main object of the other to confine his attention to the board, lest he should be disturbed by any stray sound that may filter in from beyond that door. So the other's "focus of consciousness" is somewhat less limited, and his concentration less complete, so that he is at a disadvantage, which has already landed him in difficulties, as his ear automatically strains to catch any telltale sound.

He is aware that there is a safe in that room, and that there are secret plans and drawings in that safe; plans for the construction of some mysterious engine, Hitler's secret weapon, for the destruction of Great Britain. They must be photographed, these plans, that this infernal machine may be dealt with before it comes into action. And two daring men, one dropped by parachute with the necessary apparatus, are making this desperate attempt while the attention of the German officer-in-charge is being kept down to this game of chess.

This second player is myself, a humble middle-aged tutor, engaged before the war to coach the son of a French family. I am of neutral nationality, but strongly attached to the family, and to the Allied cause, having been educated in England.

When the enemy occupied this château in the Pas-de-Calais, the family were relegated to the servants' quarters and given the privilege of attending to the needs of their unwelcome guests, who made themselves comfortable in the principal rooms.

Strange things were going on in the vicinity, secret operations on a considerable scale, involving the laying of railway lines and the wiring off of a large area.

It had been decided from the first that an attitude of seeming submission and co-operation, though hard to maintain, was likely to prove of more value to the cause in the long run than outward resistance. This proved to be correct.

One evening the German commandant entered our quarters with some demand, and found me playing chess with my pupil. He chanced to be in a genial mood, and suggested a game with himself. I complied, and an evening game became quite a regular custom. It provided him with an hour of relaxation from his strenuous duties—it provided us with a means to checkmate him while he was on the spot, so that the sentries, who were always posted when he was out, were relaxed.

How the entry into this room was to be effected I did not know. It was best that I should not. I supposed it would be from the roof, through the one window There was no other entrance. My job was to keep the enemy occupied. I was but a pawn in the greater game, where the two knights were operating, but the success of their maneuver depended upon my keeping my position.

Usually I can beat the German, but it is not politic to win often. Now, however, I am in real difficulties, owing to lack of complete concentration. I have got my pawns in a line which blocks my own free movement without hindering his, and I have lost a bishop by a careless move.

I glance at the clock. Barely a quarter of an hour has elapsed since the game started, and I have undertaken to keep him occupied for an hour. Already his attack has developed strongly. He has me in an awkward corner with most of my pieces immobile, while his are well co-ordinated. He has forced my king to move, so that I cannot castle and bring my king rook to bear.

Chessmen are like human beings. They need handling and understanding. Their material forms are immaterial, if you will excuse the play upon words, being merely outward symbols of inward potentialities which must have scope—the bishop with diagonal powers; the rook rectangular; the knight tricky and uncertain, ever changing his mind, able to overleap obstacles—like my opponent. None of my main pieces seems to be able to employ its potentialities freely. There is that line of my own pawns obstructing them all. Very bad staff work!

I seem to hear a slight sound of movement beyond that door, or is it my imagination? I look anxiously at my opponent. He, intent on his move, has not noticed it, anyway. I breathe again. He makes his move, and awaits my reply, sitting back and smiling confidently. I can see that he has his next move ready. He will not take time to consider it, unless my counter obviates it. I must not be too long. Already he is tapping the table with the fingers of his outstretched hand, a sign of impatience, dangerous as affording him time to relax his concentration.

With an effort I withdraw my attention from the outside world. I shut it out. Ah! I see what it is. I must do something, and quickly. How can I meet it? A pawn advanced will get in his way, and will also give my queen an opening to get into the field of play, but it leaves my king rather more exposed. Still I must try it. There is nothing else. It works! for the moment. He has to think again, to adjust his plan, and he takes time over it, giving me a chance to develop some plan of my own. For the moment I have staved off disaster, and see possibilities, if only he makes a certain move! He does! and I get my queen in position to attack. Check! His king must move, and I get his knight, the pivot of his attack.

We are more equal now, though my position is too exposed, but I have escaped from a precarious situation. He is deep in thought, and taking his time.

Heaven above! What's that? A sound from the outside world, quite distinct this time, a sharp metallic sound from beyond that door, as if force had been used on something that had suddenly given way. I look up at him. Has he noticed it? Thank God! He is still gazing fixedly at the board. What a relief!

He moves.

I have not anticipated that! I don't like it. My attention had been taken off for the moment, and I had not foreseen the danger of my last move. It gives an opening, and he has not missed it. My plan of attack collapses, and I must bring my queen back to a defensive position.

I am unnerved, and I have made another blunder, and a big one this time He does not hesitate. He checks me with his remaining knight, lying craftily in ambush, at the same time threatening my queen, whom I have inadvertently placed in a position of danger. The queen must go. It is a serious loss! Can I now hope to hold out; I glance at the clock. Forty-five minutes have now elapsed. Can I last another quarter of an hour? Confident of victory, he is taking less time over his moves, now.

My position is hopeless, but victory lies, not in winning, but in postponing defeat as long as possible. Looking at the board, I cannot see how I can survive for more than three moves. I might create a diversion if I could free my blockaded king rook. The pawn blocking his exit must go. I push it forward, threatening his bishop. The square is doubly covered by his men, and he takes it. I pause to think, and move the rook two squares. He is considering this for a moment, when there comes another sound from beyond the door, quite clear and definite this time, as of the shutting or opening of a window. He can hardly miss it!

"Ach, what is that!" he exclaims.

He rises and goes to the door, while I hold my breath in anxiety.

He turns the handle and pushes the door open—darkness and quiet within. He turns up the light and looks round. Thank Heaven! Nothing seems to be amiss.

They must have completed their task, and made their exit through the window, the closing of which disturbed us. What if they had been a minute later?

My opponent looks round for a minute, while my heart stands still. Seeing nothing out of place, he returns to his seat, leaving the light on, and the door ajar.

"You heard nothing?" he asks sharply.

I do not trust my voice to reply at once. I affect a fit of coughing to clear my throat. Then—"I did hear something shake. With a wind like this, it is not surprising."

He sits down and looks at the board.

"My move, I think, unless you wish to resign. You have little chance."

"No," I reply, still a little huskily. "Like the British, I fight to the last ditch."

Even now time is of value, to enable them to get clear.

There are two ways in which he can finish me off, as I see it. The one takes only three moves; the other, a little more spectacular, affords a chance for further delay. He is not the man to take the more round-about way, but his attention has been distracted and he takes the latter course, which gives me time to move my rook into action, attacking his queen. It is futile and suicidal, but he dies in a good cause, though he may not know it. Many have sacrificed themselves in this war, and we wonder why the good God should permit it. We do not see far ahead.

As I put out my hand to make my move, he says: "You are nervous, my friend, your hand shakes. You do not take your defeat with equanimity."

The rook is taken, but not before he has checked the king, and caused protraction, and it is nearly ten minutes before the final move places me *hors de combat*. The game has lasted well over the promised hour.

As I gather up the pieces and put them in the box, I try to conceal the triumph which I feel and leaving the room I bid him a dejected good night.

This story was told by one of the many thousands who regained their liberty when the victorious British* armies at last drove the hated enemy out of France.

The sequel to the episode which he narrates was that a few days later a British bomber force had come over and blasted the whole place, including the residence, into ruins, destroying the preparations which were being made for that which might well have proved our undoing.

He had been existing where and how he could in the meantime, and was in a pitiable condition, but he was full of pride at the humble service he had been able to do towards the Allied cause.

* Thus Mr. Wood's text. But "Allied" seems more courteous—and more accurate.—F.R.

How the principal actors had achieved their object, he was unable to say, as he had not seen them again before the final blow fell, which rendered him and his hostess homeless.

British Chess Magazine, 1946.

CHESS IN AN R.A.F. PRISONER OF WAR CAMP
By F. A. O'Malley

Readers of Stefan Zweig's famous story The Royal Game *will recall how a prisoner in the hands of the Gestapo occupied himself with chess to stave off madness. For many a wartime prisoner, chess, when it was available, must have been equally precious.*

The greatest of the very few pleasures left in life to the P.O.W. was in the form of sport, and it was this very important item which decided the make or break of the newly-arrived prisoner. In the early days of P.O.W. life, sporting activity was not organized; on the contrary, it was a very casual way of defeating acute boredom and the consequent breaking of morale.

In R.A.F. P.O.W. camps this state of affairs did not last very long. First football, then rugby, theatricals, bridge, etc., became highly organized, as the master of each art arrived as a guest of the Third Reich.

Chess enjoyed the most sensational transition of all, as before the master of this art arrived, chess was merely a means of passing the weary hours in locked barracks until lights out. When he did arrive in Stalag Luft 1, I had the good fortune to come in immediate contact with him as he lived in the same barracks. He was by name Novotney, a Czech, and from the day of his arrival chess enjoyed a great boost in genuine popularity. The fascination for this game became one of Stalag's miracles as the general theory and more exacting features of the game were expounded in novel, excitable English by the Czech. His first lecture on the game was to a small group of fans in the barracks, and by introducing the mysteries of recording a game, as his first subject, he enslaved us to the game there and then.

We were then encouraged to carry on playing chess in a casual way as before, but to record our games. This led to a systematic check on the amount of benefit we received from his lectures and on our progress as reasonable chessplayers. When our orders for Stalag-made chessmen were fulfilled by the camp craftsmen this system of chess education became widespread. A committee was eventually formed to control all chess matters such as tourneys, barracks matches, individual challenge matches, and playing rules.

The blow to chess fell suddenly; Novotney was moved from the camp to Stalag Luft 3. Chess was now in danger of losing some of its previous vigor, but the keenness and hard work of a few chess enthusiasts did not allow this.

The arrival of one by name Brunet, a Canadian, pushed the standard of chess quite out of our reach—he was the master of them all. The pioneer work of Novotney faded before the spectacular displays of this new prisoner. He became extremely popular in the chess world for his modesty and charming manner. Notwithstanding his shabby treatment at the hands of the Gestapo, he commenced to work hard in the interest of chess; this included patient tuition and week-end simultaneous displays (16 boards). He gave me the honor of organizing and introducing the Stalag correspondence chess between compounds. This was carried out by inter-compound communication via the camp ration party. He also introduced a ladder tourney which became very popular; this was followed by the introduction of Kriegspiel, but it did not have a chance to flourish, as the cessation of hostilities rudely interrupted all further play.

The high spot in the chess history was the important part it played in an escape bid.

It happened one day in the Stalag workshop. The German interpreter, who was a keen chessplayer, was challenged to a game by a P.O.W. The German accepted the challenge without any hesitation, as, no doubt, he wished to defend the Fatherland somehow, against this arrogant Englander. The game had not been in progress very long, when the German guard became an interested spectator, as, no doubt, he wished to witness *Sieg für Deutschland* at last, if only over the chessboard. The result was as expected, however, and quite fair —one British officer missing. So chess in a P.O.W. camp, whether played poorly or with skill, was in many ways a great benefit to the P.O.W.

British Chess Magazine, 1947.

The Golden Age

CHECK!

By T. H. Chetwynd

Her king he reigned; his queen was she,
Although not e'en a knight was he:
They in no castle dwelt in state,
And yet a bishop did them mate!

The wife once running short of cash,
Approached her spouse with speed most rash—
"Another check I'll need today,
Wherewith for household needs to pay."

"Another check!" her husband cried;
"Too far my patience you have tried;
It's 'check, check, check!' for evermore,
'Tis time extravagance was o'er!"

Then spoke the wife in somber tone—
"One thing at least you'll surely own;
If 'tis not 'check, check, check' to be,
It must be 'pawn, pawn, pawn,' you see!"

Chess, 1936.

LABOURDONNAIS PLAYS MCDONNELL

By G. H. Diggle

The four-months' encounter of eighty-five games between these two colorful figures was really the first match for the world championship. But that is something that can be realized only from the perspective of later events. There has always been universal agreement, I believe, that these two masters were the greatest of their time, but there were no rules for the handling of such a contest, and even the very concept of a world championship was still a thing of the future. The high level of the play, and the enthusiasm that it aroused, had a marked effect on future competition and on the establishment of standards of playing strength. While there has never been any doubt that the better man won, the valiant and ingenious resistance of his opponent has always equally evoked admiration. Labourdonnais has never lacked for wholehearted and even exaggerated praise; but the best proof of his genius, I believe, is the way he hammered at McDonnell's weak play in the Queen's Gambit and the Sicilian Defense. In this respect the brilliant Frenchman revealed a mature understanding of the game which was far ahead of his time.

Exactly one hundred years have passed since these memorable matches were fought out at the Westminster Chess Club. Unlike the Staunton-St. Amant contest ten years later, they did not greatly attract the attention of the outside world. But the splendor of the actual games produced by Labourdonnais and McDonnell made a deep impression on the then limited number of chessplayers capable of appreciating them. "Those with the intellect to understand" realized the difference in caliber between these struggles and all that had ever gone before. George Walker, who had regarded Philidor as unapproachable, now wrote: "I unhesitatingly pronounce the Labourdonnais-McDonnell matches to be the finest series of games, actually played, on record." A century of unbounded chess activity has since passed away—and there are many today who think that Walker's words are still as true as when he wrote them.* They have been echoed by great masters and experienced critics of every generation since his own—Howard Staunton, Paul Morphy, W. N. Potter and H. J. R. Murray are unanimous. Even Dr. Lasker, that austere abominator of loose praise, permits himself to record, in his recent great work, that the Labourdonnais-McDonnell games were "hard games," and that Labourdonnais was "an extraordinary genius."

In 1834 both masters were, as Mongredien tells us, in the prime life and at the zenith of their powers. "But there was this difference. The French champion came over from Paris flushed with a thousand triumphs, and having defeated every· rival at home, felt assured of an easy victory in England. On the other hand, McDonnell had only recently emerged from the ranks; the trophies he could show were few and merely local; his admirers rather prophesied his future than proclaimed his past glories." The inference that Labourdonnais, having beaten all his own countrymen, was therefore far too good for anybody here, shows how the supremacy of the French as a chessplaying nation had in those days become an axiom. But McDonnell's stock stood somewhat higher than Mongredien allows. By 1833, as Walker tells us, he was acknowledged to be head and shoulders above every other English player, and even at pawn and move there were not more than half a dozen who could make a stand against him. "Such was McDonnell in 1834, when Labourdonnais came to London with the roses of June."

Within a week of his arrival, the great series of games had begun "in the presence of a large concourse of amateurs at the Westminster Chess Club." They continued for nearly four months, the two champions playing on nearly every day of the week except Sundays, usually from noon till about seven in the evening. By October, no less than six matches and eighty-five games had been played, the following being the full results:

---

* Luckily, it is possible for us to enjoy the Labourdonnais-McDonnell games without taking the rather extreme view that the quality of their play has not been improved upon in the ensuing years!—F.R.

First	Match	Labourdonnais	16	McDonnell	5	Drawn	4
Second	"	McDonnell	5	Labourdonnais	4	"	0
Third	"	Labourdonnais	6	McDonnell	5	"	1
Fourth	"	Labourdonnais	8	McDonnell	3	"	7
Fifth	"	Labourdonnais	7	McDonnell	4	"	1
Sixth	"	MacDonnell	5	Labourdonnais	4	"	0

TOTAL: Labourdonnais 45, McDonnell 27, Drawn 13.

It will be seen at once that Labourdonnais won a most devastating victory in the first encounter, that McDonnell recovered himself splendidly in the second and third, that in the fourth and fifth matches the Frenchman "resumed his high vantage ground," and that his opponent rallied once more in the final contest (which, however, was never finished).

Mongredien, who was a member of the Westminster Chess Club at the time, describes the enthusiasm aroused there when the opening three games of the first match, after 53, 58, and 55 moves each, were all safely drawn by McDonnell against the foreign giant, though Labourdonnais had the move each time. (In those days it did not change after a drawn game.) "The first game was viewed with intense interest, the second with interest fermented into excitement. Surely the third game must decide the battle. Who would not be there to see? The fateful evening arrived. The moves were followed by a dozen boards in different parts of the room, each surrounded by groups of players criticizing, admiring, blaming, or not understanding each move as it was reported to them." A great burst of applause greeted both champions at the conclusion. Labourdonnais told George Walker at this point that "McDonnell was the greatest player he had ever encountered." McDonnell meanwhile was itching to get the move. "When I am able to attack with my Bishop's Gambit," said he to Walker, "then you'll see." The spell was broken in the fourth game, which the Frenchman won "hands down" in 31 moves; but McDonnell must have completely brought the house down when he not only drew level in the fifth game (one of the finest of the whole series) but actually took the lead by winning the sixth also. At this juncture, however, Labourdonnais saw fit to spoil everything by winning the next eleven games running!! This, of course, decided the match, but it being one of "twenty-one games" and not "the winner of the first eleven," the agony was prolonged until twenty-one games, exclusive of draws, had been duly played out.

McDonnell stuck to his soul-deadening task magnificently. But, as Walker points out, he had partly his own folly to thank for the turn affairs had taken. He handicapped himself "by persisting in risking openings rotten at their very cores." He invariably accepted the Queen's Gambit, and he would insist on meeting the Sicilian Defense by the inferior 2 P-KB4. "With the powers of genius, he possessed also its firmness, amounting often to mere obstinacy. Nothing would induce him to evade the Queen's Gambit." The following are extracts from a letter written during the first match by McDonnell to George Walker, who had begged him to change his openings:

"I am much obliged to you for your very friendly letter. I acknowledge I am sensitive and nervous in playing, more on account of the kind partiality of friends than from personal anxiety about the games. I cannot get over this, and I fear it will be fatal to my success. Let us not, however, underrate the Frenchman's powers. He is the most finished player of the age, and all I can expect is to play up to him after some practice. The openings may not be happy, but how can you mend them? I broke down in my Bishop's Gambit, the game of all others I most relied upon. The fact is, practice of a superior kind is indispensable to form a first-rate player."

The second match is noteworthy, not only for McDonnell's fine recovery, but for its first game, that memorable one in which he for the first time tried the "Evans" on his formidable opponent. It came off. The great Frenchman, as McDonnell and his friends had hoped, had never seen the opening before. Yet his genius nearly carried him through. He accepted the gambit, improvised Lasker's defense, but went wrong later by refusing to exchange queens, lost the game, withdrew from the arena for a couple of days, had a good look at the new opening, and reverted for a time to his "King's Pawn one."

It was in the third, fourth and fifth matches that the play reached its greatest height. "As the contest went on between these renowned artists, it was curious to mark in how much bolder style they played, than in the introductory games. Like two haughty knights, throwing away helm and shield, each appeared to disdain defense, provided he could strike his opponent a home blow with sword and ax." It was now that Labourdonnais began to play the Evans with brilliant effect, and "suffered his terrible Queen's Gambit to rest awhile." Meanwhile the incorrigible McDonnell stuck at nothing. In the third match he played the King's Gambit five times, venturing it even in the final game, when the score stood five all and one to play. In the fourth match he only won three games—but what wins! One was "the immortal fiftieth," another that brilliant Muzio in which he gave up two pieces in the first nine moves. The sacrifice merely of one piece, Walker says, "was not counted much" by either champion. Each seemed determined to "go one better" than the other in daring. Some of their complications have driven annotators to despair. Staunton himself in one case can do no more than helplessly declare: "It seems utterly impossible for either player to save the game." Even the drawn games are not the 20-move rest cures of modern match play, but great marathons of 60, 80, even 100 moves in length. "They played the endings," writes Freeborough, "as if they loved them, and never knew when they were beaten."

The sixth match had to be left unfinished. After nine games had been played, the Frenchman was compelled to return to Paris, McDonnell being at the same time called away to his native town, Belfast. They never saw each other again.

George Walker, in summing up, says:

"We cheerfully admit the superiority of Labourdonnais. His blows are dealt with greater vigor; his stratagems better timed; his powers of counterattack more forcible; his judgment of position sounder. Had they played a second eighty-five games, I believe the Frenchman would still have won forty-five or fifty against the minority. Had they played, however, five hundred games, I think there was sufficient chess in our countryman to bring him honorably and well up to Labourdonnais. The

grave, however, has closed upon these two great artists, and all speculation upon what would, might, could, or should have been, becomes
indeed 'vanity and vexation of spirit.' "

Over the board, they must have presented a contrast in every respect.
Labourdonnais was a great, boisterous, slovenly bohemian; McDonnell
was a quiet, reserved, outwardly imperturbable man, not without a due
insular sense of decorum. During the play, Walker tells us, Labourdonnais "talked and laughed a good deal at intervals, when winning,
and swore tolerably round oaths in a pretty audible voice, when fate
ran counter to his schemes." According to another observer, the Frenchman would sometimes chatter most volubly to the spectators in his
native tongue, "mainly, I *think,* about politics," and often made his
move as he was speaking. At other times, "jokes and epigrams burst
like a flood from his lips"—the evidence is conflicting as to whether
he ever attempted a song. He may well have excited the ire of Mr.
William Greenwood Walker, that fine old worshiper and "Boswell"
of McDonnell, as he sat beside the English champion "with spectacles
on nose, eagerly taking down the moves," * and "scarce daring to
breathe, lest the conceptions of his hero should miscarry." McDonnell
himself seems to have put up with his opponent's excesses with a sort
of grim resignation—after all, nuisance that Labourdonnais was, there
was no one else in the world worth playing. Moreover, there really
were extenuating circumstances for the Frenchman's behavior. For
McDonnell, Walker admits, was inordinately slow, "and sometimes
dwelt on his moves till the sense of sight in the looker-on ached with
the sickening of hope and expectation.... I have known McDonnell,
[to take] an hour and a half, and even more, over a single move." He
always sat with his legs sideways, completely absorbed in the game, as
though his soul's fate depended on the result. Frequently he would
shift his legs from one side to the other, and occasionally when doing
so would mutter to himself a formula of his own invention: "I don't
like it muchy." Labourdonnais sometimes lost temper at the prolonged

* We owe him an enormous debt for doing so. He sat out the whole 85 games, which
but for him would have been lost to posterity forever.

calculations of his opponent, and showed his impatience by "sundry very plain shrugs and gestures," augmented in extreme cases by open grumbling. "As Labourdonnais spoke no English, and McDonnell no French, they had little conversation together. The word *check* was nearly the sole phrase that ever passed between them."

No less a contrast than their habits during the play is the manner in which each master spent his time when "off duty." Labourdonnais's gluttony for chess seemed insatiable. After a seven-hour sitting with McDonnell he would snatch a hasty dinner at the side of the board, and then play games at large odds against all comers till long after midnight. A fine odds-giver, he was immensely popular with his victims; great master as he was, he had no sense of importance, or fear of making himself too cheap, but would play with the humblest novice at a moment's notice. "He played," says Mongredien, "with marvelous rapidity, yet rarely made a mistake. *'Tout ce que je demande,'* he used to say, *'c'est une petite position.'* The moment he had got his *petite position,* his opponent's doom was sealed. I could never play my best against him; his rapidity dazed me. Although talking and laughing all the time, no sooner had I made my move than his at once came down with a loud impact on the board, as though he meant to break it. I was fascinated, and fell an easy prey to the huge python."

The other side of the picture is a sadder one. Walker is convinced that it was the prolonged strain of his matches with Labourdonnais that really killed McDonnell. Though always composed and cheerful in the arena, at the end of the long struggles he would go home exhausted, yet unable to rest, "and I know that he not unfrequently walked his room the greater part of the night, in a dreadful state of excitement." There can be no doubt that, throughout that eventful summer, the "chess fever" had gripped McDonnell completely. It is only too probable that he was even then threatened with the grave organic complaint which was to destroy him within a year, that a regular life free from nervous tension was essential for him, and that those eighty-five games which have made his name immortal sealed his fate.

British Chess Magazine, 1934.

THE CAFÉ DE LA RÉGENCE
By George Walker

Few men have done as much for chess as Walker accomplished for English chess in the third and fourth decade of the previous century. He made possible the publication of a cheap chess book, collected the finest examples of master play extant in Chess Studies, *established the first regular chess column in England, founded two important clubs and did other valuable organizational work, and gave much-needed financial assistance to those two titans, Labourdonnais and McDonnell.*

Judging from the vivid and racy style of his writings—so different from the sedate pages of Dickens, Thackeray, and Trollope—Walker must have had a great, uninhibited zest for life and a boundless love for chess in all its manifestations. We are fortunate indeed to have this colorful and authentic picture of the famous old café.

"Hypolite!"

"*V'là, Monsieur!*"

"*La carte à payer!*"

And while, as MacHeath sings, "the charge is prepared," let us settle the point as to how we shall keep our veins thawed this frosty night. We have dined, and—thanks to Champeaux—have dined well; but where, in phrase of France, shall we "do our digestion"? On a Sunday evening the Paris theatres are mobbed; to dress for pretty Madame M.'s soirée, upon a ten-franc dinner, with the thermometer below freezing point, is north of inviting. I am a chessplayer; and you, my friend, ought to be so; therefore, put faith in my pilotage. We'll away to the Café de la Régence, and sip our mocha among Caissa's votaries.

The *garçon* of Monsieur Champeaux serves his writ, and fingers the cash with a grace worthy of the name he bears. We are bowed forth. Ugh! How cutting is this northeaster! and how dense the snowfall! The Place de la Bourse reminds me of an ice-plain in Russia; and the Bourse itself looks like a huge twelfthcake, plastered over with white sugar. The building was modeled after a Greek temple; it is a

temple still, the name of its god being merely altered. Tramp—tramp—
we plash through the snow and mud. The streets are desolate, to
what this part of Paris generally is at seven o'clock, and the sludge is
a foot deep. We gain the Rue Richelieu, bound like the reindeer across
the Place du Palais Royal, and first draw breath as we dash headlong
into the entrance of the brilliantly illumined salon which constitutes
the Café de la Régence.

We are in the temple of the THIRTY-TWO; and here indeed chess
"rules and reigns without control." No pen has yet fairly sketched this
celebrated locale, though many have pretended to trace its lineaments.
In that amusing work, *Les Français peints par eux-mêmes,* Méry pen-
cils the Parisian chessplayer and—the truth shall out—depicts him vilely.
Méry has a fluent tongue and a witty brain; but knows no more of
chess, practically, than the man in the moon's dog. The historian of
the Café must have mixed intimately during many years with the first
chess artists, past and present, and must play pretty well himself. Let
our own right hand crayonize the French chessmen, as they present
themselves in the year of grace 1840; and pounds to pumpkins we
beat Méry out of the field. *Voyons.*

The Café de la Régence, in its outward man, is soon disposed of.
Large, low, and in its shape resembling a parallelogram of toasted
cheese, the very antithesis of the graceful or lovely, our salon presents
nothing in its personal appearance which may compete with the glittering café of modern times. Stove-heated to suffocation—gas-lighted
to oppression—the black hole of Calcutta was his eldest sister; though
the Régence has mirrors in abundance, and slabs of marble to top its
tables. Seven days in the week, from morn to midnight, the crowd pass
over its sanded floor, like the waves of the sea on the Brighton beach;
the said floor doing double duty on Sundays. After three or four o'clock
on a winter's Sunday, happy is the man who has formed his *partie;*
room to place another chessboard, even on your knees, being out of
the question. All keep their hats on, to save space; and an empty chair
is worth a monarch's ransom.

The din of voices shakes the roof as we enter. Can this be chess?—
the game of philosophers—the wrestling of the strong-minded—the

recreation of solitude—thus practiced amid a roar like that of the Regent's Park beast-show at feeding time! Laughter, whistling, singing, screaming, spitting, spouting, and shouting—tappings, rappings, drummings, and hummings, disport in their glory here around us. Have we not made a blunder, and dropped into the asylum at Charenton? Stunned with the riot, we sigh for cotton to stuff our ears; and fight our progress into a faraway corner, in order to recover our bewildered senses. Coffee is brought. We sip, and scan the scene before us; resolving its discordant elements by slow degrees into one vast tableau. Man gets used to everything except the toothache. I know a Londoner dwelling next door to a coppersmith, who wakes in the night when the artisans cease hammering! So it is with me at the present moment. The noise is bearable, and may presently become even agreeable. Manners are to be noted, and chessmen to be sketched.

The good city of Paris, be it known, holds four thousand cafés; of which the Café Procope and the Café de la Régence are unquestionably the Adam and Eve. The Régence was established as a rendezvous for the literati of the day, under the government of the Duke of Orleans; and, like Will's in London, became, from its eligible position, the haunt of the most celebrated *esprits* of France during the eighteenth century. Voltaire, the two Rousseaus, the profligate Duc de Richelieu, Marshall Saxe, Chamfort, St. Foix, Benjamin Franklin, Marmontel, Philidor, and Grimm, are but a few of the men of note who constantly frequented the Régence in early times. The very chairs and tables acquired name and fame from classical association; and, till quite recently, the master of the establishment might be heard commanding his attendants, in tones of pride, to "Serve Jean Jacques,"—"Look to Voltaire,"—the identical tables at which this pair of philosophers were wont daily to play chess, being still at that time in existence, named from departed guests. These sacred shrines are now superseded by marble slabs; coal-gas sparkling in sun-like lusters; and Voltaire could hardly recognize his favored lounge, save from the low-ceiled room unaltered in its proportions. A dingy portrait of Philidor yet hangs, I am happy to see, against the wall. To a chess antiquary, the relic would be worth purchase at its weight in gold.

Custom soon stamped the Café de la Régence as the headquarters of chess, and the uninitiated retired from its walls. It is shocking to see the fane at the present time occasionally desecrated by draughts and dominoes; and had I my will, even the timber-framed journals should be thrown overboard. Chess is chess, and should be preserved intact from grosser material. In the French Ana exist many *mots* leveled at the Régence, in the earlier years of its existence. One of the foremost of these Parisian "Joes" runs, that a certain man was once seen, who spent daily six or seven hours at the Régence for ten years; constantly occupied in poring over the players, but refusing invariably to play himself, and never speaking even a single word. A disputed point arose; the *galerie* was thin, and the taciturn veteran was pressed into service as umpire. Sorely pushed to decide the question, Monsieur owned that, so far from being a player, he did not even know the names of the pieces! Astonished at this, the query naturally came: why, then, waste ten years of life in looking over the board? The reply was that he was a married man, and did not care to go home.

... Deputy Louvet was ardently attached to chess, and playfully hits at his brother amateurs in the following passage, put into the mouth of his chief hero:

"I enter the Café de la Régence, crammed with men deeply engaged in cooking checkmates. Alas! even they had more life about them than I had. I seat myself at a table, and look on; but my irrepressible agitation causes me to walk the floor with hurried and unequal strides. Soon one of the players exclaims with eager tone, 'Check to the king!' 'Grands dieux!' cries his opponent, 'my queen is forced! the game is gone—and such a game! *une partie superbe!* Yes, sir, rub your hands—fancy yourself a Turenne* as you will, do you know who you have to thank for the coup? This gentleman—this fool here. My curse upon lovers!' Astonished at the uncourteous manner in which I was apostrophized, I assure the losing player that I did not understand him —that I had nothing to do with the matter. 'You don't understand

* A famous French general (1611-1675), greatly admired by Napoleon—F. R.

me?' replies he. '*Eh bien;* but see, a check by discovery!' 'Well, sir, and what have I to do with the check by discovery?' 'What have you to do with it? Why, sir, for the last hour you've been hovering around us like a vulture, ejaculating all manner of nonsense about your Sophia! your beautiful cousin! I listen to all this trash, and play like a school-boy. When a man is in love, sir, he does not come to the Café de la Régence.' I was about to answer, to excuse myself; but he continued with violence—'A check by discovery! The king must be covered, and my queen is lost. A miserable *coup de mazette**—a child could have foreseen it; and a player like me (he turned again to me)—sir, under-stand me again, that all the women in the world are not worth a queen won by discovery. She is lost! no resource remains. To the devil with the lover and his miss too!'

"Now, of all that had been said, the last reproach was infinitely the most cutting. Carried away by my zeal, I rushed towards him, but catching my coat-skirts unhappily in a neighboring chess table, down goes the whole concern—the men flying over the floor. This awakens the wrath of a brace of fresh enemies, and confusion becomes con-founded. 'Sir!' cries one of them, 'are you mad? do you ever look before you?' The other screams, 'Sir, you have cost me the game!' 'You had already lost it,' observed his antagonist. 'I had won it, sir; I would have played that game against Verdoni, or Philidor himself.' 'Well; but, gentlemen,' observed poor I, 'do not all talk together. I am ready to pay the stake, if the fault were mine.' 'Pay! pay! you are not rich enough, were you to coin your brains and bones.' 'For how much then were you playing?' 'For honor—for honor, sir. I have come seven hundred miles, post, to accept the challenge of Monsieur here, who fancied himself invulnerable; and but for you I should have given him a lesson—I should have taken down his pride!' 'A lesson! What do you mean? You ought to thank the young man for coming to your assistance as he did. I had your queen won by force in 18 moves.' 'Absurd! ridiculous! I should have mated you in 11. I had looked through it.' 'Mated me? Can you dare to say so! You it is, sir, I am

* A duffer's move—F. R.

to thank for this gross insult. Learn, young man, that people don't run in the Café de la Régence.' Up jumps another player. 'And learn you yourself, sir, that people don't shout in the Café de la Régence, and that they have no right even to speak here.' The hubbub rises; but one resource remains. I rush forth from the café and take refuge in the Palais Royal."

Fashion varies, but man changes not; customs alter their complexion, but human nature runneth in a circle, like the squirrel on its roundabout. Louvet's description of the old café, fifty years back, would hold equally good this evening; the individuals being a different set, and clothed in garments of other cut and pattern. Still, when we read the roll inscribed with the names of those who have been great in chess, can we forbear responding to the heartfelt exclamation of the limner, on viewing the works of Raphael, "I too am a painter"? Fruitless were it, however, to dwell over-long on the past, to the neglect of that which moves and breathes and walks among us. Bootless is it to ponder exclusively on that which we know but in spirit; and not to appreciate and admire that which comes home to us as in the form of living excellence. As I sit this night in the Régence, shall I suffer my contemporaries all to pass away like a vision, without a faint attempt at least to catch and embody their leading features on the canvas—or the page? The greatest living chessplayers are around me at this moment—men linked to me in the strong bonds of our magic masonry; and I catch the inspiration imparted by their presence. That which man has done, man may do. Were Philidor to come again in his strength, like the Cid who rose from death to smite the Moors for Spain, is it altogether certain that we could not find a champion to meet him in the lists?

One, ancient of days, walks quietly across the floor, and hats are raised in token of respect at the coming in of M. Boncourt. Seventy years and more have passed over him; but their weight has not bowed down his light and even spirit. To this simplicity of the dove, as regards his dealings with the world, Boncourt unites in chess, the veriest serpent guile. Inferior to none save Labourdonnais in skill, there breathes not the mortal more free from arrogance or vanity than this our venerable professor. Attired in an old-fashioned frock-coat which sweeps the ground, with a vest of scarlet or perchance grass-green, Boncourt placidly smooths down his silver locks, as he drops mechanically into his seat before the chessboard. Eccentric in some of his habits, Boncourt in his old age keeps hours which render it difficult to secure him as an antagonist. He delights in dining at ten o'clock at night; and he'll then mate you till cock-crow. Having a comfortable pension as a retired government clerk, he takes the world as he finds it, and practices the true philosophy of resignation under every stroke of fate, whether in life or in chess. He receives beatings better than any Frenchman of his day, shrugging up his shoulders and replacing the men when defeated, with a nonchalance perfectly edifying. His favorite companion is a little dog, well known to the chess circle, and a frequent visitor at the Régence. Boncourt has never been in England, which, considering the present facilities of traveling, is remarkable; and evinces total disregard as to fame, whether present or posthumous.

Boncourt's style of play is *the correct,* rather than *the brilliant.* Comparatively weak in the mechanical openings and endings, Boncourt has no superior in the capacity of piercing through the intricacies of positions of intense difficulty. "In the twenty-five years I have played chess," said Labourdonnais to me, "never did I see Boncourt commit an error in a crowded situation." His favorite *début* is the Giuoco Piano; in the early stages of which he almost invariably drives up his queen knight pawn and queen rook pawn two squares. I must add that Boncourt has not the usual rapidity of the French school; but is to the full as slow in digesting his chess calculations as *nous autres* in the London Chess Club.

And that young man, Boncourt's present antagonist, who is he? Did you ever see a more pleasant smile, a more intellectual countenance? How smart his dress! How becoming that budding mustache! He is engaged in a match of long standing with Boncourt, and they are to play a game this evening. Rivals in reputation, their respective partisans press around, like Homer's myriad warriors to view the encounter of Hector and Achilles. Youth has the call, and Boncourt by the mob is set down as *passé;* but the elect deem otherwise. The free, gallant bearing of the younger combatant is much in his favor. He has a *bon mot* for each, a smile for all. His eagle eye darts at once over the position of the men, and grasps fully the difficulties and capabilities of the array. He delights in danger; and the excitement of peril lights up his brow with increased expression, and tinges his cheek with deeper hue. At one time spoken of confidently as the successor to Deschapelles and Labourdonnais, St. Amant may still be styled the favorite of the Café de la Régence. Certainly, no other player in the world is more agreeable to look over. It is a matter of universal regret that St. Amant has in a measure fallen away from his allegiance to the chequered flag he once followed, by night and day, through France and England, and now confines his chess to Sunday evenings.

St. Amant's game unites the dashing style of Greco with the ingenuity and steadiness of a veteran chief. Young in years, he is aged in chess. Quick as lightning in commonplace situations, St. Amant takes a full measure of contemplation in positions of difficulty. In play with me, I once timed him three-quarters of an hour on a single move! None of the French players approach St. Amant for courteousness of demeanor and readiness to oblige. He never sneers at a bad player; never taunts the unfortunate, nor insults the conquered. St. Amant visited England upon the occasion of bearing Deschapelle's proud challenge* a few years back, and had a decided advantage in chess over our best practitioners. He has beaten, in fact, every player but Deschapelles, Labourdonnais and Boncourt. Rather a stickler for reputation, St. Amant declined risking his laurels upon the occasion of Szen, the Hungarian, visiting Paris in 1835, and refused to accept his challenge; but the feeling is unfortunately but too common among fine players.** St. Amant and Boncourt have played in all about 35 games; and Boncourt stands at present, I believe, with the majority

---

* It seems that someone in England started a rumor that in 1806—some thirty years earlier!—Deschapelles had been unsuccessful in giving rook odds to Berlin players. This report, so the story goes, infuriated Deschapelles to such an extent that he sent St. Amant off to England offering anyone odds of pawn and two moves in a match for £1,000! All of which indicates that Deschapelles was far more money-minded than the modern master.—F.R.

** St. Amant was a "stickler for reputation." His modern imitators are "rotten sportsmen."—F.R.

of three. Signor Calvi is spoken of latterly as the equal of these two heroes, but does not play at the Régence.

The Régence represents the sun round which the lesser spheres of light revolve. It is the center of civilized Europe considered with regard to chess. As Flanders in days of yore was the great battleground on or at which nations engaged in the duello, so for above a hundred years has this café served as the grand gladiatorial arena for chess-players of every country and color. Stamma the Moor came hither from Aleppo; and more than one bearded Turk and copper-skinned Hindu have worshiped chess within its walls. The Régence is the "central flowery land," receiving courteously, but with dignity, such "outside barbarians" as approach the celestial kingdom, "looking upwards with reverential awe." The Rialto of Venice, in its most palmy hour, presented not a greater mixture of garbs and tongues than does the Régence at the present time. Szen, from Pesth, came down here one day like a meteor; traversing Calais Straits to London and back to Poland in his flying visit of three months. Labourdonnais himself could hardly yield Szen the pawn; and the second advent of the Pole, it is presumed, will be to aim at taking the proudest ground. It is the Régence which places French players so high, giving them opportunities of encountering every great artist on earth by turns, and thus obtaining a varied and beautiful style of game.

To find a chess amateur of a certain force who has not visited this locale, no matter in what clime his residence, were as great a wonder as to fall in with a London Cockney in Rome who had not scratched his name, whether Noakes or Hoakes, upon the crumbling Colosseum, or the pillars of St. Peter. Be it recorded, however, that despite the fact of ten thousand Englishmen playing chess constantly in the Régence, the frames of its mirrors are guiltless of their initials—the glasses themselves are pure of the diamond-carved "Jack" and "Tom" which, like the S.P.Q.R. of the Roman nation, serve as a line of beacons, traced upon the face of the whole earth, to assure travelers that a Briton has passed that way.

It cannot be supposed the Régence could so long have held sway without attempts having been made from time to time to throw off

"Rat" Chess Set (see 4, page 303).

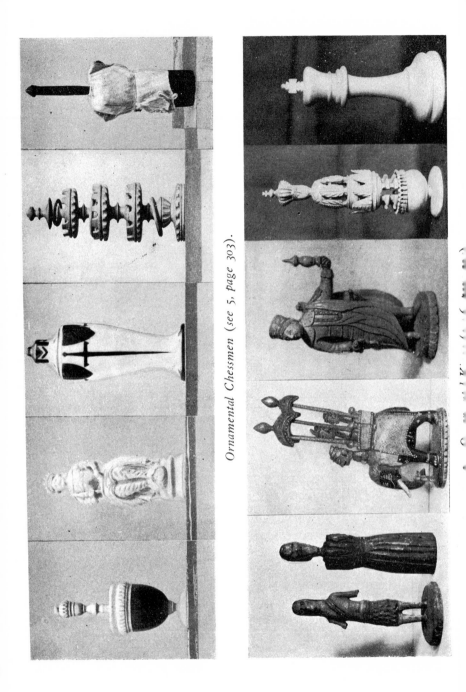

Ornamental Chessmen (see 5, page 303).

its authority. Man is a restless being and not too prone to let well enough alone. At one time the Café de Foi drew many of the elect aside from the right path. At another period Alexandre, with his Paris chess club at the Café de L'Echiquier, presented himself in open rebellion, and warred against legitimacy. Knocked down, as the Titans were by Jupiter, the club-men have tried again and again to establish themselves, but ever without success. No Paris club, exclusively devoted to chessplayers, exists at the moment of my writing; and such aristocratical amateurs as turn up their noses at the Régence are wandering about the metropolis, like the condemned in Vathek's hall of Eblis, without refuge or resting-place. For a variety of reasons, I do not believe an exclusive chess club will ever establish on a large scale in either Paris or London. Chess was once the game of the aristocracy. It has been wrested from them, with other feudal rights, and is now the recreation of the million. A chess-room, to prosper, must be open to all classes of comers—free as the air of heaven—accessible, at small cost, to every man who can afford the luxuries of hat and coat. Chess, like the tomb, levels all grades of conventional rank and distinction and reserves its high places for the best players.

Compared with the other cafés, seldom is the Régence graced with the presence of the fair sex; although women may be seen within its walls. Three ladies are of the company at this very moment, and apology is due for my not having earlier noticed their existence. The lady, number one—she with the crimson bonnet, scarlet gown, green feathers, and yellow *Ternaux*—is evidently lost in surprise at the scene. She has dropped in—good soul!—with her husband, to thaw their feet, and share a bottle of *very* small beer on their route home, after a Sunday campaign unusually fatiguing. The lady has never seen chess played before, although in her sixtieth year; and classes the men as a species of skittles, cut down in dimensions to suit the degeneracy of modern muscle. She gapes around in mute ecstasy of wonder, with a look of unequivocal contempt for the poor creatures who can express so much enthusiasm over a few toys of wood. Little drinking, and less eating, is going on, which adds in no inconsiderable degree to Madame's astonishment at the enjoyment the party appear to take in their occupations. She has always respected dominoes, she will henceforth venerate them. She nudges her *caro* to empty his glass, before the lunatics around begin to bite!

Our dame, number two, a hale *bourgeoise* of forty-five, has been excepted by number one from sweeping condemnation; for this fair person, *très comme il faut,* is actually engaged at dominoes with her beau: filling up the intervals between the games by stuffing herself with savory biscuits steeped in sugared Madeira. Number two is shrill of voice, hearty of laugh, lusty as the Swiss giantess on the Boulevard du Temple. She is merry with wine and compliments and shouts in the battle like the Mohicans raising their war-whoop. When she gives a yell of victory, her voice, like an essential distillation of the lungs of twenty Grisis,* rises sublimely above the surrounding orchestra of sounds.

The chessplayers glance growlingly from their boards at the annoyance, the more intolerable as not coming from one of their own corps; and the profane term of *grosse vache* is unhesitatingly muttered as applicable to this, one of the women of France, by a *vieux moustache,* my next-table neighbor, with most un-Paris-like *politesse.* The French, however, are not always particular about doing the pleasing, if their personal comforts are entrenched upon—but let that pass. The fat lady cares little for aught save herself and her friend. If they don't like her laugh, they can leave it; there is room outside, although inside places are the more comfortable on a snowy night. Number two is engaged in a domino-party of one hundred games, of which there are not above seventy-eight yet to be played out. The wily spirit of the sex teaches her that she is at present a nuisance; and she fancies herself a Joan of Arc in the species of warfare carrying on. Let her alone, silly Frenchman, you ought to know woman better. Cease your murmurings! appear not to be aware of her presence; and triumph will open her gentle heart to the softer emotions of pity. It will cost her contented beau another glass of Madeira, which she will drink in token of a general peace, and many a day hence will she laugh exultingly at

---

* Giuditta and Giulia Grisi, sisters and famous nineteenth-century opera singers.—F.R.

the recollections connected with the night on which she gave the chessplayers their own—and something more. Good evening, Madame, and pleasant slumbers! The youngest of the fair trio awaits her profile.

Number three presents, indeed, a study for an artist; for not only is she playing chess, but playing it well. Her bonnet of beaver, and quiet cloak of gray, cannot conceal a face replete with beauty and intelligence. A mere girl, you can read in her expressive eye that the mind within answers to the grace without. A suffused blush is on her cheek, and the smile of conquest plays tremblingly around her lip. Her antagonist, a fine young fellow rather overdressed, is clearly her lover; and instead of calculating his moves he has been looking in her bright eyes to the very verge of checkmate, happier in defeat than any other chessplayer present in the height of triumph. The youth is nothing more than a small clerk, with a yearly salary of twelve hundred francs; the damsel, a superior kind of sempstress, just redeemed by chess from the class, *grisette*.

I can read their whole history at a glance. He has rented an apartment adjoining that of her parents; and cultivating the intimacy, has taught her chess and love. Papa and mamma have consented, and the wedding will take place in the spring....

The great variety of character developed in the Café de la Régence is not the least interesting feature of the picture. The French are the worst losers in the world; in more ways than one. I have seen them, when checkmated, dash the men about the floor, with as many *sacré tonnerres* as would sink a seventy-four. They are moreover not *too* exact in the settlement of certain small debts of honor. A very small stake is necessarily risked at the Régence, it being the custom that the loser on the balance pays the sixteen-sous tribute levied by the *garçon* for the use of the chess equipment for the sitting, no matter how long. A half-franc or franc is occasionally wagered on the game, in addition. While you go on, game after game, dropping your coin kindly and readily, Monsieur is funny and gentlemanly enough; but turn the tables upon him, and the *pestes* and *sacrés* break bounds audibly. "Base is the slave who pays" is often the maxim.

I once played, when a youngster, in the Régence several days constantly with a regular old soldier, at half a franc the game, and departed after each sitting, minus some two or three francs. Now it happened that upon one glorious occasion, rising to leave, I found myself to be for the first time on the credit side of the account. One half-franc was the sum due me; and I could not forbear smiling at the rueful look of my very respectable friend on casting up the score. Poor fellow! deeply, and slowly, and vainly, did he dive for the needful. The silver would not come; the pockets were free from encumbrance. Feeling pity for the man's position, I turned to quit the café, saying, "Never mind," and all that. "Monsieur," cried the gentleman gravely, *"je suis Français—je suis homme d'honneur*—what do you mean by going thus without your money?—*rendez-moi un demi-franc."* Of course I complied, handing him the change I supposed him to require, and presenting him my palm, to grasp the larger piece of silver in return. "Now, sir," quoth Monsieur, dropping the cash into his pocket with a low bow, "now, sir, I owe you a franc, which I shall do myself the honor to pay at the earliest opportunity."

The game we are looking over is done; Labourdonnais gives checkmate, and the noise becomes positively infernal. Not only do all chatter at once, but, like the talking bird in the Eastern tale, each man appears endowed with twenty different voices. A rush is made towards the chessboard, and a dozen hands snatch at the pieces, to show what the unfortunate loser could, would, should, or might have done. Thus was Job comforted of old, and thus do the tormentors attack a man already suffering sufficient disgust in being beaten.

The English are the best lookers-on in the world, the French the very worst. They do not hesitate, during the most interesting crisis, to whisper their opinions freely; to point with their hands over the board; to foretell the probable future; to vituperate the past. It is hard to play before such critics; and rather trying to the nerves to hear yourself styled, perhaps, an "ass," for what you thought a neat bit of play; or to see lips curling, and sneering, and smiling contemptuously at your proceedings, knowing that the scorners in a similar case would play ten times worse than you have done. When your move is made, half a dozen voices are loudly raised to demand *"Pourquoi diable,* you didn't do this?" or, "Why you overlooked that?" I have lost many games in Paris through similar impertinences, and have all but vowed that when next I played chess there, it should be in a barricaded room.

Talking of barricades, I may remark that never was the Café de la Régence more thronged with chessplayers than during the three glorious days of July, 1830. Speak of parting lovers! Why 'twere easier to sunder Romeo and Juliet, than two staunch chessplayers over a good game. Ten revolutions working at once around—the sun and moon dancing the *chakut,* with the stars whirling by in joyous gallopade—no wreck of worlds or systems could, I say, sever two real chess enthusiasts in the heat of battle.

To those who think I exaggerate the noise of the Régence at the close of the evening, I can only say, witness it before passing judgment. In singing and spitting its intimates are particularly strong; would they all sang the same time, and spat only, as French lady-vocalists do on the stage, between the verses. I know Frenchmen who, at chess, expectorate airs with variations, and are quite surprised we do not sanction the custom. Cigars are forbidden at the Régence. This is as it should be. The same moral rule which permits one individual in a public room to blow second-hand tobacco smoke in your face, should be equally lenient to the smokers of opium, valerian or asafetida. Eat, drink, or suck what you will yourself, but do not force me to go shares against my will.

Labourdonnais and his illustrious staff have left the Régence; the players are thinning rapidly off; the drums have beaten the round— and the good wives of Paris are airing their husbands' nightcaps. The *garçons* yawn and sigh as they watch the termination of the last domino party. Even that comes to its end, and the Régence is nearly vacant; the counter is abdicated; the café is cleared; my friend has gone, and the gas seems going. I am alone in the field of battle—the last man of the campaign. Midnight has struck its long, long bell, and I reluctantly prepare to face the cold. Farewell, at least for a season, to the Café de la Régence!

Chess and Chessplayers.

THE FIRST INTERNATIONAL CHESS TOURNAMENT
By Paul Hugo Little

As the first event of its kind, the celebrated tournament at London in 1851 marks the opening of the grandest epoch in the age-long pageant of chess. Aside from the lasting historical interest of this event, it had many curious and picturesque features which deserve to be remembered. Incidentally the tournament marked the downfall of one great star—Howard Staunton—and the emergence of a far greater master—Adolf Anderssen. Only a few years more, and both men would seem small indeed in the presence of Paul Morphy. But meanwhile Anderssen was to enjoy his great victory—over the chessboard—and Staunton was to have his revenge—in the Book of the tournament.

The scene is London, that fabulous city with its colorful contrasts of Piccadilly and Soho, of Whitechapel and the majestic House of Parliament on the bank of the stately, impassive Thames. Massive, sprawling like an ancient giant, London has fashionable homes and grubby slums in this year of 1851. Victoria, not yet the "Widow of Windsor," rules over all the land. A great exhibition of art and science is in progress this spring. What could be more natural than to have the greatest chessplayers of the day assemble in a grand congress? Although never before has there been an international chess tournament, that is not to say that rivalry among European players is lacking.

In 1834 Parisian chessplayers and those of the Westminster Club engaged in a correspondence match. The leader of the victorious French forces was Pierre Charles Fournier de St. Amant.

Of noble birth, he was trained as a soldier but drifted into journalism and at one time was even a wine merchant. A powerful chessplayer, St. Amant first visited England in 1836 when he defeated George Walker, a prominent English master, in a match.

Seven years later, St. Amant played a short match with Howard Staunton who had just defeated Cochrane to take his place as the leading British master. St. Amant won by a narrow margin, $3\frac{1}{2}$-$2\frac{1}{2}$. In

November of that same year, Staunton journeyed to Paris to claim his revenge. He earned it after a fierce battle in which he won eleven, lost six and drew four games. The encounter produced some of the finest chess seen up to that time.

This last match crystallizes the desire of the English players to meet the best available opponents in serious and conclusive combat. The St. George's Chess Club to which Staunton belongs begins to make extensive plans. A committee enters into correspondence with Jaenisch and Schumoff in St. Petersburg, Szen in Budapest, Kieseritzky—a Livonian player who has risen to the rank of French champion after St. Amant's withdrawal from competition, Anderssen who is considered second best player in Germany (der Lasa stands first), Mayet, Horwitz, and Lowe. Subscriptions for the tournament fund come pouring in. The locale is to be 5 Cavendish Square, the spacious rooms of the St. George's Chess Club itself, not far from the Great Exhibition.

On May 26th, 1851, the Committee of Management, led by Staunton, calls "for the assemblage of all those who proposed to take part in the general *mêlée*," to quote from the official tournament book by Staunton himself. Unfortunately Petroff, der Lasa, Major Jaenisch, and Schumoff, as well as St. Amant, are missing. This first day of the congress is used to draw up the rules of play. They are curious in the light of our own practice. There is no time limit—even the use of sand glasses in tournament play is years from realization. It is to be a knockout contest; it remains for a later generation to discover the superiority of round-robin play. After the first-round matches, the winners will play winners and so on until a single victor remains. There is heated discussion as to the length of the elimination contests. Originally the winner of three games out of five—draws not to count except to reverse pieces—was to go forward. However, by a close vote, the number of games is reduced to two wins out of three.

The prizes in this first international tournament are wonderfully enticing. As described in the prospectus of the event, the first prize is to consist of "a sum not less than one-third of the net amount of the funds collected." Second prize is a tenth of this revenue which is derived from a $25 entry fee levied on each contestant as well as the subscriptions. The cash awards are graduated down to a fortieth of the net amount for sixth place.

The entrants are as follows: Anderssen, Horwitz, Kieseritzky, Loewenthal—who has come from America to take part, Lowe, Mayet, and Szen are the foreigners; Staunton, Wyvill, Captain H. A. Kennedy, Williams, a young accountant named Henry Evelyn Bird, Newham, and an unknown provincial player named Mucklow. As Jaenisch and Schumoff may come any moment, Brodie and E. S. Kennedy, two skillful English amateurs, enter as "provisional competitors" to facilitate an even pairing of eight against eight.

To determine the pairings for the first round, the Committee now puts eight white and eight yellow tickets in a ballot box. Each set is marked with the numbers 1 to 8. The white tickets are further marked "choice of chessmen and first move"—presumably the holder of a white ticket can request the black pieces yet still make the first move! Such were the carefree days of yore.

The shortcomings of this haphazard system are at once apparent when the first-round pairing brings Anderssen and Kieseritzky face to face. No matter what the result one of the best players is certain to be eliminated from the tournament. The match is a conflict between vastly different personalities. Adolph Anderssen has a broad, placid face framed by scrubby chin whiskers and a receding hairline. His manner is serious yet kindly. Basically a sound player, he reserves "brilliant" chess for offhand games. Lionel Kieseritzky has a pale, unhealthy face and his manner is "melancholic and afflicted." Speaking of Kieseritzky's chess, Reverend Wayte says "he is essentially a gallery player, dealing chiefly in fireworks against weak opponents." Such a man can not stand up against the Professor from Breslau. Anderssen wins two games and draws one to advance to the next round.

Marmaduke Wyvill, taking time from his duties in Parliament, scores in two straight games against "Old" Lowe. Young Henry Bird, pitted against the veteran endgame composer Horwitz, begins splendidly by drawing the first game and winning the second with a slashing attack. His crafty adversary rounds into form, however, wins the next two games and the match.

The English champion, Howard Staunton, has an easy time with the reserve player Brodie. Two games are enough to settle that struggle. Staunton is a man of imposing appearance. He has a high arching forehead surmounted by a mane of curly hair. His eyes are piercing; his mouth small and prim; and, in keeping with the day, he has a fringe of beard along his chin. A renowned Shakespearian scholar in his day, Staunton is equally famous for his *Handbook of Chess*. Ironically, it is the latter by which future generations will know him. Today, Staunton's critical writings are the property of pedants, but his chessbooks have influenced uncounted thousands of chess enthusiasts for the past one hundred years.

Josef Szen, the swashbuckling Hungarian, polishes off Newham in two straight games. An unexpected result occurs in the match between Szen's countryman Loewenthal and Williams. Staunton characterizes the latter as "unquestionably Loewenthal's inferior in every point. Yet, overtaxed by the ardors of his journey from America—and it must be realized that in 1851 sailing the Atlantic sometimes takes as long as two months!—Loewenthal loses the first game, manages to retrieve the second, but is eliminated by dropping the third and final game. Meanwhile, Captain H. A. Kennedy defeats Karl Mayet in two consecutive encounters.

The final match of this first round is between Mucklow and E. S. Kennedy. Staunton acidly notes that the former is "a player never heard of until his appearance in the lists...persisted in refusing the advice of those who wished him rather to join the Provincial tourney" —a minor event held for weaker players. Mucklow wins two games by simply outsitting his rival. Of this, too, Staunton has something to say: "Mr. Kennedy in his ordinary play is rarely guilty of the errors which, worn out by the intolerable and incredible slowness of his adversary, he fell into in this match."

In the second round, the eight winners again ballot to determine the pairings. Ruefully noting the elimination of strong players, the Committee of Management reconsiders its original decision to make matches hinge on two out of three games. Henceforth, the best of seven games, not counting draws, will decide.

Wyvill defeats Captain Kennedy four to three while Staunton wins four, loses two and draws one to down Horwitz. Williams takes four straight from the intruding Mucklow...but not without effort. The time of this match is not recorded but the secretary makes a significant notation to the score of the first game: "both players almost asleep."

In the middle of the Anderssen-Szen match, there is an unusual and highly unethical bargain between the players: it is agreed that if either wins first prize, he will pay one-third of it to the other! Surely, we must blush at such perfidy in this first of all tournaments.

Play goes on: Wyvill meets Williams and loses the first three games, then recovers magnificently to win the match by allowing Williams only a draw. Against Anderssen, Staunton loses the first three games, scores in the fourth, but bows in the fifth and deciding one. Friends of the English champion excuse his poor showing on the grounds that the arduous work of arranging the tourney plus his editing and publishing chores have undermined his health.

In the consolation matches, Szen scores in four straight games over Horwitz while Captain Kennedy does as much for Mucklow, who continues to show his lack of class.

The last round leaves Anderssen and Wyvill in the center of the stage. On the side lines, Williams and Staunton will fight it out for third and fourth; Szen and Kennedy for fifth and sixth; and Horwitz and Mucklow for the last two awards. This last match does not take place since, owing to a misunderstanding, Mucklow fails to appear. Again Staunton has a barbed comment: "This is not much to be regretted, for what can be looked for in an *even* match [that is, without odds] between a player of first-rate skill against one to whom he can give rook odds?" So Horwitz gets seventh prize by default and the unknown Mucklow—who, fortunately, will never be heard from again in serious play—gains eighth place with a final score of two wins and eight losses in addition to four games forfeited!

Five games are enough for Szen who allows Kennedy only one draw while relegating him to sixth place. The Hungarian, of course, is fifth.

Staunton suffers another setback as Williams defeats him four games
to three with one draw. While castigating some of his own moves as
"imbecilic," Staunton plaintively reiterates his argument against the
injustice of being "outsat." Says the English champion: "When a player, *upon system,* consumes hours over moves when minutes might suffice, and depends, not upon outmaneuvering but outsitting his antagonist, patience ceases to be a virtue and one cannot help expressing
deep regret that there is not some legal or moral force which may be
brought to bear upon the offender." Staunton reflects that he can nor-
mally give his unchivalrous rival odds of a pawn and two moves! Is
it any wonder clocks are used today?

The brilliant Parliamentarian Wyvill faces Professor Anderssen in
the final and most vital match of the tourney. All England is arrayed
behind Wyvill and he makes a gallant fight. After losing the first game,
he draws the second and wins the third! Anderssen is relentless: his
steady play earns for him the next two games. The Englishman struggles against fate and, after a seesaw battle, wins the sixth game. Then,
in the seventh, Anderssen has White and for the fourth time Wyvill
adopts the Sicilian Defense. The game proceeds: 1 P-K4, P-QB4; 2 B-
B4, P-QR3; 3 P-QR4, N-QB3; 4 N-QB3, P-K3; 5 P-Q3, P-KN3; 6 KN-
K2, B-N2; 7 O-O, KN-K2; 8 P-B4, O-O; 9 B-Q2, P-Q4; 10 B-N3,
N-Q5; 11 NxN, BxNch, 12 K-R1, B-Q2 (Wyvill errs; this loses at least
a Pawn); 13 PxP, BxN (this saves the Pawn but leaves Black's King-
side hopelessly weak); 14 BxB, PxP; 15 B-B6!, B-K3 . . . and now
Anderssen finishes off nicely . . . 16 P-B5!, BxP; 17 RxB!, PxR; 18
Q-R5, Q-Q3; 19 Q-R6, QxB; 20 QxQ . . . here Wyvill offers his resigna-
tion: Anderssen wins first prize.

Thus ends the first international chess tournament. Rich in drama
and the personalities of its competitors, this event leaves an indelible
mark. Its very mistakes provide the foundation for enlightened tournament play. The mistakes may be forgiven. It is enough that London,
1851 begins international tournament play for the delight of chess
fans the world over.

Chess Review, 1949.

"AH, THE GOOD OLD DAYS!"
By Fred Reinfeld

At the time I wrote this article I was nettled by the disparagement of modern masters which flourishes side by side with unthinking praise for the ancients. My views are still the same, although my approach to his type of controversy has mellowed considerably!

It is unfortunate, but true, that a sizable proportion of amateurs find modern chess dull. "Ah, the good old days!" This is based on what is for the most part an imaginary kind of chess which is supposed to have been peculiar to any age but our own. If the good old chess was really so interesting, we should expect it to have flourished in the first international tournament at London in 1851. If we turn to the Book of the tournament, however, we discover that it is an epochal collection of the most dreary, tedious, witless, planless, slovenly, and inept chess that has ever been assembled between the covers of a book. Of the 85 games in the main event, not more than five could be described as brilliant by the most charitable man in the world; and he would be hard put to it to find ten games that were worth looking at.

It is impossible to retain any more illusions about the chess of this period as one reads Staunton's peppery philippics against his bumble-fingered colleagues. (And since he was much inferior to present-day analysts, he leaves myriads of blunders untouched!) Listen to him: "In some respects these players were well paired, not for equality of force, indeed, Mr. Williams being by far the stronger, but because each in his degree, exhibits the same want of depth and inventive power in his combinations, and the same tiresome prolixity in man-euvering his men. It need hardly be said that the games, from first to last, are remarkable only for their unvarying and unexampled dull-ness" (p. 88).

And: "P-KB5 might have spared both parties some hours' tedium" (p. 90).

And: "Mr. Horwitz has now an undeniable superiority, but in these games, he only gains advantages to throw them away" (p. 127).

And: "Would it be credited by anyone unacquainted with the names of the combatants, that the White men in this game were conducted by Mr. Horwitz? Would a player to whom Mr. Horwitz, when himself, could give a knight, play in a style so utterly wanting in all that constitutes good chess, as Mr. H. does in the present termination?" (p. 128). Poor Horwitz has just capped a number of previous blunders by putting a piece *en prise!*

And: "Contrary to all expectation, Black was enabled to bear up against the intolerable tedium of his adversary to the end of this trying game, but the effect of his exertions was painfully evident in the after *partie*" (p. 155).

And: "Mr. Szen is evidently not so well acquainted with the openings as with the endgames; this move ought to lose him a pawn" (p. 168) and on the *fourth move*, at that! And his opponent, in turn, overlooks it! Master chess, indeed!

And: "It can hardly fail to strike the most unobservant reader that in this match there is scarcely any combination on either side. Mr. Williams, with his habitual imperturbability, contents himself by keeping his game together, and exchanging his pieces as opportunity serves, satisfied to await the chances which a twelve or fourteen hours' sitting may turn up. The Hungarian, in despair of infusing anything like fire into such an unimaginative opposite, resigns himself to the *far niente* tactics of the enemy, and like him resolves to wait and watch also. The remarkable thing is, that with all this wariness and lack of enterprise, with hours upon hours devoted to the consideration of the shallowest conceptions, the games abound with blunders. In a game shortly preceding this one, Mr. W. leaves a bishop *en prise.* In the present, we find Mr. L. very generously giving up his queen, and in the very next game Mr. W. loses his queen in a similar manner!" (p. 277).

But enough of these melancholy reminders of crass mediocrity. Let us examine another popular belief: what was the average length (in number of moves) of the 85 games contested in the main section of the tournament? Tabulation of the game lengths shows that the formal average duration is 42 moves, but quite a few games end with the cryptic remark "and wins." Either the secretary fell asleep, or the loser continued to play on out of pique when his material disadvantage was colossal. It is therefore safe to assume that the average length was at least 45 moves. Now in modern tournament play, this would require an average of from four to six hours, which to the amateur seems inordinate; yet in 1851 there was no time limit, and we know that players took anywhere from half an hour to *two and a half hours* on a SINGLE move! Even offhand games were long drawn out, hence it is doubly certain that serious games proceeded at an even more funereal pace. We may therefore conclude that the average game of 45 moves in the London tournament took (at least) eight hours! I have purposely made my estimate a conservative one, for the chances are that the average length was much nearer to ten hours a game! Who would prefer this to modern chess?!

Chess Review, 1940.

PAUL MORPHY: KING OF CHESS
By John C. Rather

Even after the passage of a century, Paul Morphy still remains the most glamorous figure in the annals of master play. His career at serious chess lasted only three years, and he was through with tournament and match chess when only 23! Morphy's life is more thoroughly documented than that of any other master, yet it remains a tragic riddle to this day. John Rather has chronicled the events of Morphy's life succinctly without minimizing their dramatic impact.

The spectacle of disillusioned genius is pathetic and provocative, for an aura of mystery clings to the man who abandons his success with the applause of the world ringing in his ears. In one of his poems, Edwin Arlington Robinson echoes our bewilderment. "Richard Corey," the poet tells us, is envied by all who know him, yet one night this man with everything to live for goes home and kills himself. In a very real sense, this is the pattern of Paul Morphy's tragic career.

Morphy was born in New Orleans on June 22, 1837 and from the very beginning his life was an easy one. His parents were cultured, well-to-do people, prominent in the social life of New Orleans. His father, Alonzo Morphy, was appointed a judge of Louisiana's Supreme Court at the age of 42, in 1840. Paul grew up in an atmosphere of genteel manners—an important factor in shaping his attitude toward chess in later life.

He was given a sound education at the Jefferson Academy and, later, at St. Joseph's College near Mobile. In 1855, he received his M.A. in law with highest honors, having a mastery of three foreign languages. Apparently he had a phenomenal memory as well for he was reputed to be able to recite from memory nearly the whole text of the Civil Code of Louisiana! A year later, when he was only 19, Morphy was admitted to the Bar on the condition that he would not practice until he came of age. With a two year vacation to spend before he could begin his legal career, Morphy turned again to chess.

He had learned the game when he was about ten and, even in his first experiences with amateurs at his father's home, his genius was apparent: he beat them easily. By the time he was twelve, he had defeated Rousseau and Stanley, at that time considered to be among the country's leading players.

His uncle, Ernest Morphy, wrote enthusiastically to the editor of *La Régence,* describing the youngster's aplomb:

"The child has never opened a work on chess; he has learnt the game himself by following the *parties* played between members of his family. In the openings he makes the right moves as if by inspiration; and it is astonishing to note the precision of his calculations in the middle and endgame. When seated before the chessboard, his face betrays no agitation even in the most critical positions; in such cases he generally whistles an air through his teeth and patiently seeks for the combination to get him out of trouble. Further, he plays three or four severe enough games every Sunday (the only day on which his father allows him to play) without showing the least fatigue."

Young Paul's greatest test came in 1850 when he contested two games with Johann Loewenthal, a master of international repute. The first encounter was a draw, but Paul won the second in convincing style. Loewenthal took his defeat with good grace and, according to legend, embraced the boy and predicted that he would become the greatest player the world had ever seen.

School occupied the boy for the next few years and most of his play was confined to odd games with his friend, Charles Maurian. After his passing the bar examination, Morphy felt justified in giving more attention to the game.

American chess was just struggling from the doldrums and visionary organizers had formulated plans for the First American Chess Congress to be played in New York during the latter part of 1857. Morphy was among those invited to compete.

It is popular to suppose that Morphy arrived on the scene like an unheralded knight and took the scoffing multitude by surprise. Actually, Morphy was well known and the January, 1857 number of *Chess Monthly,* published in New York, had called him "the most promising player of the day." If there were any lingering doubts, he quickly dispelled them on arriving in the city. Before the tournament had begun, he had decisively trounced most of the players in offhand games. It was clear from the beginning that 24-year-old Louis Paulsen of Dubuque was his only serious rival.

This prediction was correct: in the preliminary rounds, consisting of the best of five games in match play, the two young men made equal scores, winning nine games and allowing only one draw. But there was an obvious difference in quality: Paulsen was a plodding player whose chief talent lay in outsitting his adversaries; Morphy was an exponent of cut-and-thrust: he moved rapidly and won quickly. There would be no justice if the end had been other than it was. Morphy won five games, lost one, and two games were drawn. Thus, Paul Morphy of New Orleans became the first U. S. Chess Champion.

No sooner had he returned home than his admirers began talking about a match with Howard Staunton, the English master, author of the famous *Handbook of Chess,* and, as Morphy had already noted, "some devilish bad games." That Staunton occupied such a prepossessing position in the chess world must be considered as proof of the power of publicity. Actually, his one material success was victory over the French master St. Amant in 1843. Yet so carefully had he nurtured this triumph that, despite his failure at London, 1851 he was still considered one of the world's best players!

Staunton could not be lured to the United States for a match with Morphy so the young American resolved to journey to England. As far as meeting Staunton was concerned, he might just as well have stayed home: the Englishman skillfully avoided the challenge and at the same time implied that Morphy was little more than an irresponsible chess professional. Now, considering Morphy's background, Staunton could have found no blow more telling. Morphy fiercely resented any such imputation. Whenever possible, he disposed of his winnings in a manner that left no doubt that he had no interest in the money. For instance, while waiting to play Staunton, Morphy scored an easy match victory over Loewenthal. The stakes were $500 a side. Immediately after the match, Morphy presented Loewenthal with $600 worth of furniture for a new residence!

The closest Morphy ever came to playing Staunton was in two consultation games and they were definitely not the hand-to-hand encounters Morphy craved. However, for what satisfaction it gave, his side won both games.

Traveling to Paris, Morphy met Daniel Harrwitz in an on-again off-again match which the American finally won 5-2. Then, Morphy arranged a match with Adolf Anderssen, winner of the great London 1851 tournament.

Like Staunton, Anderssen had been out of practice. Despite this and the evident inconvenience of journeying from Breslau, he agreed to meet Morphy in Paris. The result was another decisive victory for Morphy, this one by seven wins, two losses and two draws. Still, the games themselves raise doubts. Anderssen handicapped himself with miserable opening variations and he made obvious blunders in simple positions, some of them won for him. Morphy himself must have been objective enough to see this and it may have increased his dissatisfaction at not meeting Staunton.

While in Paris, Morphy played one more match, this one with Augustus Mongredien early in 1859. He won seven games and drew one. This was the last serious contest of his brief chess career.

Returning to London, he gave a remarkable simultaneous exhibition against five masters (Barnes, Bird, Boden, Loewenthal, and de Riviere). Morphy won two games, lost one, drew two. Then he left for New York with a secret resolution forming in his mind.

In New York, he was received royally and given a triumphal banquet. Trophies were showered upon him. Morphy's speech of acceptance showed the direction his thoughts were taking: "Chess never has been and never can be aught but a recreation. It should not be indulged in to the detriment of other and more serious avocations— should not absorb or engross the thoughts of those who worship at its shrine, but should be kept in the background, and restrained within its proper province. As a mere game, a relaxation from the severe pursuits of life, it is deserving of high commendation...."

That evening Morphy played several games with Frederick Perrin at knight odds, having announced that he would never play any American at lesser odds. Subsequently, he defeated James Thompson, another of the competitors in the First American Congress, 5-3 at these odds!

After touring New York, Philadelphia, and Boston and playing a great many offhand games, Morphy returned to New Orleans. There he issued a final challenge, offering to give the odds of a pawn and move to any player in the world. When he received no response, he declared his career as a chessplayer finally and definitely closed.

We have become so accustomed to an endless procession of beaten champions attempting to make comebacks that we stand in awe of the man who rejects success at its peak. Where the "has-been" only emphasizes his frailty, the retiring champion seems to establish his invincibility for all time. Never was this more true than in Morphy's case.

His career was scarcely three years in duration. He participated in only one tournament and a handful of serious matches. Yet, on the strength of these sixty-odd games together with some three hundred offhand games, chess fans have sworn that Morphy was the greatest player in the history of the game. Masters like Emanuel Lasker and Wilhelm Steinitz held the world championship for more than a quarter of a century but, when we recall them, it is as beaten champions, fighting a losing battle against youth. As Jacques Mieses says, "Morphy performed the magician's feat of forcing on his generation and posterity, the unshakable conviction: this man would never have been beaten." And he did it by the simple expedient of retiring in his prime.

If this were all, the picture would be a happy one. But the other side of the mirror is dark and somber. Morphy's retirement as a player was motivated by his distaste for chess professionalism, yet he could not escape his fame. He failed as a lawyer because people recalled him only as a chessplayer. The Civil War further compromised his position, for while he would not turn against the South, he could not support its cause. During part of this time, he lived in Havana and Paris. Gradually, signs of acute mental disturbance appeared. He had delusions of persecution. Still, when his family tried to have him committed to an asylum, he argued so rationally that they were fearful of making a mistake.

About that time a project was broached to publish a work on famous citizens of Louisiana; Morphy was to be included as "the most celebrated chessplayer in the world." When Morphy was informed of this, he wrote angrily to the *Turf, Farm and Field;* he pointed out that his father had left an estate valued at $146,162.54, and that he himself had no profession, but that he had a lawyer's diploma.

Release from this tragic life came on July 10, 1884 when Morphy died in his bath. The cause was congestion of the brain, following the shock of cold water to an overheated body. The man was dead, but his games lived on.

Chess Review, 1949.

MORPHY'S ESTIMATE OF STAUNTON

His knowledge of the theory of the game was no doubt complete; his powers as an analyst were of the very highest order; his *coup d'oeil** and judgment of position and his general experience of the chessboard great; but all these qualities, which are essential to make a great chess-player, do not make him a player of genius. These must be supplemented by imagination and by a certain inventive or creative power, which conceives positions and brings them about. Of this faculty I see no evidence in the published games of Mr. S.

In a given position, where there is something to be done, no matter how difficult or recondite the idea, Mr. S. will detect it and carry out the combination in as finished a style as any great player that ever lived, but he will have no agency in bringing about the position.

Therefore, in his best day, Mr. S. (in my opinion) could not have made a successful fight against a man who had the same qualities as himself, and who, besides, was possessed of the creative power above mentioned. Such were Anderssen of Germany, McDonnell of England, and Labourdonnais of France.

British Chess Magazine, 1891.

EVANS GAMBIT DECLINED AND ACCEPTED

The origin of the names of many chess openings is shrouded in mystery. Equally sad is our ignorance of the temperaments and biographies of the men who originated these lines. All the more interesting, therefore, is the following anonymous article about the discoverer of "that most beautiful of all chess openings," the Evans Gambit.

The Evans Gambit, of which so much has been heard lately, was casually discovered by Captain William D. Evans, R.N., of Milford, about the year 1834; the exact date is uncertain. He was an officer in the

* Literally glance, look—F. R.

British Navy, holding a captain's commission. He lived to a ripe old age, and for many years lived a quiet life somewhere in France or Holland, subsisting on a pension which he held from the British Government. The following anecdote is told by a gentleman about Captain Evans having met and defeated in a game of chess the Grand Duke Nicholas of Russia:

I was personally acquainted with Captain Evans. His son had served in the same regiment as I, and that was how I came to know his father. The old man was living in Ostend in somewhat straitened circumstances with his daughter and the son already mentioned. This was just before the Franco-Prussian War broke out in 1870.

During the season of that year the Grand Duke Nicholas was on a visit to Bruges, which is about sixteen miles from Ostend. Hearing that the inventor of the Evans Gambit was in Ostend, and being himself a warm devotee of the game, the Grand Duke sent an invitation to Evans to come over to Bruges and play him a game. Captain Evans was of a very independent turn of mind and, taking the fancy, refused to go. Perhaps this refusal was in consequence of something which will be explained directly. However, the invitation came a second time and was a second time declined. On the third occasion, when the Grand Duke gave a special commission to one of his aides-de-camp to bring the old man whether he would or no, Captain Evans, for some reasons best known to himself at that time, consented to go to Bruges.

The old salt and the brother of the greatest of autocrats met and fought a stubborn game, which lasted for three days. Of course they played without time limit. The Grand Duke was counted a fine player, but the old Welshman got the better of him in the end. When the fight was over—Captain Evans told me the story himself—the Grand Duke turned to his adversary, and, addressing him in French, said:

"I believe you invented the Evans Gambit?"

"Yes," replied the Captain, "and it is not the only thing I have invented for which you have not paid me."

"What is the other?" asked the Grand Duke.

Captain Evans then explained that he was the inventor of certain ships' lights—the red and the green for "port" and "starboard" I believe it was—which have since been almost universally adopted. The Grand Duke Nicholas was at that time the Admiral of the Russian Navy, which had just begun to use the lights to which Captain Evans referred. Nothing more was thought about the matter at the time, and Captain Evans continued his quiet life at Ostend. Some months later, however, he received a letter from the Russian Consul in that city asking him to call at the consulate. When the old man reached there the Consul handed him a letter from the Grand Duke Nicholas, in which that great man, in very complimentary terms, told the Captain in French how happy he had been to meet him and play with him a game of chess.

When the inventor of ship lights and the Evans Gambit had finished his perusal of this letter, the Russian Consul said that was not all he had to give him, and thereupon he handed to Captain Evans a magnificent gold chronometer. Upon the obverse side of the case was an inscription in Slavonic characters in these terms: "To the great and good man, William Evans," while on the reverse were engraved two ships, with their lights represented by precious stones. Accompanying his appropriate gift was a valuable gold chain, each link of which represented the link of a ship's anchor, and the holder a ship's lantern with a brilliant for its light. And finally, to make the thing complete, there was a draft for £2,000 from the Grand Duke Nicholas to Captain Evans, ostensibly in payment for Russia's rights to use the Captain's invention on her ships.

British Chess Magazine, 1891.

SIMPSON'S DIVAN

By Charles Tomlinson

Those who complain about the alleged cupidity of the chessmasters, glide rather easily over the distressing fact that three World Champions, Steinitz, Lasker, and Alekhine, died under conditions of undeserved poverty. In the glamorous days of the Golden Age of chess, the chess professional's life was often even more wretched.

...On entering the Divan [the visitor] was surprised to find long rows of sofas, the smell of tobacco, many chessboards and shelves full of books. A civil old waiter brought him his coffee, together with Blackwood and some newspapers, and enquired whether he would like a game of chess, which was declined; when lo! a musical clock was set going, which could be heard in every part of the large room.

My recollections of the Divan extend back to the twenties of this century.* As its interests in chess were more and more developed, it became less literary, that is, fewer books and papers were taken in, and the musical mechanism was removed altogether, as it tended to disturb the royal game. I remember on one occasion, when the Divan was being cleaned and redecorated, that the proprietor carried out what he conceived to be a clever idea in the interest of the chessplayers. He caused to be sunk into each marble table a mosaic chessboard, the squares of marble being of opposite colors. When the room was re-opened, the players would not use these stone squares. We must, they said, have a board raised from the table, with a terrace round it; for these marble things, being flush with the table, a dishonest player might easily coax with his sleeve a captured piece or pawn back again on to the board.

Simpson's in its best days was a pleasant place. It was the resort not only of well-known chessplayers of London and the provinces, but also of authors, actors, artists, and men about town. In cold weather there was a large fire at each end of the room, and we used to congregate about the one farthest from the door for a chat and a smoke. All sorts of subjects were more or less discussed. When Sir Robert Peel introduced his income tax measure, it was frequently talked over. An old gentleman remarked that he remembered it in Pitt's time, and how it led to a remarkable case of fraud in the town where he resided. A dashing young fellow engaged the best lodgings, lived in good style and got into society. He returned his income at a very large figure, and soon after paid his addresses to the daughter of the surveyor of taxes. This worthy fellow told his friends how good a match it was,

* Nineteenth century, of course!—F. R.

"Because," said he, "I know what his income is." After the marriage it was discovered that he was a mere adventurer, and his income return a fiction.

Buckle would occasionally join in the talk; he was always very positive, and few cared to contradict him. His rapid talk was not like his play, for this was very deliberate. On one occasion, when playing against Stanley, he occupied upwards of an hour over a single move. When he did move, Stanley said, "Yes, I thought that the knight would be the right move!" "You only thought so; I know it," retorted Buckle.

Buckle would sometimes invite a player to visit him at his house for a game. He was fond of giving pawn and move, or pawn and two, to a strong player, and the game would usually last late into the night. Next day, Williams, who edited a chess column, would look out for Buckle's antagonist, and get him to go over the game of the night before, which was then taken down. In this way some of Buckle's games were preserved, which otherwise would have been lost.

I was talking with Mr. Lewis* on the too great length of games, when he stated that the practice of long pauses was introduced by Staunton. "In the old Westminster Club," he said, "if a game lasted three hours, it was matter of talk for a fortnight. In my match with Deschapelles, all three games were played before dinner. Also with Cochrane's games on the same occasion. But one of Staunton's games may last twelve or thirteen hours, and even then be adjourned." At the time when Harrwitz and Loewenthal played their match, a time limit had frequently been discussed, but not agreed on. Staunton directed Loewenthal on at least one occasion when I was present, if not oftener, to take a quarter of an hour for every move. But Nemesis pursued even Staunton. He told me that in a match, a professional antagonist, whom I will not name, coolly said to him in answer to his remonstrance to his slow play, "I can't afford to lose this: I must sit you out!"

Staunton was not a favorite at the Divan. His chess column in the *Illustrated London News* was made the vehicle for many a stinging satire on well-known players. He always called himself an amateur,

---

* A leading English player and writer of the early part of the nineteenth century.— F. R.

and professed to despise those who played for money. But one of the professionals said to me, "I knew him when he was glad to play for threepence a game." This was probably true at one time; but Staunton rose above the position in which Fortune had placed him. He cultivated literature with some credit: he was a successful student of Shakespeare, and edited a well-known edition of the works of the great dramatist. His books on chess are admirable examples of sound exposition, judicious arrangement and selection, and good editing. During several years he was the leading player in Europe, and engaged in matches at odds with men of position, for money, it is true, for this was his chief means of support. He also played correspondence games for a stake, and I thought it somewhat unreasonable when the members of a provincial club complained to me bitterly that Staunton asked for the money as soon as he obtained what he called a winning position.

After his defeat by Anderssen in 1851 he became, as Boden termed it, "decorticated"; that is, more sensitive to every touch of Caissa, more irritable, and, if possible, more unfair. But he maintained his pompous manner, and his love of armorial bearings and sealing wax, which might appear ridiculous to a sober man, but were sources of irritation to those who professed chess and nothing else. One of his publishers told me that Staunton informed him that his family objected to his mixing himself up with chessplayers and chess divans. But it may be fairly enough suspected that Staunton's family was a myth, and that "Howard Staunton" a part thereof, however aristocratic the sound. Rumor, however, assigned a different name to our hero when he appeared first as an actor and next as a chess amateur. But to return to the Divan. This was in a state of excitement at the end of every week, when the *Illustrated London News* came in, and the notices to correspondents were eagerly examined. I remember that much indignation was caused by the reference to a "certain player named Williams," that player being as well-known in the chess world as Staunton himself; and also a contemptuous reference to Lowe, "that Professor!" when it was notorious that Staunton had a match in hand with Lowe at the odds of pawn and two; but finding his antagonist too strong for him at those odds, refused to go on with the match, and abused him in print. This will explain a remark of Buckle's, when someone asked him if he had ever engaged Staunton in a match. "No!" was the reply. "I was always careful to maintain friendly relations with him."

But the excitement at the Divan was, perhaps, at its height during the match between Harrwitz and Loewenthal. The former repaired to the Divan after the day's play, and went over the moves of the game before an admiring host of friends. Harrwitz was so elated at having won the first two games that he declared in my presence that Loewenthal should not win a single game. Boden encouraged him by saying: "I had rather throw a five-pound note into the gutter than that you should lose this match." Staunton, who got hold of everything that occurred in the chess world, got hold of course of this boast of Harrwitz's, and in his next chess column remarked, "We understand that Mr. Harrwitz intends his contest with Mr. Loewenthal to be a maiden match." The players met in a private room in an hotel near Spring Gardens, and in the following week I was present when Staunton dropped in, and Harrwitz went up to him and denied ever having made the remark which called forth Staunton's sarcasm. Staunton simply smiled, and said nothing. Of course I was equally silent, from a reluctance to get into hot water with the Divan party. Here the feeling ran very high, and it became so embittered as to lead to very discreditable conduct on the part of some of its inferior members. As the match inclined decidedly in favor of Loewenthal, one man said, in my hearing, that he had sent an organ boy to play before the window, so as to distract the attention of Loewenthal, who was known to be very nervous. He also did not like smoking and had stipulated beforehand that visitors should not smoke; but some of the Divan party had made it a point to smoke as near to Loewenthal as possible, and I even saw one man light his cigar at Loewenthal's candle, and puff the smoke into his face. I was never more convinced of the necessity for a chessplayer to be a gentleman.

But to return to more genial reminiscences. Among the players at the Divan were some very pleasant men. I do not think that I ever got over the odds of pawn and two, which these gentlemen gave me;

but I played even with Captain Evans, whose game was not, I thought, equal to his reputation.

Little Alexandre, who had worked the automaton, and talked pleasantly of Mouret who had preceded him, and also of some other earlier players, said he could not give me pawn and two; but he had become old and feeble, and was probably in bad circumstances, his *Thousand Chess Problems* and *Encyclopedia of Chess* having but a scanty sale.

Williams was a pleasant, gentlemanly antagonist, and he published some specimens of his Divan play in a little volume which he sold to the benignant amateur. It is entitled *"Horae Divanianiae,* a selection of one hundred and fifty original games by leading masters, principally played at the Grand Divan." It was published by the author at the Divan, in 1852, and it has a long list of subscribers, showing how greatly Williams was respected. The book, we say, was purchased off the author by the benignant amateur. I have seen a man take the odds of a knight, and score game and game and a draw, and then retire well satisfied with himself. One day when this occurred, Williams protested that he could not afford to give a lesson in such terms. Of course, under such a protest, none but a shabby man would refuse to pay the fee.

Daniels was also a most pleasant antagonist, he was chatty and intelligent, and his game had a flavor of originality about it which was rare among the professionals. There was a man named Finch, for example, whose moves were all stereotyped, as well as his traps and catches. He generally tried to evade giving odds by complimenting the amateur on his strength. On one such occasion an incident occurred which became a standing joke in the Divan. A clergyman introduced to Finch by Simpson, sat down before him and assented to the customary "Play for a shilling?" He lost about a dozen games, and then got up and deposited a shilling on the board, and would not be persuaded that a shilling a game was intended.

Daniels died early of consumption, and was greatly regretted.

Williams also died early. A subscription was got up in the Divan for the benefit of his widow and children, and I hope it was liberally supported. He had been a medical man in Bristol and was a distinguished member of the chess club there. Williams became so fascinated with the game that he gave up his practice for a precarious seat in the Divan.

I have also a melancholy recollection of Labourdonnais, who, broken in health and in fortune, was engaged by the proprietor of the Divan, at two guineas a week, to play all comers. The engagement did not last long. He was attended in the kindest manner by George Walker, who, when he died, conducted his body to its last resting place in Kensal Green Cemetery, near the remains of his old antagonist McDonnell. The last illness of Labourdonnais was said to have been occasioned by the great mental strain of a blindfold game with Boncourt. He said he felt as if something had given way in his brain. What a contrast between this single game and the twelve simultaneous blindfold games which I saw conducted by Blackburne in the old Divan!

The professional players were subject to a somewhat heavy tax about Christmas time. They had to subscribe each a sum of about two guineas to the waiters' fund. As the players were more or less dependent on the waiters for their customers, no one dared to put his name down for a smaller sum.

British Chess Magazine, 1891.

"MODERN SIMPSON'S"
By A. G.

This description of Simpson's Divan in the '90s is redolent of the snug, leisurely atmosphere of a bygone age. Incidentally, a pretty theory could be evolved about the relationship between London weather and the development of nineteenth-century chess in England. Another theory: the exclusively male atmosphere of Simpson's fitted neatly into an age of male domination. Perhaps the decay of Simpson's was but an episode in the male's fall from grace during the past 60 years. Wanted: women chessplayers!

The weary wayfarer, crossing the Strand on one of the sloppy days of early spring, cannot but admit to himself that he has a "bad game." The position is somewhat complicated. He has stepped up to his ankles in mud, and placed himself *en prise* to an omnibus. With the true instinct of a chessplayer he at once recognizes the perils of his situation. Nothing but a master-stroke can avail him. He therefore makes a combination to dash across the roadway, and after a narrow escape of being taken *en passant* by a hansom, he castles safely into the Divan.

And truth to tell he could hardly have found a more comfortable place of refuge for a wet afternoon. The very atmosphere of the place is inviting. Delicate fumes of tobacco mingle with the aroma of coffee, and there is moreover the sound, pleasant to a chessplayer's ear, of wooden pieces being placed more or less emphatically on their squares; while seated at the tables there are experts engaged in the rigor of the game, but not so deeply absorbed as to prevent them from chatting with the bystanders and making chaffing observations to their opponents. Certainly the writer in the *Daily News* who recently displayed his ignorance by asserting that chess is a melancholy game, chiefly practiced by old men at clubs, could never have been to Simpson's Divan. For here is good-fellowship and good temper, occasionally diversified, it is true, by the passing shade of sorrow that indicates the loss of a queen, or the impossibility of avoiding mate—misfortunes which are soon forgotten in the excitement of another game.

For the benefit of those who are only able to regard a visit to Simpson's as a pleasure to come, it may be well to briefly describe the room, which being undoubtedly the chief chess rendezvous of London, may without presumption be designated as the headquarters of the world. If any justification for this title be required, it is only necessary to remark that chess has made more progress in this country than in any other, and as a consequence there is frequently more chess talent gathered together on a single afternoon at Simpson's than could be found in the whole breadth of some of the continental countries. The room, which is fairly spacious, is situated on the second floor of the building occupied by Simpson's. The lower floors are devoted to dining rooms, and there is a cigar shop on the street level.

The chess divan is a lofty apartment, with three high windows looking out upon the busy Strand, and under these windows there is a row
of tables provided with boards and men of a somewhat antiquated and
peculiar pattern. In the center of the room is another row of tables
similarly provided, and at the back is a recess containing a library which
includes much useful literature, as well as many interesting works on
chess. The tables in the recess are piled with current magazines, and
this part of the room, it may be observed, is principally frequented by
non-chessplayers, who here indulge in coffee, cigars and philosophical
conversation after lunch. Indeed it is not until after the luncheon hour
that the Divan begins to assume anything like an animated aspect.

A few early comers drop in and look over the papers, the most
notable of these usually being the gentleman familiarly but not dis-
respectfully known as the "Old Frenchman." Whether he is really old
or not is probably unknown to anyone but himself. The writer has
known him by the same sobriquet for the last fifteen years, and is prepared to vouch that his appearance has undergone no change within
that period. M. Fevrett, for that is his name, has come to be regarded
as quite an institution at Simpson's Divan, where he generally practices the calling of a professional chessplayer. He is a little man, with
bent shoulders, iron-gray whiskers, and wide felt hat. It is curious
that notwithstanding his long residence in the country, he has never
acquired a knowledge of our language. He has the mercurial disposition common to his race, and under the exciting influence of the
game he causes a good deal of amusement by his running comments
in his own language. In fact he has excited the emulation of many
imitators, and one of his favorite expressions: *"Voilà ce que je n'aurais
pas voulu"** is very commonly heard on the lips of London chessplayers
when they get into difficulties.

Of late, three of the most notable frequenters of the room have been
absent, namely Bird, Blackburne, and Gunsberg. The former is only
just recovering from a very serious illness, Blackburne has gone to
Havana, and Gunsberg has been engaged at New York in a contest

* "Just what I didn't want!"—F. R.

with Steinitz. The absence of these gentlemen is greatly felt, but none of them has been so keenly missed as the veteran champion Bird. Probably he has enjoyed more games at Simpson's than any other living player; enjoyed we say advisedly, for if there is one thing more remarkable than another about Bird's play, it is the keen sense of enjoyment with which he enters into the excitement of the game. His broad good-humored visage reddens, his eyes grow keen, and evidently as far as his own feelings are concerned he might be once more the elegant youth of forty years ago, elaborating brilliant combinations for the overthrow of Boden or Staunton.

Perhaps this is one reason why his games always excite so much interest. The beauty and ingenuity of his play are well-known, and so it comes about that whenever Bird sits down to a game at Simpson's Divan, there is sure to be a goodly crowd of bystanders to watch his intricate maneuvers. We all hope soon to see him back in his old place again. Blackburne and Gunsberg also will receive a welcome at Simpson's on their return from the West. But even with these three giants away, there are still plenty of leading masters to be seen at the Divan, by anyone who cares to spend an afternoon in the fascinating atmosphere of that establishment.

There is James Mason, with his imperturbable face, playing in his usual sound and solid style against a hapless amateur, who vainly struggles for a draw. Mason is remarkably quiet while playing at chess, all his energies being obviously devoted to the game, and in this respect he differs from many other noted masters, who are apt to assume an air of carelessness and indifference which disconcerts aspiring beginners by giving them the idea that they are undervalued. Under other circumstances Mason is quite a different individual, being very fond of animated and convivial conversation. He is also capable of giving sound views on the political questions of the day, in which he takes a great deal of interest. I remember some time ago introducing an artistic friend to the mysteries of Simpson's Divan; he had hardly been there five minutes before he called my attention to Mason and asked who he was. The information being given, he exclaimed: "I should like to paint his head, it is one of the best I have ever seen."

Indeed one can easily understand that the keen dark eyes and intellectual contour of Mason's head would make a very interesting study for a painter.

No less picturesque is the massive brow and plentiful gray beard of the Rev. G. A. MacDonnell, who often comes to Simpson's whenever he can snatch a brief respite from his clerical duties. Mr. MacDonnell has for a great many years been a prominent figure in the chess world, and his brilliant weekly comments on the progress of the game, under the *nom de plume* of "Mars," are well known to the public. It is no exaggeration to say that he is one of the most popular men at the Divan. Besides being an exceptionally fine player, he is gifted with an inexhaustible fund of humor, and there is no man who more frequently "sets the table in a roar." Mr. MacDonnell has endless anecdotes to tell of the players of the last generation—Boden, Buckle, Falkbeer, and Staunton, and those who have heard him imitate the pompous manner of the latter, cannot but admit his dramatic ability. So life-like, in fact, are Mr. MacDonnell's impersonations of these former masters, that one seems actually to know them from his descriptions.

Another remarkable man who frequently appears at Simpson's is James Mortimer. His history is a romance. A former secretary of the American Legation in St. Petersburg and Paris, the friend of Paul Morphy, the editor and proprietor of the *Figaro,* as well as several other journals, and the author of several plays, Mr. Mortimer's experiences have been exceedingly interesting and varied. He is an enthusiastic chessplayer, and has taken part in every first-class tournament held in this country for many years past. Mr. Mortimer's games are well worth watching, for even in those that he loses he almost invariably produces some ingenious or brilliant combination. He has an impetuous disposition and is occasionally irritable under defeat; but this slight infirmity is easily condoned by those who know and esteem him.

Among the other frequent habitués of the rooms are Mr. Lee, Mr. Van Vliet, and Mr. Muller, all of whom are comparatively new recruits to the ranks of the masters. Besides these, it frequently happens that continental, American, and provincial celebrities are to be seen at Simpson's, for it is seldom indeed that any chessplayer comes to London

MR. STAUNTON.　　　MR. BODEN.　　　HERR LÖWENTHAL.

(*See 7, page 304.*)

HERR ANDERSSEN.　　　M. SAINT AMANT.　　　HERR HARRWITZ.

Paul Morphy

(*See 8, page 304.*)

without making a point of visiting the classic Divan. With such an array of talent as an attraction, it is not surprising that a great number of amateurs are continually finding their way to the room. These include men of every degree and representatives of every class of life. Men distinguished in various professions are often to be seen: comedians and clergymen, journalists and doctors, elderly merchants and youthful clerks, pompous family lawyers and briefless barristers, all animated by the same desire, either to see the masters play or to try their own skill against them at the modest outlay of a shilling. That small sum is all that it is customary to stake upon the games, so that it is open to anyone to obtain the best possible practice without the smallest chance of being accused of extravagance.

It has often been suggested, and not without justice, that the masters would better consult their own interests, as well as their dignity, if they did not make chess so cheap.* One cannot well understand how a shilling can repay them for all the mental labor needed in a contest with a strong amateur, especially as there is always the possibility of making a slip and losing the game. And yet it is a fact that the unfortunate Zukertort was playing for a shilling at the time when he was seized with the apoplectic stroke that led to his decease. It is, however, needless to recall this sad event. The chessplayer is, as a rule, endowed with the artistic temperament, thinking but little of tomorrow or yesterday, and enjoying himself in the present, amid the endless complications and delights that his chosen pastime never fails to afford.

...An eccentric gentleman, I will call him Mr. C., used to cause a great deal of amusement by the extraordinary velocity of his moves; he boasted that he had won every game he had played with Zukertort, the fact being that he had played only one, which by some accident he had happened to win, and after this he steadfastly refused to play Zukertort again.

"I have beaten you every game," he used to say, "and if I played you again, I might not be able to say so any more."

---

* Did A. G. really imagine that sellers can establish the going rates in a buyers' market?!—F. R.

One day he was playing Blackburne, and the latter somehow got into a hopeless mess. Mr. C. was boiling over with excitement, and Blackburne, seeing that there was nothing else to be done, had recourse to a little artifice. He took up his opponent's bishop and put it down with a bang, exclaiming "Check!"

"I take it off," said Mr. C. excitedly.

"You can't take your own piece," retorted Blackburne.

"Oh, of course not," said the bewildered C., who thereupon moved his king and was mated, amid the laughter of the bystanders.

I remember an equally amusing incident which happened when two beginners came in and sat down to play. I was occupied at a board close by, and an occasional glance at their proceedings showed me that their skill at chess was confined to a knowledge of the moves. Their game proceeded quietly and laboriously for some time, until at last one of them remarked: "I think you are mate. You can't go there and you can't go there. You can't move at all, you *are* mate."

"So I am," said the other, after carefully scrutinizing the board, and then taking another look at the position he added: "But you are mate too."

"Well, I mated you first," said his opponent.

"No, that you didn't," was the reply.

On this a dispute arose, but how it was eventually settled I do not know, for just then my own game required so much attention that I was unable to notice anything else....

British Chess Magazine, 1891.

PURSSELL'S

In this article, the anonymous author evokes the genial atmosphere of another famous Victorian haunt of chessplayers. Reading these lines, we cannot help but feel that the present diversity of available amusements has had a harmful effect on the existence of chess clubs.

...Outside there is little or nothing to distinguish Purssell's from the many other places where city men get their chop or luncheon; certainly there is nothing to suggest the proximity of one of the greatest chess rooms in the world. Pass upstairs, however, and after two short flights of steps, there you are. The room may at first appear not very inviting. It presents a somewhat somber appearance, especially if you come—a not very probable supposition by the way—from the bright sunlight without. It is large, indeed very spacious for the city, considering the enormous rentals hereabout. But skylights are impossible except on top floors, and the view from top floors, and the view from side windows is only what you may expect if you know the city. You can call for what you please; for unlike the Divan, where you can get nothing substantial to eat in the room, here you can obtain almost anything in the shape of refreshment for the inner man, the cellar being especially well furnished.

Who are the frequenters of the room? Stock Exchange men, and city men of business generally, with a good sprinkling of foreigners, lawyers and other professional men, and occasional visitors from all parts, including a large proportion of really strong chessplayers. Loafers are here almost unknown. It is a place frequented by *gentlemen;* cool, calm, quiet, hard-headed men of business, of the sort that have made England, and especially the City of London, what it is. Some select a quiet corner and spend their midday rest over a newspaper or magazine; a few play dominoes; many discuss the latest chess news eagerly; a very large proportion enjoy a game themselves, and all are interested in chess generally, and especially in any good games in progress.

If you arrive early you may find the room nearly empty; but as one o'clock approaches, one after another comes in, for about this time is the city man's leisure hour, and the room will soon be full. After a time many leave for afternoon work, returning after business hours to enjoy a game of chess before leaving the city for home and evening engagements.

... Blackburne was once playing here with a very irascible old gentleman, who was most particular in enforcing all rules of the game, and when in a certain humor, could not take a joke. It was his own first move, and he played ... P-K3. "Ah," said Blackburne, "now I resign." "All right," said his touchy opponent, "that's one game to me!" and nothing, as Blackburne knew, would alter that determination, so it was duly scored. This is the shortest game on record. Blackburne was beaten in one move!

...Fenton has been an institution at Purssell's for no one knows how long. No one knows his age, and no one knows, accurately, his real strength. I remember him as long as I can remember anything of chess matters, and I solemnly declare he is now looking at least as young and blithe as when first I saw him. He plays at least as well as he ever did. To him, twenty or thirty years seems to make no difference. He is always there. A day at Purssell's seems like drawing a blank. Chess tournaments have no attractions for him; nothing lures him from his den, except one or two days' good cricket in the very hot weather, "but it must be a really fine day if I go." I have a shrewd suspicion that one reason for this is that it pays him best to remain where and as he is. He possesses more than any other player I ever saw, the faculty of getting good customers and keeping them; and many believe (rightly or wrongly) that no player has at times done better by chessplaying, pure and simple, than R. F. Fenton.

Not that there is anything brilliant about his play. His maxim—one of his many maxims I should rather say—is "Never try to checkmate your opponent, but try to win the game!" Hence he tries to *win,* and to this end plays a safe careful game, according to the good old rule, the simple plan,

> Keep yourself safe, all other graces
> Will follow in their proper places.

So he plays for safety, picks up "a little stray pawn," and wears you down until you surrender.* It is his boast that his style is perfect; he never hovers over the board, and no one, he says, ever saw him take a move back. "A man that will take a move back at chess," he sometimes says, "will pick a pocket." When the end approaches, if by chance he is losing, he gives in without submitting to the last indignity of the game, and he freely advises his opponents to do the same. "Never allow yourself to be checkmated," he often says. "No human being has

---

* So that's how they played chess in the good old days!—F. R.

ever seen me checkmated yet." If the game is equal, or thereabouts, he will offer to turn the board round if you don't like your game. I never yet saw anyone accept the offer, though there is a story of someone who did so and won the game!

In the end Fenton generally wins; but he has so many ways of consoling his opponent, so many good stories and sayings, and is so intelligent in conversation that you can't feel angry. He tells you, for instance, that at a certain point your ideas were very good, etc., etc. (only overlooking that a certain piece or pawn was left *en prise!*), that one man is just as good as another at this game, and that you only need a little French polish to make you first-rate. Altogether you are convinced that you are getting on; and you pay the small stake and go away with a light heart, feeling that you have spent a pleasant hour, and firmly persuaded that your friend who has beaten you so often will not have such an easy thing on hand when next you meet. Fenton is one of the few men who appear to have no enemies.

Tinsley belongs to another school, being brilliant, daring, dashing; not so sound as Fenton, but more dangerous, and not by any means rash. He appears at first sight to be getting on in years, but is in reality comparatively young. Coming to London at a very early age, fresh from the plough tail and the agricultural wilds of one of the home counties, with much less than the proverbial half crown, and no scrap of education or knowledge of the world, Tinsley has had to buy experience and knowledge dearly, and it has told on a high-strung, sensitive disposition, but his spirits are ever buoyant and juvenile.

His first chess experiences were acquired in a good school. Who remembers the Divan thirteen or fourteen years ago? "All the talents" were there daily, and Saturday afternoons were especially attractive. Steinitz, Zukertort, Blackburne, Potter, Hoffer, Mason, Bird, Boden, and MacDonnell—really those were palmy days! What warm discussions there were on positions, endings, problems, games, and all sorts of chess matters; and how frequently Zukertort, Steinitz and Hoffer quarreled and made it up in five minutes! How heartily Boden enjoyed a game with Bird or MacDonnell!

Tinsley was a pretty frequent listener and spectator, and having a retentive memory and an insatiable thirst for knowledge of all kinds, it is not to be wondered at if he picked up a few good chessy ideas under such favorable conditions. In offhand play he holds with giving your opponent a chance, and cannot bear the idea of a humdrum, dead-level solemn game, lasting for an hour or two without a whisper or a murmur, as if it were a matter of life or death; unless indeed you profess to play a serious match game. He is fond of a trap, and it will not be wise to rush at once to the conclusion that any particularly obvious line of play will be to your advantage. He is usually careful and deep, and sees far ahead in a short time, and few can beat him at the pace. That at Purssell's he is popular is obvious. He says many cutting things, but the Purssellites know him and make allowances, feeling that he has their interests at heart, and is strictly impartial.

It is notable how many who do not addict themselves to strict chess, never make any real progress. Some play several games regularly every day, but not having schooled themselves into an exact system go on year after year and show no sign of improvement. This is one very strong argument for the profession in chess, and for having a small stake on a game, and it cannot well be answered. The smallest stake will, ninety-nine times at least in one hundred, be an incentive to unusual care; and I should fancy any man who hates gambling need not, in chess, object to having something on.

In regard to carelessness—and going westward for one moment—I remember an old gentleman, Mr. A., who used to drive up regularly, Sundays and weekdays, to the Divan, who rarely spoke a word except by way of a mumble, and who sometimes played a few games. At that time, perhaps fifteen years ago, the late M. Dellannois, of Paris, was in London. He was a brilliant, eager, effusive skittler, very old and white, with prominent eyebrows. Over the game his head would be bent forward, all attention to the game, but utterly regardless of the way the pieces were placed on the squares. He met the gentleman referred to above, and they skittled away. Presently in castling, Mr. A., unconsciously of course, brushed his king off the board altogether, an incident which the few onlookers noticed much amusement, but no one thought of speaking. Dellannois went on, of course quite oblivious,

until, presently, he brought out his bishop to B4 with a *check;* when
lo and behold there was no king to administer the said check to. His
majesty was, in fact, on the floor, amongst cigar ashes and other refuse,
and had to be brought up on to the table to be checked!

Purssell's has, then, players of all grades; some who play so carelessly
as to rarely win. In leisure intervals Tinsley often watches such games,
and if such and such a player by any chance scores a game, promises
to make a note of it in his diary, as an unprecedented circumstance; a
remark that is by no means resented, for the reasons already stated.

One popular character at Purssell's is Mr. Manley, a good old Purs-
sellite, who is best known by his "rat" openings (P-N3 and B-N2). He
takes much care of, or rather sets much store by, his bishops. One of
his peculiarities is to give audible expression to his feelings at the
sight of "featherbed soldiers," *i.e.,* pieces undeveloped. What a pity
it is we have not someone in every chess room to go the round of the
boards and say, "For heaven's sake, gentlemen, don't keep that knight
at home any longer!" Here one could moralize for a very long time
upon the games lost through not bringing out the queen knight alone.

Everyone remembers, kindly, "Old Roby." He is gone. Ten or twelve
years ago I knew him well. A fine, gentlemanly, clever man, with
soft gentle manners, much respected and greatly missed. He had come
down in the world, I hope not through chess, and was capable of better
things. He is often mentioned with evident interest.

Perhaps one of the most interesting and popular characters at Purssell's within living memory, was an old white-haired gentleman of
striking features, best known as "His Lordship." He has also gone over
to the majority. He possessed the faculty of giving all frequenters of
the room some appropriate nickname, and of making 'cute and
peculiar remarks, during play and in conversation, that are treasured
to this day. One of these, often repeated, is remarkably suggestive of
the difficulty of seeing everything clearly: "Why, sir, you want eyes
all over your head, like a bluebottle, to play this game." This was
trotted out every time you were simple enough to make a more than
usually stupid oversight. Neither he nor Roby was very strong, but
Roby was the better player of the two.

There is a good story told of how one of the Paulsens* came in, was challenged, and offered the odds of a knight by His Lordship. The odds were accepted, needless to state with what result, and Paulsen returned the compliment with success, greatly to His Lordship's disgust. He had a peculiar habit of taking a knight up in his left hand and, twirling it over his head when in a difficult position, bringing it, spinning, down on to the intended square with a bang and another twist. If he had a knight left on the board on this occasion you may be sure he did the same with great energy; but history does not say. Anyhow, it is certain the incident had a mutually agreeable termination.

One of his clients was a gentleman who was spending his substance too freely, and played at one time for more than the usual small stakes; the result being a balance in His Lordship's favor of, I think, nearly £10. Now this was a most unusual amount and was paid by check, and there was a shrewd suspicion that it would be wise to get the cash speedily. So down the stairs His Lordship rushes, goes to the bank, gets the money in breathless haste, returns with almost equal speed, calls for the best port in the house and says, 'How delightful it is to live at the rate of £10,000 a year for five minutes!"

Roby was ingenious, imaginative, inventive, scientific. He devised an infallible plan to win money at Monte Carlo, in fact, to break the bank there. He firmly convinced himself of this by mathematical calculations. What is more, he unfolded his plan to a gentleman with whom he played, and convinced him, too, that there was something in it. They both went to Monte Carlo, Roby supplying the plan and his client the cash. The Monte Carlo tableites were, meanwhile, in blissful ignorance of the catastrophe that was looming. Arriving there the two went to work and experienced, I suppose, much the same as others have done before and since. Roby explained that the reason his plan did not work at once was that there were so many absentees; a little later he wrote that "the long absentees came tumbling in"; but unfortunately by that time all the money had tumbled out of their pockets, and they went back home and to Purssell's, sadder, but probably not much wiser

* Louis Paulsen was one of the great masters of the century. His brother Wilfried was only a moderate player, but doubtless capable of trouncing His Lordship.—F. R.

men. At all events, Roby was still as firmly convinced as ever that with "sufficient capital" they could still have "broken the bank."

Roby invented another system, one that is still in vogue at Purssell's at least. It may be explained in this way: the usual stake or fee is one shilling per game; which means, presumably, that if the professional wins two out of three games he gets one shilling Now three games may last for two or three hours, and Roby saw the injustice of spending so much time for such small remuneration. He therefore proposed, when playing with fairly strong amateurs, that he should be paid one shilling each for every game he won, irrespective and not deducting those he lost. To this arrangement many gentlemen readily consented, and hence the adoption of the "Roby system" or the "Roby irresponsible system." I fear the above explanation is rather elaborate; it may be put in fewer words—heads, I win; tails, you lose. Without some such arrangement, however, it is not at all uncommon for a strong amateur to occupy a professional's time, win a majority of games, *and take the money.*

There was much of the Micawber spirit in Roby. Conversing with him frequently, I always found he had just matured some plan for making a good income, apart from chess, and was going the very next day to set about it, until a fatal illness overtook him and he died in the hospital. Roby was not singular in respect to what I have just stated; Bird, who, until his much lamented illness, was very active in disposition, always spoke in the same strain. Fortunately for chess, and perhaps unfortunately for themselves, these good resolutions are not always adhered to, and the best players do not carry out their frequently-repeated determination of "retiring definitely and finally from chess."

Purssell's varies little as years roll on. Every chessplayer visits it at one time or another, some more or less regularly. The same faces are seen day after day in the accustomed places, and at set times, all the year round. The City is conservative, changes are abominated, and the proprietors of this establishment seem to fully share this feeling. This may account in some measure for the fact that few special efforts are put forth here in the interests of the game.

Unlike most popular chess resorts, Purssell's closes for incomers at eight, and for outgoers at nine. But long before this, except for the street traffic, Cornhill is deserted; and though there always is in every chess room that one last lingering game, Karl usually has no great difficulty in getting rid of the last couple of enthusiasts, and the day is done.

I am sorry to close in so prosaic a fashion; but I am no poet, and appropriate quotations do not seem to come at the bidding. Moreover, at Purssell's we are not very sentimental or poetical, but sober everyday people, who have to meet life as it is, and who find that life greatly relieved by a moderate indulgence in the purest and most ennobling of all amusements, a game of chess.

British Chess Magazine, 1891.

The Modern Masters

HASTINGS, 1950

By Lord Dunsany

Silence. And silence still.
Then one long roller breaks
And Hastings' houses fill
With the wild sound it makes.

Silence again. The sea,
Though it may seem to sleep,
Is still the vast and free
Inscrutable deep.

Who shall entirely scan
All its mysteriousness?
Even the mind of man
Has deeps beyond our guess.

So, when a move has brought
Some strategy in sight,
We cannot plumb the thought
That brought that move to light.

And, small although it be,
And missed by careless eyes
A chessboard, like the sea,
Has unplumbed mysteries.

British Chess Magazine, 1951.

UNCONVENTIONAL SURRENDER
By Hans Kmoch and Fred Reinfeld

When this article was first published, Chess Review *commented: "Messrs. Kmoch and Reinfeld possess between them a great store of chess experience: curious caissac episodes, amusing anecdotes, and reminiscences garnered from personal contact with the immortals of the game. The following examples, all slanted to a certain end, seem designed to point a moral. As to what that moral may be, each reader will best form his own judgment. Our guess: You, too, can be a chessmaster! The need to score points and win tournaments seems highly overrated. What you really need is to be able to resign impressively."*

There are many ways of resigning a game of chess.

You can resign with an almost happy smile, congratulating the winner with a hearty handshake. This is the British style, best illustrated by the almost superhuman sportsmanship of Sir George Thomas.

You can resign with a poker face, registering undiminished calm (the Rubinstein manner) or undiminished friendliness (the Euwe manner).

A man mounting a table, however, and yelling at the top of his voice, "Why must I lose to this idiot!" (*Gegen diesen Idioten muss ich verlieren!*) would be following the example of Nimzovich, who thus vented his rage—after losing in the last round of a great rapid transit tournament in Berlin and so missing first prize.

Resignation in the style of David Janowski is suitable for the more modest man who contents himself with describing his opponent as the greatest patzer in chess history and then denounces the committee for inviting people whose chess is so wretched that it sickens a real master.

When Spielmann reached the point of resigning, he never uttered a word—certainly not the fatal word. Instead, he indicated his overwhelming disgust by grimacing distastefully, closing his eyes, shaking his head violently, turning aside, and pushing the chessmen away from him as if they were poisoned.

Resigning *à la* Capablanca calls for the hauteur of a millionaire giving a dime to a beggar.

Gruenfeld's method is to stop the clock and leave the table without even looking at the winner.

Leaving the table, departing from the tournament room, and absenting oneself until the game is officially scored as a forfeit is still another way of resigning. The most famous instance is that of Bardeleben at the Hastings tournament of 1895. Just as Steinitz was approaching the crucial point of one of the "grand combinations" of chess history, Bardeleben found it convenient to retire. This was the situation on the board:

BARDELEBEN

STEINITZ

Once Bardeleben's departure had been recorded in the score table, 60-year-old Steinitz rattled off the following famous win after Black's virtually forced reply:

1	. . . .	K-R1		7	Q-N7ch	K-K1
2	RxPch!	K-N1		8	Q-N8ch	K-K2
3	R-N7ch!	K-R1		9	Q-B7ch	K-Q1
4	Q-R4ch!	KxR		10	Q-B8ch	Q-K1
5	Q-R7ch	K-B1		11	N-B7ch	K-Q2
6	Q-R8ch	K-K2		12	Q-Q6 mate!	

During the Kecskemet tournament of 1927, Hans Mueller hit upon a novel method of resigning which saved his dignity, if not the point. Mueller's method was—complete secrecy! The game was adjourned, and, only when Tournament Director Maroczy opened the envelope, was Mueller's sealed "move" revealed: *aufgegeben!* A little study of the position shows the way Mueller came to hit upon his "innovation."

YATES

MUELLER

White's trouble is that he has no good square for his attacked knight. Thus, if 1 N-K2?, P-Q6. If 1 N-N5 (or 1 N-R2 or 1 N-N1), B-K6ch; 2 K-B1, P-Q6! Finally, if 1 N-R4, P-B6!; 2 R-N1, B-K1; 3 R-R2, P-B7!

So we see that Mueller really could have resigned at once. But perhaps the idea of being questioned was too much for his vanity!

Alekhine hit on still another way of resigning during the Vienna tournament of 1922. Gruenfeld had played what was then his new defense. Alekhine had tried to refute it and had failed. The game was adjourned in the following position (*see diagram on page 131*):

Alekhine naturally realized that he was lost but was still curious to know whether his opponent might have sealed a mistake. So, when play was resumed after dinner, he appeared in the tournament room. Wearing his hat and overcoat, he went to his table which happened to be located near the entrance. When he saw that Gruenfeld had sealed

54 ... Q-B6 (the strongest move), Alekhine resigned—by taking his king and throwing it across the room.

GRUENFELD

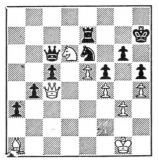

ALEKHINE

And so it goes. Nobody likes to lose a game. When they lose, few people have the ability to hide their disappointment. And then, as Tartakover says, "Nobody has ever won a game by resigning."

Chess Review, 1950.

PRONUNCIATION

By Nat Halper

Halper is a player of near master strength. He is also gifted with a glib pen and a pleasant sense of humor. Under the guise of being helpfully pedagogical, he manages to get in some good-natured digs at the masters. But if you're troubled by the often mouth-breaking syllables that make up the masters' names, you'll find these verses quite useful, at that!

Chessplayers' names are often hard to pronounce. Many readers have declared they would like a handy guide to their proper pronunciation. It happens that I have such a guide in my possession. This is how it came about.

A couple of years ago, I taught chess to a girl whom I was wooing. I did my job too well. I found, all too soon, that I had created a *Frankenstein*. For my pupil fell in love—not with her teacher but with the game that he was teaching. I had thought I was building a stepping-stone to her heart. But, instead of this, the chessboard became a barrier I could not cross.

Like many another man, frustrated in my love, I turned to writing poems. My verses were not about bees. They were not about flowers. In my songs, I sang about the many, many, many men for whom my girl had spurned me—namely, the many, many immortal Masters of the Chessboard.

Now I was forced to learn how to speak their names before I could fit them into my rhythms and my rhyme. If you, in your turn, study my rhythm and my rhymes, you will learn the pronunciation of more than three-score names.

To get the maximum benefit, I really think you ought to read these little songs. You should read them with expression. You should read them with emotion. You should caress every sound.

> Oh! she is the Tarrasch
> Of this parish.
> Tartakover
> Is her lover,
> And Ragozin
> Is her cousin.
> When I gaze upon her ankle,
> All her thoughts are Capablanca-l.
> When I look upon each knuckle,
> All her reveries are Kmoch-al.
> When I dote upon each freckle,
> Her ideas are Charousek-al
> And a trifle Golombek-al!
> She's a girl who stoops to folly
> Only if you are a Colle.
> She will always take a night off

For a Miguel Moishe Najdorf.
She will be your hotsy-totsy
If you are a G. Maroczy,
    A. Yanofsky!
    D. Janowsky!
       Koltanowsky!
       Romanovsky!
          Znosko-Borovsky!
          Bonch-Osmolovsky!
Oh—
An' what of
Kotov?

Ah! she thinks there's nothing freer
Than a Tony Santasiere.
She thinks there's nothing grander
Than an O'D. Alexander.
She thinks there's nothing finer
Than a Rubinstein or Steiner.
Ah! she thinks there's nothing higher
Than a Breyer, a Bisguier,
In a pinch—
A Leonard Meyer!
Since she played with Georgie Kramer
All the other men seem tamer.
For her little toe gets wiggly
Every time she thinks of Gygli.
She will play the hurdy-gurdy
With a Reinfeld or a Purdy
And will dance a hot kazatsky—
If a man is Ulvestad-sky!
She will spurn a Tyrone Power,
A Van Johnson or a Gable,
For a Cenek Kottnauer
Or a man like Dr. Treybal.

For she henkers
After Denkers,
And the thing that she is wantin'
Is a Pilnik or a Staunton
    A Reshevsky!
    Bondarevsky!
    Ilyin—X. Y. Z.—Genevsky!
Ah!
An' what of
Kotov?

Will she, will she
Always Flohr me?
Will she never
Phil-adore me?
Will she never
Care a damn bit
For my Center
Counter Gambit?

She's a lady
Who will get rough
If you are not like a Petroff.
She will be a lot of trouble
If a fellow is not Grob-al.
She's a baby
Who's as mean as
Twenty wildcats and as heinous
If you are not a Mikenas!
She is very
Very bitchy
If you are not Nimzovich-y.
She is very
Very ritzy
If you are not Horowitz-y,

    Ebralidze,
    Goglidze.
No! she will not
Be your woman
If you are not a Ryumin.
She will say, "Bo!
Go away, Bo!
Leave my portal!"
If you are not like a Szabo,
If you are not Zuketort-al—
      If you aren't a Koshnitsky!
      A Levitzky!
         Kieseritsky!
Yes—
An' what of
Kotov?

She'll be
All milk and honey,
If a man is Simonson-y.
She'll give you all the gravy,
She will be your faithful slavey
If you are a Maxie Pavey!
For
A Keres
Is the berries,
And a Dake
Takes the cake,
And a Schlechter
Is like nectar,
While a man like Przepiorka
Is a double-barreled corker.
She'll be
Your sweet golubchik,
She'll be your Betty Boop-chick

Only
If you are a Kupchik!
She is daffy
About Jaffe.
She thinks that a Lisitsyn
Is the only one who fits in!
This little miss is partial
To no one but a Marshall.
This little miss is matey
With no one but a Reti.
This little miss'll marry
No one but a Milner-Barry.
Yes, yes—
She is marryin'
No one but
A Kasparyan!
She will even take a gonef
If he is a Makagonov
    John!
    Kahn!
    Bolbochan!
    Spielmann!
    And Sultan Khan—
An'
An' what of
Kotov?

I will have to pull my neck in
For she dotes upon Alekhin[e].
I will have to pull my oar in
For she dotes upon Tchigorin!
How I pine,
How I yearn,
But my girl,
She wants a Byrne!

Oh! I'm at sixes, I'm at sevens
For she's crazy about Evans.
All I can do is grovel
When she gets Bogolyubov-al.
And the Euwes
Make me nervous.
I am fevered, I am famished
For a little girl who's Saemisch'd.
Her desire for Botvinnik
Makes me sour. I'm a cynic.
I will go
Into a clinic!

*   *   *   *

Here my manuscript ends.

As I read this poem, I feel once again the emotion and the pain that I felt at that time. Oh, how odd it is to think that out of my agony there came a handy guide to a proper pronunciation!

Well, that is the way it is. That is how our world runs! Here is a handy guide. I offer it for your use.

P.S.—I married a woman who doesn't know how to play chess.

Chess Review, 1940

LAST ROUND

By Kester Svendsen

In the United States, in Australia and in Holland, Last Round *has been acclaimed as one of the best stories, if not the best story, ever written about chess. For dramatic tension and for its uncanny insight into the "grandeur and misery" of a chessmaster's life, this story unquestionably deserves a high rating. The fusing of the action, interior monologue, and the actual moves of a real game is a remarkable achievement. It is a pity that Black's moves are not of grandmaster caliber, but this flaw is well disguised in the masterly narrative.*

The Old Master looked down at the board and chessmen again, although he had seen their stiff pattern times out of mind. While the tournament director was speaking he could wait. And as he waited the old questions rose once more in his mind. Could this be it, the perfect game, the thing of beauty, the work of art? Could there come out of this tension of minds, this conflict of wits, anything more than victory and defeat? This unknowing search for secret beauty! What was the perfect game of chess? Was Capablanca right? Was it a draw, with the board exhausted of pieces? Was it a smashing victory? Was it a thing of small advantages multiplied into attrition?

The director's voice seeped into his reverie.

"Final round . . . Rolavsky the Russian champion leading with seven points . . . draws against Henderson and Zettler . . . then six straight wins."

The thought of a perfect game faded. Win? Could he even draw? Could he hold off the faultless Rolavsky, whose countrymen had for years pooled their incredibly patient testing of every defense to the Queen's Gambit and the Ruy Lopez?

"His opponent half a point behind . . . no one else close enough."

The Old Master looked up at the other playing areas roped off in the center of the ballroom. Epstein and Creech, poised, repeating a tableau older than memory. Batchelor, bushy-haired and nervous, glancing at tiny Zeitlin, prepared to play as if the title were balanced. The others farther away, still figures drawn sharply together over the subtlest challenge in their lives. The huge demonstration boards against the wall, runners and movers waiting to record the play in each game. The crowd, impatient for the director to finish and for this game to begin.

"Ten years since he won a tournament . . . his entry invited frankly as a sentimental gesture to the spirit of his long career—now his amazing comeback against eight of the world's best . . . world's championship vacated by the death of Alekhine . . . assured of second place, he has already done better than the old Lasker at Moscow . . . can this grand old man of chess snatch a full point from his ninth and last opponent, the unbeatable Russian? . . . He needs a win, Rolavsky only a draw."

Could he win? He lingered a moment over what a win would mean. The cash prize. Exhibitions. Tours. New editions of a champion's works. Contracts for others. No more the poverty of a chessmaster's life, articles and annotations for short-lived journals, books that barely paid their way, lessons to sharkish amateurs who wanted only to beat each other. How many masters, having given their lives to the game, had died penniless, like Alekhine?

"Additional drama ... youth and age ... the only player in the world with a plus score against Rolavsky ... that famous fifteen-move surprise win of his at Bitzer Lake ten years ago." Bitzer Lake! The Old Master looked at the board again and wondered how he should open this time. Queen's Gambit?

"Like his countryman, Frank Marshall, he has never played to the score, but has always sought to make each game a work of art."

A Lopez? Had Rolavsky been saving a defense for the Lopez ever since that savage encounter at Bitzer Lake? Could he meet it cold as Capablanca did Marshall's at New York and smash it? What to play? King pawn or queen pawn?

The voice stopped. The director was at his table, starting his clock. Two hours for thirty moves. The photographers near his table poised themselves as he moved his arm. He lifted his eyes to Rolavsky's face and saw etched in it the sharp memory of that defeat at Bitzer Lake.

Suddenly he felt tired, remembering the dilemma in which he had spent himself so many times in fifty years. Play for a win or play for perfection? There rose against him the ghosts of a hundred games and a dozen tournaments lost because he could never decide which he wanted. The clock at his elbow ticked insistently. King pawn or queen pawn? And, as ever, in a corner of his mind, the same old question. Could this be it, the work of art? He thought of Kieseritzky, remembered only as the loser of that ever-famous *partie* to Anderssen.

Rolavsky twisted a little, and somewhere out of the thousands of games and hundreds of players in the old man's memory there stirred a spark. The immortal Lasker playing his fourth move at St. Petersburg. Bishop takes knight, most drawish of all the variations in the Lopez, and there was Lasker needing a win but playing bishop takes knight against Capablanca. Psychological chess. Capablanca sweating away at the thought of a new wrinkle. Lasker sitting like a stone. Rolavsky twitched again and suddenly the Old Master wasn't tired any more. Conviction freshened him like wine. He felt again as at every game, before the first move. He smiled at Rolavsky—and moved his pawn to king four. Photographers' flashes sprang at him. The audience riffled forward as Rolavsky duplicated the move. With no hesitation, the Old Master moved his queen pawn beside his king pawn and listened for the buzz from the spectators.

"Center Game!...is he playing the Center Game?...Mieses used to try it...but the queen moves too soon...hasn't been played in a tournament since Tartakover tried it at Stockholm against Reshevsky ...is he crazy? Rolavsky will smash it to bits."

There was no good way to decline the capture even if Rolavsky had wanted to, but the younger man seemed a little slow as he took the pawn. The old man caught his eye again, smiled again, pushed his queen's bishop's pawn forward a square, then leaned back and waited for the avalanche.

It came with a rush, as of collapse at a distance. Rolavsky half rose from his chair.

"Danish Gambit?...Danish Gambit!...two pawns...who can give Rolavsky two pawns, development or no development?...what does he think this is, a skittles game?...Danish...not in a tournament since Marshall drew one with Capa twenty years ago."

Rolavsky stared across the board, tight-lipped in contempt. Then he took the second pawn.

For a moment the old man's mind drifted back to other ballrooms and hotels, the Crystal Palace, chop houses and concessions, the thousand places where he had paused before a board and moved a pawn or knight. The simultaneous play where he walked forever within a horseshoe of tables—fifteen, fifty, a hundred sometimes—moving a piece or being waved by, ever returning and ever wondering with each move if somewhere, in some single play, even on a greasy board with clumsy pieces, he might pluck the secret. The thick smoke, the bad food, the hours of walking, the stale people behind the tables straining for a win or a draw against the master and playing on even though a queen or a couple of pieces down. He remembered too the glittering tournaments at Margate, Hastings, San Remo, Monte Carlo, with jeweled women and royalty looking over his shoulder. He lived again that moment at Breslau when Marshall plunged his queen into a nest of Lewitzky's pawns, and the spectators, caught up in the excitement of the most elegant move ever made, showered the table with gold pieces. Slowly he forced these memories from his mind and, as he looked out over the spectators, moved his bishop to queen bishop four.

The crowd stirred uneasily, waiting for Rolavsky to take the third pawn and then hang on through the attack. The Old Master wondered a little too. Rolavsky always took the pawn in the Queen's Gambit, probably because it wasn't a gambit at all. In the Danish he had to take the first and could take the second, according to the books. Schlechter had always taken the third, too. But how lately had Rolavsky played against a Danish? He was taking too long, that young wizard. Now it came: knight to king bishop three. Development. Playing safe. The old man advanced his knight to king bishop three and tapped the clock, as after every move.

Rolavsky studied the board a long time. Again the spectators shifted about. A few moves more, thought the Old Master, and he would know whether to hope for a draw or a win. With an edge of sudden fear he remembered that Tchigorin had once lost a game in eight moves, Alapin in five. He jerked his mind about and worried the chessmen as they waited for his turn. But Rolavsky was plainly hesitating now, as if trying to recall the best line. Surely the pawn was not poisoned. Yet, one piece out to White's two. Even before Rolavsky's fingers touched the bishop, the Old Master moved it mentally to bishop four. There it rested, and a surge of power flowed into his mind. His reply was obvious, but he lingered over it a while, probing with his imagination the mind of his antagonist, that mind crammed with encyclopedic knowledge of standard openings, hundreds of variations in the Queen's Pawn. Was it shaken a little now, that fine machine? The crowd seemed to think so. A half caught whisper: *"Why didn't he take the pawn? ... why not?"*

Why not? Was Rolavsky thinking of Bitzer Lake and the thrust of rage with which he had swept the pieces to the floor at the fifteenth move? Now the Old Master lifted his knight and removed the Black pawn at bishop three. Rolavsky moved pawn to queen three; and as the old man castled, it was obvious that White had ample compensation for the pawn sacrificed. Again the muttering. *"Seven moves and Rolavsky on the defensive ... unheard of .. a Danish Gambit!"*

After long thought the Russian castled, and now the Old Master felt himself moving into that strange trance of chess intuition. Attack. Tempt a weakness. A combination, with the pieces piling up at one spot, cleansing the board of each other's presence. Lines of play ran through his head. The pieces on the board swirled into patterns, blended, and stiffened into place eight or ten moves on. Tempt a weakness. But would Rolavsky move his pawn? His whole queen-side undeveloped? The Old Master put his hand to the king's knight and a small sigh went up from the spectators. *"One move ... a single tempo ... and Rolavsky's even ... why didn't he pin the knight?"* A moment's hesitation, and then he placed the knight at knight five. There. Now would Rolavsky move the pawn? The precisionist wouldn't. The arrogant refuter of gambits would. Did there linger still a trace of something from the third move? Would this Russian weaken? Rook and pawn, did he think, for bishop and knight?

Rolavsky studied the position almost interminably. Then he pushed his pawn to king rook three—then dropped his hand as if burnt, as if too late he had seen beneath the surface of the board a steady fire. And now the crowd was quiet, waiting, and there began to break into the Old Master's brain a long shaft of light. A combination, the moves tumbling over one another with sweet promise. A game of equilibrium, a perfect tension of pieces, everything held in suspense by a perpetual check from Black, a fantasy of eternal motion caught in the flowing lines of a knight's pendulum move. The perfect game of chess! He could force Rolavsky to play for a draw. Eagerly the Old Master took the bishop's pawn with his knight and waited for Rolavsky to retake with the rook. The combination was irresistible. But would Rolavsky see the knight check he himself would have to give, five moves later, to hold the draw? Would he take the draw that would give him the championship of the world?

Rolavsky retook with the rook, and the old man moved the king pawn down. The crowd, sensing something in the quick replies after so long a series of waits, rippled with comment. *"Why didn't he retake with the bishop? ...if pawn takes pawn, the queen is lost...what's the old man after? ...no, the rook is pinned ...it won't run away."* At last Rolavsky switched the threatened knight to knight five. The Old Master moved the pawn to king six and found himself praying that Rolavsky would not take it with the bishop. The continuation darkened his mind: he takes with his bishop, I'll take with mine; he threatens mate, queen to rook five; I take the rook and check; he takes the bishop with the king; I check at bishop three with the queen; he goes to the knight square, then pawn to king rook three and he's lost. But lost in a brutal way after a blunt struggle. No charm there, no beauty, only a win. For a moment the Old Master cursed this insane undesire to win that had cost him so many a tournament; and he hoped that Rolavsky would take with the bishop. The pull of the title spun the chessboard before him as he thought of the fifty years he had divided his heart between fortune and perfection. He searched Rolavsky's face as the clock ticked off minutes. Two hours for thirty moves. Only a third of them made, and Rolavsky still looking at the board. Too long.

But now Rolavsky was moving his queen, and the old man saw it glide to rook five. The dreaded and then hoped-for continuation vanished from his mind and in its place came a sense of lightness and power. The pattern was forming. The tensions, threat and counterthreat, were moving toward that poetry of perpetual motion he had anticipated. He took the rook with his pawn. The Black king moved under it. He played his bishop to bishop four, covering the mate at rook two. The clock ticked as he listened for the beating of Rolavsky's heart and in a minute or two they seemed to focus, rising in tempo until at thunder pitch the Russian pulled away the bishop's pawn and dropped his knight on the square. The old man moved his queen to king two. The perfect game! He ran through the moves. Black knight to knight five, check. White king to the rook square. Black checking again with the knight. How tense the pieces looked! What a balance between White's accumulated force and the gyrations of the Black knight!

Rolavsky was sweating now, and the crowd was quiet. Twice the Russian's hand strayed to the board and twice he withdrew it. The old man went through the moves again. Then he looked up again from his dream to see in Rolavsky's eyes something that wrenched him. Bitzer Lake! The eagerness for revenge across the board shook him. Something in the game crumpled, and with it something in the old man's mind.

Rolavsky was bending over the board, demanding a win of his pieces. He didn't want a draw. The crowd jabbered, unmindful of frowns from the director, piecing out the perpetual check.

"Sure it's a perpetual ... knight just moves back and forth ... old man must be crazy ... giving the championship away ... why doesn't Rolavsky move?"

At last Rolavsky did, knight to knight five, discovering check. The Old Master pushed his king aside, and with it the illusion of fifty years. Rolavsky could check once more, demonstrate the perpetual to the referee, and then sweep the pieces into confusion as he rose. The Old Master waited.

But Rolavsky did not check. Slowly the old man's eyes moved from Rolavsky's face to the silent chessmen. They blurred; then the Russian moved—bishop to queen two.

As he stared at the move, the Old Master recognized a new defeat. There was no perpetual check. There never had been. Blindness! As if seeing the position for the first time, he painfully picked over the moves, resisting each pull into the combination that deluded him. Had Rolavsky checked with the knight, Black would have lost. Knight checks, rook takes knight, and if Black retakes, White mates at king eight. The Black bishop had to move to queen two to protect the mating square. The old man looked up again; and as he stretched his hand to the board, he sensed rather than saw something else at the edge of Rolavsky's eyes. He stopped his hand, and the gesture released the breath of the crowd in a quiet sigh.

Once more he searched the position, wondering why he continued, deaf to the reawakened swell of flurry beyond the ropes. Suddenly he saw it and everything else faded except the patterns of force formed by the pieces as they moved into their predestined places. Again the testing of each move, racked by the error of the first delusion, soothed by what he saw unfolding on the board. Finally he pulled his queen rook to king square. Rolavsky hurried his other knight to queen bishop three. And now it was as if some inevitable force suddenly set in motion were lifting the game away from both players. Or perhaps the old man had realized that Rolavsky was but a chess piece too, to be moved and used. Whatever the reason, only the moves remained. The Old Master traced the final position in his mind. The rooks, side by side, one checking, the other covering an escape square. The bishops, one checking, the other covering an escape square. The rook on white and the bishop on black, checking together, one from afar, the other only a diamond from the Black king.

Here...here, this was it. There could be no mistake now. Out of defeat, victory. Out of death, life. Out of the tangled emotions of this fleeting game a beauty to endure forever. Those fifty tortured years of his had not been in vain after all. This was perfection, a work of art, an abstraction of force into an eternal tension utterly withdrawn from its creators, from the moment, from the unmoved chessboard itself. A superb sequence of power begun by the most daring stroke of all chessdom, the sacrifice of the most powerful piece, the queen. No...no, not one queen but two! One queen, combiner of rook and bishop in its motion, to die; from its sacrifice to come a new queen, itself to die stillborn, then the mate to be delivered by its divided functions, by bishop and rook. Surely, the old man told himself, there was no greater beauty than this. The victory was his. He had but to take it. With trembling fingers he lifted his queen, moved it steadily down the file to king eight.

Someone in the crowd gabbled in astonishment. *"His queen? ... he's crazy ... that square's twice covered ... I can't see ... no, Rolavsky's time is almost gone ... it's a trick ... Bitzer Lake ... remember Bitzer Lake!"*

Rolavsky, with a wild look at the clock, swept the queen from the board with his rook. The old man took the rook, queening the pawn with the check. Rolavsky's hand faltered, moved again, and the bishop captured the second queen. Then with a loving movement, a long caressing gesture, itself somehow a part of the final position, the Old Master drew his bishop up to the queen pawn, removed it, left the bishop, and whispered, smiling gently above the file of the unmasked rook, a single word.

"Mate."

[The moves in ordinary notation were: 1 P-K4, P-K4; 2 P-Q4, PxP; 3 P-QB3, PxP; 4 B-QB4, N-KB3; 5 N-B3, B-B4; 6 NxP, P-Q3; 7 O-O, O-O; 8 N-KN5, P-KR3; 9 NxP, RxN; 10 P-K5, N-N5; 11 P-K6, Q-R5; 12 PxRch, K-B1; 13 B-B4, NxBP; 14 Q-K2, N-N5ch; 15 K-R1, B-Q2; 16 QR-K1, N-B3; 17 Q-K8ch!!, RxQ; 18 PxR(Q) ch, BxQ; 19 BxP mate. Charousek-Wollner, Kaschau, 1893.]

Chess World, 1947.

THE MIND IS QUICKER THAN THE EYE!
By Fred Reinfeld

Some aspects of chess which seem astounding to the layman are often pooh-poohed by the expert. Not so in the case of blindfold chess. No matter how often blindfold chess is explained "very simply" in rational

*terms, it still retains an aura of the fantastic. And so the following is
an attempt to highlight, rather than "explain," some of the most remarkable aspects of this type of chess.*

Do you know how many ways there are to play the first four moves
in a game of chess? Each player has 16 units at his disposal. Offhand,
you might say there are 100 or 200 different ways to play these units in
the first four moves. Yet the mathematicians tell us that the number of
possible ways is no less than 318,979,654,000! But that's nothing. By
the time you get to the problem of how many different ways there are
to play the first *ten* moves, the number has risen to the staggering
figure of 169,518,829,100,544,000,000,000,000,000! Even if the experts
have dropped a logarithm or two and are out by a few billion possibilities or so, they have succeeded in making their point: chess can be
a mighty complicated game.

Yet, for at least *800* years, there have been experts who could play
chess blindfold! This doesn't mean, of course, that they were actually
blindfolded when playing. They sat with their back to the games,
calling out their moves, which were made for them on each board;
then their opponents made their replies, each calling out a move in
turn. This process is of course made possible by the chess notation,
which gives every square on the board a distinctive name.

Even a non-chessplayer can realize that blindfold chess requires a
combination of several remarkable qualities. The most obvious is a
vivid imagination: right at the start, a player must be able to visualize
the 32 men as they are placed on the 64 squares. From then on he must
keep track of the changes, some of them far-reaching, that occur from
move to move.

The blindfold player must have a tenacious, infallible memory. If
one little detail is "blacked out," the whole mental picture of the game
is spoiled. He must have the ability to concentrate: let his attention
wander for a while, and God knows what may come into his mind
instead of that chessboard with its numerous pieces jumbled "haphaz-
ardly" in every sector.

So you can see that it is quite a chore to play a game of blindfold chess. But what do you think of a man who can play *two or more games blindfolded, simultaneously?* That is surely one of the most phenomenal mental feats in the history of mankind; in fact, when the great Philidor managed to play three games simultaneously in 1782, the newspapers raved, affidavits were prepared, chessplayers and laymen marveled. Yet the modern chessmasters have steadily increased the number of games played blindfold simultaneously until the record now stands at *forty-five!*

Let's be clear about just what is involved in the performance of such a stupendous feat. Assume that a player is conducting a single game blindfold. If he "sees" all the board and chessmen as one composite image at any given point, and the game goes 35 moves, that means that while the game is in progress, he must "see"—and remember perfectly!—70 such images! Now if he plays 30 games simultaneously, and we again assume 35 moves as the average length, we find that he has to deal with 2100 such images during the exhibition. And at any given moment, he must keep 30 images in mind at the same time. Of course, as the number of games gradually tapers off, he has less to think about; but on the other hand, his fatigue begins to tell on him.

So expert are the blindfold geniuses that at the end of a performance, they are able to rattle off all the moves of every game, in their exact order with the most astonishing glibness! It sometimes happens during an exhibition, that there is a dispute as to the correct position. In such cases, the blindfold player will settle the matter conclusively by calling out all the previous moves; it will be found that he is right, and that his opponent, moving the men on the board, is wrong!

One feature of blindfold play that arouses our curiosity is this: at what rate of speed does the expert play? Does he stew over his moves, averaging say five or so minutes per move? Or—and this is inconceivable, considering his burdens—does he play very rapidly?

Well, suppose we consider a concrete example. The wonderfully gifted British master, Blackburne, gave a simultaneous exhibition on ten boards only two years after he had learned the moves! He won five games, lost two, and drew three. (This was in 1862, when ten games was the unsurpassed limit for blindfold play.) Blackburne played

St. Petersburg International Tournament, 1914 (see 9, page 304).

ADOLF ANDERSSEN

WILHELM STEINITZ

JOSÉ RAOUL CAPABLANCA

Three World Champions (see 10, page 304).

292 moves in his ten games, which lasted six hours. Assuming that Blackburne and his opponents played at the same rate of speed, and making no allowance for time consumed in announcing moves, we can make a rough estimate of the time spent per move: 36 seconds for each move! So we see that the speed with which the master makes his moves is perhaps the most remarkable feature of his phenomenal skill.

Some masters have specialized in fascinating byways of blindfold chess. Pillsbury, the great American master who lived about the turn of the century, is considered by some the greatest player who ever lived. He did a great deal to advance the art of blindfold chess, and the feat which particularly delighted his audiences was to play 12 games of chess, six games of checkers and a game of duplicate whist at the same time!

An onlooker recalled in later years that "While conducting the card game with all the precision of a fairly good player, he would keep the ever-changing chess and checker positions at his back clearly in his mind's eye, and call off his moves at each board with an accuracy and promptness that looked little short of miraculous. He could break off a seance for an intermission and upon resumption readily call up the positions on every board at will, and, when requested, would announce the moves in any particular game from the beginning."

Pillsbury's most remarkable blindfold performance was his exhibition at Hannover, 1902, against 21 *minor masters*—naturally a far more impressive feat than a contest with 21 carefully selected wooden soldiers. An even more astonishing aspect of this exhibition is that Pillsbury gave it on his bye day in an international tournament, playing his regular tournament games the day before, and the day after, the exhibition!

In more recent times, Newell D. Banks, noted American checker master, has played ten games of chess, ten games of checkers, and a game of billiards. Even more astounding in some ways was the feat of the nineteenth-century organist, Sir Walter Parratt, who made a habit of playing Beethoven sonatas on the organ while conducting two games blindfold.

Authorities and onlookers alike are baffled by one feature which is common to all these prodigious feats: the apparent, or relative, absence of strain. This is borne out by the steady rise in the number of games played simultaneously. Morphy and Blackburne played ten games at a time in the '60s. Blackburne soon raised his total to 16, a figure also attained by Zukertort. At Moscow, in 1902, Pillsbury hit 22. For a while there was a lull in record-breaking.

Then at Haarlem, in 1919, Reti played 24; Breyer went on to 25 in 1921; and Alekhine played 26 games in New York in 1924. The following year Alekhine went on to 28 games in Paris, but to no avail, at Reti played 29 the same year at São Paulo. The succeeding changes have been: Koltanowski, 30 (1930); Alekhine, 32 (Chicago, 1932); Koltanowski, 34 (Edinburgh, 1937); Najdorf, 40 (Rosario, 1943); Najdorf, 45 (São Paulo, 1947)!

Incidentally, an achievement which compares with the best that has been accomplished in this field is Reuben Fine's performance of playing four games blindfold, simultaneously at the rate of *ten seconds per move!!*

How do they do it? So far no one has given a fully satisfactory explanation: geniuses are notoriously better at doing wonderful things than at describing them clearly. Another explanation of the mystery is doubtless that no master likes to give away his "trade secrets." There has been no dearth of sensational revelations—Damiano tried that as far back as 1512. But the explanations have been ridiculously inadequate. One expert, for example, claimed that he had painted a chessboard on the ceiling over his bed, and that every morning, when he awoke, he would school his blindfold skill by alternately looking up at the board and then closing his eyes to train his visual memory.

However, we all know that most of us ordinary mortals would make no appreciable progress with such "training." Apparently the faculties needed for blindfold play on a large scale are innate. What are they?

It is a matter of common observation that skillful blindfold players have astonishing memories. It is said of Blackburne that when he was shown games in 1899 that he had played in 1862 and had not seen in the intervening 37 years, he readily remembered all the details and effortlessly pointed out mistakes and better lines of play. Pillsbury regularly performed even more remarkable feats of memory. Irving Cherney tells of an occasion on which two professors gave Pillsbury a grueling memory test. Pillsbury offered to memorize any 30 words read to him once. These were the words selected:

Antiphlogistine, periosteum, takadiastase, plasmon, Threlkeld, streptococcus, staphylococcus, micrococcus, plasmodium, Mississippi, Freiheit, Philadelphia, Cincinnati, athletics, no war, Etchenberg, American, Russian, philosophy, Piet Potgelter's Rost, Salamagundi, Oomisillecootsi, Bangmamvate, Schlechter's Nek, Manzinyama, theosophy, catechism, Madjescomalops. "Pillsbury repeated them in the order given, and then in reverse order, and had no difficulty repeating them the next day!"

The second quality is vivid imagination. Blackburne had an image of every single piece on every single board. A friend said of him that "he thinks in pictures."

The third quality is almost superhuman concentration. When Blackburne played blindfold chess, he concentrated so profoundly that he lost the senses of touch, taste, and smell.

The fourth quality, and perhaps the most important of all, is "simultaneous alternation." The same friend of Blackburne described this as the power "to remember every detail and then to forget it, to concentrate all one's energy on one point and then shift it like a searchlight to another."

So there are the four necessary qualities for blindfold play. A fifth quality, which is not necessary but generally accompanies them, is a fantastic degree of absent-mindedness in everything else but chess!

Some day our greatest psychologists will devote exhaustive studies to blindfold chess. Meanwhile, if you want a unique kind of entertainment and a thrilling insight into the unplumbed capacities of the human brain, pay a visit to an exhibition of blindfold chess. Yes, indeed, the mind is quicker than the eye!

Chess Review, 1951.

THE DREAM OF THE TACTFUL CHESS REPORTER
By "Chielamangus"

The Australian author [Purdy] of this mordant piece derived his pseudonym from a line of Robert Burns: "A chiel's amang ye takkin notes." What chess journalist has not toyed, in his wildest dreams, with the nightmarish notion of describing players and games with unfettered frankness?

The eleventh and final round (thank God) of the State chess championship was played last night. The results were: Gadzooksky beat Shoestrings, Crakanut beat Pastings, Greenhorn beat Wurdy, Brass beat Growl, and Mukall beat Praughan; Eelskin had the bye.

The spectators were treated to the usual display of thud and blunder.

Gadzooksky's game was the first to finish. Gadzooksky evaded Scholar's Mate, and thereafter never looked like losing, Shoestrings refusing to give him the slightest chance. With ordinary skill Gadzooksky would have forced a decision even earlier.

Crakanut's game with Pastings was the cynosure of several eyes. It was a crucial one. Crakanut rose to the occasion in characteristic style. After being completely outplayed by Pastings, little more than a tyro, he won a piece by accident, and thereafter the result was never in doubt, Pastings for once coming out in his true colors and piling blunder upon blunder till interrupted by mate.

The spectators then moved over to the Greenhorn-Wurdy encounter, which was expected to result in a triumph of mediocrity over muddling. Greenhorn was playing as though inspired, not once having left a piece *en prise*. The result was inevitable. Wurdy registered his tenth successive loss, but had the consolation of knowing that he had struck Greenhorn in such form that several of the other competitors might almost have lost to him in the same circumstances.

Tenth and eleventh place being now decided, interest centered on the destination of first prize. Growl was still playing for the title though seven points down; he was opposed by Brass, who is the "baby" of the tourney, having attained his third birthday less than twenty years ago. The colt made a pathetic attempt at brilliancy, and had he been meeting one of the strong competitors (if any), its childish unsoundness would have been demonstrated in humiliating fashion. But before Brass could reach the point of his combination—if point—Growl, who had already made his usual quota of blunders, played himself into a *Zugzwang* and resigned.

Everything then hung on Praughan's game with Mukall. From Praughan's play, it appeared to the onlookers—the few that had the remotest glimmering of the rudiments of the game—that he must inevitably lose in the first hour, but naturally every time Mukall found himself with a winning advantage, he contrived to find the only possible way of losing it. Praughan, however, finally hit upon a way of forcing a loss. He had conducted both the opening and middle game with deadly inaccuracy. There was no endgame.

Eelskin for once managed to avoid a loss by having the bye. He slipped away.

The result is that all the competitors, except about three, tie for first place with $5\frac{1}{2}$ out of 10. This score is no indication of the strength of their play, but due purely to the mathematical impossibility of winning a tournament with a score of less than fifty percent.

The Champions' Career

Messrs. Mukall, Praughan, Gadzooksky, Brass, etc., were born in various places some years ago. This is the first occasion that they have won the State championship all at once, but several of them have sprung surprises before. They learned the moves between the ages of two and twenty, but thereafter their progress was comparatively rapid, and it was not many years before they were heard of in first-class handicap events, often taking a high place at the odds of queen.

This is the greatest success of their career to date, and many critics think—and hope—that they will go far.

Among These Mates.

CHESS OF THE FUTURE
By Dr. Siegbert Tarrasch

In 1890 Steinitz began a two-game cable match with Tchigorin—the stakes were $750!—to test his fantastic theories in the Evans Gambit and Two Knights' Defense. In the latter opening he held out fanatically for the weird gyrations of his King Knight to KB3 and KN5 and KR3 and KN1—all in 13 moves! Tarrasch was impelled to write the following satire.

Played in the International Masters' Tournament, Magdeburg, July 20, 1920.

IRREGULAR OPENING

White	Black
1 N-KB3	....

Introduced by Zukertort, in honor of whom the opening is named. But as he never hit upon the correct continuation, it is better known at present as the Four Knights' Game.

| 1 .... | N-KB3 |

Zukertort's opponents used to play 1 .... P-Q4, showing but a superficial knowledge of the true science of chess by moving pawns which they could not retreat. The text move is the only correct one.

| 2 N-B3 | .... |

An excellent move, demonstrating powers of deep strategy. A novice might be tempted to play 2 P-Q4 instead of the text. It cannot, however, be sufficiently impressed upon the mind of the student that a pawn when once moved cannot be retreated, and that it forms a target for attack by the opponent's pieces.

| 2 .... | N-B3 |

The opponent also displays great generalship.

| 3 N-KN1 | .... |

A masterly conception! Threatening to obtain considerable advantage by also retiring the other knight, and thereby preventing his pieces from being molested by hostile pawns for a long time.

 3 ....   N-KN1

Perceiving the danger at the right moment. This maneuver leads to at least an even position.

 4 N-N1! N-N1!!

The spectator sees—doubtless with admiration—two masters of the highest rank thoroughly acquainted with all the most subtle points connected with the game of chess. Both sides are guarding against weak spots created by pushing pawns rashly. In former days experts used to move these pawns for the purpose of developing pieces. But as early as the end of the last century it became more and more obvious that this is a mistake, for if once moved they may be attacked by hostile pieces, and even captured if not properly taken care of.

 5 N-KR3 ....

An ingenious attempt to gain an advantage in another way. That the knights are better placed here than in the center of the board where they command too many squares was equally well known at the end of the last century.

 5 ....   N-QR3!!
 6 N-R3!!! N-R3!!!

It would be difficult to imagine play on either side more precise or more accurate and entirely in accordance with the accepted rules laid down by the masters of the present day.

7 N-KN1   N-KN1

Both of these moves were originated by the greatest master of the last century, who played them in a celebrated correspondence match. He was the only chessplayer of his time who had penetrated so deeply into the theory of the game. He was considered the father of modern chess.

8 N-N1   . . . .

At this stage Black offered a draw. White has a momentary advantage in having a piece less developed than his opponent. But this, perhaps, is not sufficient to win. The draw was therefore agreed upon.

[The game which Tarrasch was spoofing started out like this: 1 P-K4, P-K4; 2 N-KB3, N-QB3; 3 B-B4, N-B3; 4 N-N5, P-Q4; 5 PxP, N-QR4; 6 B-N5ch, P-B3; 7 PxP, PxP; 8 B-K2, P-KR3; 9 N-KR3, B-QB4; 10 P-Q3, O-O; 11 N-B3, N-Q4; 12 N-R4, B-Q3; 13 N-N1, P-KB4 etc.]

British Chess Magazine, 1891.

THE RED AND THE BLACK
By Frank James Marshall

Marshall and Janowski were gamblers par excellence at the chessboard. They had a habit of sacrificing first and looking afterwards. No wonder they succumbed to the lure of the roulette wheel!

In the chess tournament I was doing well, very well, and I really believe that I would have captured the first prize had I not been so wrapped up in roulette. During the day, while sitting at the chess table, contesting with some clever expert, my mind would constantly revert to red and black, eagle bird and double O, and of course, my play was ragged enough.

The games over, I would hurry to the pavilion and play roulette with feverish excitement. Did I win? Yes, I won, that is, at first, and was maybe several hundred dollars to the good, but I hadn't the sense to quit and kept at the thing evening after evening, until I was shy about $2,000, and barely had railway fare to Paris and expense money home.

And, worst of all, I lost the tournament, when I should have won it, all through my lack of attention to the games. I was a sore and sorry individual when I landed in Paris, and although the thing is past and gone now, I still look back and say what a fool I was.

Janowski had an awful run at Monte Carlo. He captured the first prize of 8,000 francs, and realizing his weakness for roulette, sent all of the money to friends in Paris to keep for him, with the exception of about a thousand or so, and also sent instructions to his bankers, doubtless seeing what might come, not to send him the money under any circumstances, should he wish it.

Janowski bucked the tiger, and the tiger clawed him in fine shape with the result that in a little while the French champion hardly had cab hire. He wired to Paris to his friends to send him his money, but they refused, following his instructions.

Janowski had the gambling fever right, and fired another, and this time peremptory, order for his wealth. His friends sent him a few thousand francs, and Janowski dropped the coin in one night at the game. He wired for more money, another refusal came, then Janowski, waxing wroth, threatened suit, arrest, and everything else dire, if his money were not forwarded to him.

The friends in Paris sent the money on, and poor Janowski gave it away to the men who sit behind the green-covered table, and having no more resources to fall back upon, left Monte Carlo very much poorer in purse and spirit than when he arrived there.

I believe every chessplayer of note who has visited Monte Carlo, with the possible exception of Pillsbury and Blackburne, has been bitten by the game at the pavilion. I lost out all right, but I gained a new experience, and sometimes, even though considering myself a fool. I think it worth the money.

We went against the game for a little relaxation, and, of course, we had to pay for our fun. There are lots of poor devils who start out as we started and end up penniless....

THE TRIUMPH OF UNREASON
By Hans Kmoch and Fred Reinfeld

Of all the many misconceptions about chess, the most remarkable is the fallacious view that this game requires exact calculation and scientific thinking from its devotees. The fact is that even master chess evokes such responses as prejudice, impulse, bad temper, and fatalism to an astonishing degree. Observe, for example, how Rubinstein, one of the greatest precisionists in the history of the game, stakes his first prize in a famous international tournament on a flimsy whim!

All the international contests held at Carlsbad have produced wonderful chess. In some ways, the first Carlsbad tournament, played in 1907, was the most exciting of the lot; for it was the scene of one of those dramatic struggles between the older generation (those players who had made their reputation in the '90s, if not earlier) and the younger players, who were just making their presence felt in the first decade of the new century.

The veterans included the great Mikhail Tchigorin (born 1851), already a legendary hero because of his famous matches with Steinitz, Gunsberg, and Tarrasch, famous as a notable analyst and opening theoretician and the founder of a school which was to produce many great masters. (He died the year following this tournament, and the St. Petersburg tournament of 1909 was conceived as a memorial to him.) Tchigorin, who had started his career as a Romantic fascinated by the attacking possibilities of the King's Gambit and the Evans Gambit, made chess history at Carlsbad by boldly experimenting with the King's Indian Defense. To answer 1 P-Q4 in those days with the "irregular" reply 1 ... N-KB3, took courage of a very high order!

Jacques Mieses (born 1865) could always be relied upon for colorful games arising from his unorthodox adoption of the Danish Gambit with the White pieces, and the Center Counter with Black. There seem to be only two recorded instances of Mieses' ever adopting the perennially fashionable Ruy Lopez—against Emanuel Lasker and Janowski at Cambridge Springs, 1904—and he lost both games!

Geza Maroczy (born 1870) was a world championship contender in those days, noted for his conservative though forceful style. He had an innate hankering for defensive play, but he knew how to attack on occasion. His games had a quiet elegance which was very appealing, and he had an unequaled knack of deriving some advantage from the Four Knights' Game. Maroczy's unique combination of slickness and artistry was seen at its best in his fabulous mastery of queen and pawn endings, in which department he was supreme.

Carl Schlechter (born 1874), the greatest master of the Vienna School, was nicknamed "the Drawing Master" for very good reasons. In an individual game, he was as dangerous as any man living, and he produced more brilliancies than most of his rivals. Like Maroczy, he was a contender for world championship honors. Unlike Maroczy, he got a chance at the title (1910). He drew the match, and hence lost his chance to gain the title. The way in which this happened remains a psychological puzzle to this day: Schlechter, the Drawing Master, needed a draw in the last game of the match to become world champion (the score was 1-0, with eight draws, in his favor). Instead, Schlechter elected to play for a win—and lost!

David Janowski (born 1868) was another world championship contender, but his quicksilver temperament was hardly suited to the role: he was a gambler at the chessboard (and elsewhere), always seeking risks and complications, always more interested in palpably unsound sacrifices than in steady point accumulation.

Just as dashing as Janowski—and almost as unpredictable—was his American rival, Frank Marshall (born 1877), endlessly inventive in brilliant attacking play and capable as few have been of marvelous flights of imaginative genius. The brightness and charm of Marshall's play made him a welcome figure at every tournament in which he participated. Janowski and Marshall must have played a good hundred clock games with each other, and many a time Marshall heard Janowski offer him a knight—this was Janowski's somewhat oblique formula for making the public realize that he was resigning.

Another member of the "older" generation was Richard Teichmann (born 1868), whose sharp mind was a veritable treasure house of chess knowledge and skill. The unfortunate Teichmann had two handicaps: he lacked the vision of one eye and he was undoubtedly the laziest man that ever lived. Many of his games are unbearably lethargic, but when the slumbering chess genius of Teichmann roused itself he was capable of superhuman achievements. This he proved when he won the great Carlsbad tournament in 1911.

All these older players were at the height of their fame and powers in the Carlsbad tournament. But their lot was not an easy one, for they had to contend with a new generation that was ambitious, aggressive, somewhat cocksure and bursting at the seams with new ideas.

There was, for example, Rudolph Spielmann (born 1884), a specialist in every form of gambit but the Queen's Gambit. He finally took up 1 P-Q4 in a serious way at the Carlsbad tournament of 1929, when he was 45, and came within an ace of winning the tournament! Spielmann was then a younger edition of Tchigorin, ever on the lookout for attack, sound or unsound. He was a latter-day Don Quixote, devoting a lifetime to the rehabilitation of the King's Gambit.

Oldrich Duras (born 1882) had already achieved fame as a composer of elegant endgame compositions. Duras was one of the few masters who have managed to carve out an illustrious career without ever bothering too much about opening theory. His opening play, not to put too fine a point on it, was frankly sloppy. But he had bulldog tenacity and was capable of hanging on to a lost position until his fatigued opponent let the win (and the draw, too) slip through his tired grasp. This is how *The Fireside Book of Chess* describes his game with Wolf in this tournament: It "lasted 168 moves! Duras lost a pawn in the opening, at his *seventh move* but hung on grimly through six sittings ($22\frac{1}{2}$ hours of playing time) until he was checkmated by Wolf, who had *two queens*. Duras, who had only his king on the board, must have been hoping for an earthquake." That was one time the Duras technique failed, but look at the fun he had! To complete the picture with an incredible touch, we must add that Duras played some extraordinarily brilliant games.

Aron Nimzovich (born 1886) was already setting the chess world on its beam ends with the fantastic logic of his apparently eccentric play. Amazing as it seems, Nimzovich had already articulated most of the basic ideas of his famous system. Universal ridicule merely had the effect of sharpening his sarcastic tongue and pen. He did not flinch from matching insults with the mighty Tarrasch, whose chess teachings were the Law and the Prophets in those days. Nimzovich played many delightful games in this tournament and was a contender for a high prize throughout, despite the fact that his moves were as intelligible as Choctaw.

If Nimzovich was a rebel, Milan Vidmar (born 1885) was definitely of the orthodox persuasion. A good all-round player with an even temperament and a genial attitude, Vidmar never had the chance to study theory with quite the thoroughness needed for grandmastership, and he never obtained the practice and training required for big tournaments. Vidmar's tournament appearances were always subordinated to his career of university professor, and that is why his games have a certain improvisatory air about them. He often starts in a tentative mood, begins to gain assurance and, somewhere between the twentieth and sixtieth moves, shows his real capabilities.

Dus-Chotimirsky, then in his twenties, was a fiery Russian player with a brilliant, unstable style—very much like Marshall, but far from his equal in ability. The following story, no less delightful for probably being apochryphal, conveys Chotimirsky's qualities admirably: in the St. Petersburg tournament of 1909, Chotimirsky defeated both Emanuel Lasker and Rubinstein...and managed to come thirteenth in a field of 19! Regarding his win against Lasker, it is said that he infuriated the world champion by pretending to be deeply absorbed in a Japanese translation of *Also Sprach Zarathustra* during their game!

Paul Saladin Leonhardt, a German master then also in his twenties, was a highly capable player with a fine knowledge of opening theory.

His besetting sin, however, was fantastic time pressure, which finally proved his undoing. His performance in this tourney was the best of his career.

Savielly Tartakover (born 1887) did not have his doctorate at this time, but he did have a fine head of hair. (Both of these conditions changed with the years.) Even at this time, Tartakover was already famous for his venturesome, highly unorthodox style. His unconventional games and tricky surprise moves have often dismayed opponents and always delighted the chess public.

Should Georg Salve (born 1860) be counted among the "younger" players?! Perhaps, on the ground that he started his tournament career rather late in life. Salve was preeminently a practical player who had made his way up to the championship of Lodz, a city noted for its passionate addiction to chess. To become the best player in Lodz was quite a feat. Salve, as may be guessed, was a rough and ready player who ignored the fine points of opening theory. He relied on a simple homemade Giuoco Piano of a slyly innocent cast, good enough, for example, to beat Schlechter and Duras in this tournament.

Did we say that Salve was the best player in Lodz? We should have said: *had been* the best player in Lodz. For the best player in Lodz, and some thought, in the whole wide world, was Akiba Rubinstein. Starting as a neophyte who received enormous odds from Salve, the studious, artistic, austere apprentice eventually left his master far behind. Although Rubinstein had come to Lodz as a poor Talmudic student, his exquisite games had an aristocratic stamp which made him world-famous in a few years. And now the great tournament at Carlsbad posed the burning question: could young Rubinstein (he was then 25) hold his own against the famous older masters? It soon became clear that his leading rival was Maroczy, and the two staged an embittered race which has never been surpassed in thrilling struggles over the chessboard.

After the twentieth (last but one) round, Maroczy, with a score of $13\frac{1}{2}$-$5\frac{1}{2}$, was ahead of 19 of the 21 participants. Most of the chess fans present hoped that he might win the first prize by coming out victorious in his last-round game. This desire was rooted not only in Maroczy's well-established fame and the dignified manner for which he was noted, but also in their intensely patriotic attitude; for Maroczy, like Carlsbad, represented the Austro-Hungarian monarchy.

Unfortunately, level-headed critics had to admit that Maroczy's winning chances were rather dim, for the young Polish player, Rubinstein, who had become a master only two years earlier, was a clear point ahead of the Hungarian grandmaster. To win the first prize, Rubinstein needed only to draw. And, even if Rubinstein lost, the worst that could happen to him would be a tie for first prize. But Maroczy's fanatical partisans would have been happy to see him tie for first prize.

To bring about a tie, two things were necessary. First, Maroczy had to beat Janowski. This was not too difficult: it had happened several times previously, and Maroczy was confident that it would happen again. (It did happen, in a brilliant game in which Maroczy played the flashy Moeller Attack in the Giuoco Piano and rocked Janowski back on his heels.) Much more difficult, however, was the second requirement: Wolf had to beat Rubinstein. True, Heinrich Wolf was a player of better than average strength. His score after the twentieth round was a respectable 10-9. It was not too implausible to hope that he might beat Rubinstein. Yet this hope was silly in view of Wolf's style and temperament; excelling in steadiness, Wolf, despite his ferocious name, almost loathed imagination and courage.

As he was a representative of the Austro-Hungarian Empire, however, and a close friend of Maroczy as well, Wolf was well aware of the honorable task which confronted him, and a miraculous courage suddenly inspired him with the conviction that he was going to beat "that Polish upstart."

Maroczy was of course delighted with this attitude. The night before the last round the two friends and compatriots had a long talk, in the course of which they happened to use a chessboard. When they parted, Wolf had so far outgrown his normal proportions that he solemnly promised to beat Rubinstein.

A good night's sleep is a blessing. Ask any man who frequently drinks more than he should, and he will tell you. The feeling of being reborn is wonderful.

Presumably Heinrich Wolf took no alcohol that night before the last round, but he had a very refreshing night's sleep, and the next morning he felt reborn—reborn, alas, as the Heinrich Wolf he had always been. After ten moves or so, he intimated that he would not be averse to a draw.

Rubinstein should have accepted and thus made sure of the first prize without any further risk. Every other chessmaster would have done it—probably with the exception of Janowski, who could never resist a gamble, and certainly with the exception of Capablanca, who had a habit of anticipating such offers with a still earlier bid of his own.

But Rubinstein refused the draw!! The tournament room buzzed with excitement.*

It soon became evident that Rubinstein was not crazy. He steadily strengthened his position until at move 24 he reached a position in which he had a forced win. While he studied his next move a little longer than was his custom, the news spread through the playing room that Rubinstein was about to win. There was a little combination available which was as cute as it was obvious. The kibitzers rushed over to watch Wolf get slaughtered.

But this time they were again disappointed. Instead of playing the anticipated 24...R-KR4, Rubinstein astounded everyone by playing 24...B-R3. "But why? Let's see: his move must be even stronger." Rubinstein gave the kibitzers no time to check. Two pairs of pieces were quickly exchanged, bang, bang, and a little later there was a draw by repetition of moves. At move 31, the game was over: draw! "Incomprehensible!" the kibitzers muttered and grumbled. "I told you he's crazy!"

As he left the table, Rubinstein was stormed with questions from all sides. "Didn't you see the win? It was so easy!"

---

* In the Leipzig tournament of 1888, Schottländer had refused Mieses' offer of a draw in identical circumstances, eventually losing the game—and the undivided first prize!—F. R.

Rubinstein smiled. "Yes, of course I saw the win. But I needed only a draw!"

"Only a draw?! Nonsense! But why then did you refuse his offer of a draw in the first place?"

Rubinstein laughed. "Because...with Wolf I make a draw when *I* want to—not when *he* wants to!"

And that is how unreason triumphed over Rubinstein's fabulous self-discipline.

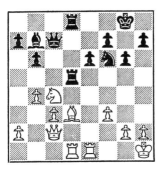

This is the famous position in which Rubinstein could have won brilliantly by 24...R-KR4! If then 25 P-KR3, N-N5!!; 26 PxN, RxPch; 27 K-N1, Q-R7ch; 28 K-B1, Q-R8ch—and mate next move.

Another possibility is 24...R-KR4!; 25 P-N3, QxP; 26 B-K4, RxR; 27 RxR, NxB; 28 PxN, BxPch, etc.

Instead of this, we get a sedate finish that indicates a meeting of the minds in a non-aggression pact:

24	B-R3	28 N-K5	Q-B2
25 N-N2	BxB	29 N-Q3	Q-QB5
26 RxB	RxR	30 N-K5	Q-B2
27 NxR	Q-QB5	31 N-Q3	Q-QB5

At this point, the game was called a draw, giving Rubinstein the first prize after all!

Chess Review, 1950.

EMANUEL LASKER: PHILOSOPHER

By Edward Lasker

All who knew Emanuel Lasker have testified to the unusual force of mind and character which distinguished him from other mortals. His namesake has conveyed Emanuel's unique qualities in a very attractive way.

. . . At the time when we were engrossed in this analysis Emanuel Lasker returned to Germany from America, and meeting him was one of the high points of my life. The striking difference between him and the other masters was that he hardly ever spent any time at the chessboard, unless he had to do it for professional reasons, that is while writing a chess article, or in the midst of a match. He seemed always preoccupied with problems of mathematics and philosophy. When he learned that the brother of the famous philosopher Ernst Cassirer was married to a cousin of mine, he did not rest until I had arranged a meeting with Cassirer. Lasker explained to him certain ideas he held on the problems of cognition and on which he proposed to write a book. Out of the first meeting developed a series of long walks which Cassirer, Lasker, and I took together, and during which Lasker expanded his strange mathematical approach to the concept of free will and automatism. Encouraged by Cassirer, who was impressed with Lasker's original ideas, the latter pursued his task with tremendous energy for five years, interrupting his work only for short periods in order to play his world championship matches with Tarrasch and Schlechter, and in 1913 his book appeared, under the ambitious title: *Das Begreifen der Welt* (*The Comprehension of the Universe*). I actually saw Lasker's hair turn gray while he was laboring over his book. It never occurred to him that clarifying the problem of causality and free will, which had defied the philosophers of two millennia, might be a task beyond the capacity of the human mind, and he persisted until he thought he had established the mathematical proof that the will is free.

An attempt to give even the merest outline of Lasker's 500-page book, would be beyond the scope of the brief sketch I would like to draw of Lasker's impressive personality. Let me mention only one of the original thoughts he introduces in his remarkable book. This thought will be of especial interest to the chessplayer, and no doubt also to the scientist. It is the concept of what Lasker terms the "Macheïde," an ideal being which has so far advanced on the ladder of biological development that it has almost reached the status of an automaton.

The term "Macheïde" is derived from the Greek μαχη, the battle. The Macheïde is the "son of battle," a being whose senses or mental abilities have been so sharpened by millions of years of struggle in the battle of life, that it chooses always the best, the most efficient method of perpetuating itself. On the chessboard, the Macheïde would always make the best move, with the regrettable result that the game would cease to exist after two Macheïdes played their first match. The best moves for White and Black would become common knowledge once and for all, and no problem, no challenge to the mind would remain.

This concept of a Macheïde is by no means artificial. In chess, even the average player finds his choice of moves in any given position very much limited by considerations of usefulness. Among masters, this restriction of choice is greatly increased, and it continues to increase as our knowledge of the game widens.

Without being illogical, we can think of this process of gradual perfection as continuing indefinitely. The being thus developing will ultimately have no more choice. It is compelled to act the way it does, because it is governed by the postulate of maximal usefulness for the purpose in hand. The Macheïde represents the limit of this infinite series of development, the threshold between life and automatism.

Ernst Cassirer, in discussing Lasker's book with me, made a comment on Lasker's approach to philosophical problems which will be interesting to chessplayers familiar with Lasker's games. He said that Lasker had brought some remarkably original thoughts to the subject, but that he had a certain naïve manner of expounding well-known old ideas together with his new ideas without making any distinction between them, obviously due to the fact that he was not familiar with the enormous philosophical literature of the past. Lasker did his original thinking from the foundation up, and he did not know how much of what he found had been discovered by others before him.

Lasker was not very familiar with chess literature either. He did not think it was worth spending time on reading chess books, because he felt that a thorough understanding of the general principles was the best guide in the struggle over the board. The chess world owes to this attitude many original contributions which Lasker made to opening strategy. But Lasker himself sometimes suffered from his attitude, particularly in his later years, because the scientific analysis of the openings had made enormous strides and familiarity with this analysis sometimes gave an opponent an advantage difficult to overcome.

Chess Secrets.

LASKER ENTERTAINS TWO CHESS "WIDOWS"
By Beatrice Reinfeld

For the chessmaster, a formidable tournament is an ordeal; for his wife it is an ordeal of a different, perhaps even more difficult, kind.

My husband was one of the contestants in the 1940 U.S. championship which was being held in a subterranean room in the plushy Astor Hotel at Times Square in New York. It was stuffy there, and the only sound was the murmur of the spectators as they analyzed the positions on the large wallboards. This half silence was broken every few minutes by the muffled clacking of the subway trains that ran under the room.

The heavy humming quiet, the dimmed lights, and the stuffy atmosphere made me feel so bored that I allowed myself to be drawn into a game of chess with Mrs. Kashdan, who plays a good deal of chess. As for me, I know the moves and dimly recall some rules I learned while typing my husband's earliest books, many, many years ago. Also, I know how to count the pieces in my husband's games, to see if someone is ahead in material. Does that make me a chessplayer?!

Mrs. Kashdan and I played in what we hoped was a quiet, inconspicuous nook away from the contestants and spectators. I was blundering as usual, trying hard not to shame my husband by losing too many pieces gratis, quaking whenever I heard a footstep! The game was almost over and I was getting ready to flee when a pale, courtly, gray-haired, genially smiling old gentleman with a merry twinkle in his eyes and a smelly cigar in his hand, stopped at our table and placed his hand on a piece. It was the famous Dr. Lasker, about whom I had heard many charming anecdotes, and of whom I stood in great awe. Naturally he was surrounded by a crowd of admirers. He proceeded with the greatest of good nature, with flashing fingers, to show us how the game might have been played, and what beautiful combinations were inherent in the position, not failing to assure us courteously that we were playing admirably.

He went on with, "If here, then here, winning this that or the other...." and "on the other hand, if..." Perhaps Mrs. Kashdan, an old hand at playing in ladies' tournaments, could follow; but I was horribly embarrassed at the thought of such a brilliant light being cast on the game which we undertook only to alleviate our boredom while our husbands were struggling in a really important match.

I had forgotten this incident, but recently my husband reminded me about it and asked for my impressions. In spite of my embarrassment, I recognized then, and still feel, that this great personality was not making fun of us; he was having a wonderful time, without any feeling of condescension. He was merely entertaining us, helping to while away the weary hours of waiting.

A MASTERLY EXAMPLE OF MY SYSTEM
By Hans Kmoch

Kmoch admired and esteemed Nimzovich as a great player and a profound and original thinker. Yet he could not help poking sly fun at Nimzovich's often pompous and bombastic manner. Luckily, this rollicking parody is so good-natured, with a few grains of sense artfully concealed in a farrago of nonsense, that Nimzovich himself was vastly amused.

Anderssen started the sacrificial style, Morphy and Gruenfeld the pure attacking style, Steinitz the positional style, Tarrasch the scientific style, Lasker the style of styles, Capablanca the mechanical style, Alekhine a style as brilliant as sunlight. But it is a generally known fact that originality and modernism were introduced by me as my own personal inventions, and enthusiastically imitated (without being fully understood) by the whole world of chess. For the ridiculously small sum of ten marks, the reader can confirm all this in my monumental work *My System,* published by B. Kagan.

Before my time chess was so naïve and undistinguished! One or two brutal opening moves, each one involving a vulgar, obvious threat, a common, banal sacrifice, a painfully elementary, bestially raw checkmate—such, more or less, was the course of chess games before my heyday set in.

Then I appeared on the scene and the chess world paid heed. The hegemony of matter was shattered at a stroke and the era of the spiritual began. Under my creative guidance, the chessmen, hitherto nothing but highwaymen, pirates, and butcher boys, became sensitive artists and subtle instruments of immeasurable profundity.

But why waste words!—come, soar to the dizzy heights of the following game:

FRENCH DEFENSE

Copenhagen, 1927

Notes by me

White	*Black*
NIMZOVICH	SISTEMSSON
1 P-K4	P-K3
2 P-KR4!!	. . . .

My very oldest and latest thought in this opening! To the chess addict nurtured on spineless convention, this move comes as a punch in the face—but calmly, calmly, reader; after all, you cannot be expected to understand such moves. (Forgive me—it is not your fault, until now no one has opened your eyes and ears.) Wait just a little while and there will pass before you a miracle of overprotection of more than earthly beauty. (I assume that I rightly assume that you are quite familiar with my theory of overprotection.)

    2 ....   P-Q4

Black of course has no suspicion of what is coming and continues serenely in classical style.

    3 P-K5!   ....

A move of elemental delicacy. (We detest, as a matter of principle, such words as "power" and "strength"; in the first place, such banal expressions make us uncomfortable, and in the second place, we like even less the brutalizing tendency which such words imply.)

Wherein lies the beauty of 3 P-K5 ... ? Why is this move strong?

The answer is as simple as it is astonishing. The move is strong because it is weak! Weak, that is, only in the traditional sense! In reality, that is to say, it is not *the move P-K5*, but *the pawn on K5* that is weak—a tremendous difference! In former times, it is true, it was customary to reject any move which created a weakness. Today, thanks to me, this view is obsolete. *The fact that the pawn on K5 is weak, obliges White to protect the pawn more and more until at last the state of overprotection arises as it were of itself.* But as we have seen (cf. *My System*), overprotection is practically equivalent to victory. Hence it follows automatically that the "weak" move 3 P-K5 is a certain road to triumph. The rest is more or less a matter of technique.

    3 ....   P-QB4

All according to famous precedent.

    4 P-Q4   ....

Here it is quite clear that it is more profitable for White to provoke ... P-QB4 and then play P-Q4, rather than the other way round, which is the customary course. For if White first plays P-Q4, there follows ... P-QB4 and White's queen pawn is under attack. But my clever transposition of moves changes the situation completely. For now Black's queen bishop pawn is suddenly attacked by White's queen pawn!

    4 ....   PxP

What else can Black do?

    5 P-R5!   ....

All very clever, original, and decisive! Of course the ordinary run of people who envy me every spark of my genius but cannot follow my line of reasoning for even three paces, outdo themselves in sneering at me with the poison-dripping epithet "bizarre."

The text move creates confusion in the whole Black army and prepares for the annihilating invasion by the queen 18 moves later.

    5 ....   Q-N3

Naturally not 5 .... N-QB3?; 6 B-QN5! etc. Why should Black play the French Defense only to allow the Ruy Lopez bishop move after all?!

    6 P-R6!   ....

An avaricious dullard would never hit on this deeply considered pawn sacrifice.

    6 ....   NxP

After 6 .... PxP White has an even more comfortable game.

    7 Q-R5!!   ....

The reason for this becomes clear after White's next move.

    7 ....   P-N3

Threatens to begin a successful siege of the weakling at K5 with .... B-N2. But White forestalls this.

    8 Q-R2!!   ....

To every fair-minded observer this move must come as a revelation! All the previous maneuvers now become clear! White has completed his development brilliantly and proceeds to overprotect K5. Against this Black is helpless.

8 ....   N-B4
9 B-Q3   ....

Note the splendid cooperation of White's forces: while the king pawn and the king bishop completely blockade Black's position, the development of the overprotective forces takes place behind the broad backs of these sturdy blockaders.

9 ....   N-B3
10 N-KB3   ....

As a rule this is a routine move. But here it is strikingly original and as such occupies a place in the storehouse of my intellectual property.

10 ....   P-KR4

Old stuff!

11 P-QN3   ....

A deep trap, as will soon become apparent!

11 ....   B-N2

How Black must have rejoiced when he anticipated his formidable opponent's occupation of the long diagonal. But...

12 B-KB4!!   ....

...how bitterly disappointed he must have been to realize that 11 P-QN3 had only been a trap and B-N2 had not been intended at all. The position of Black's bishop at KN2 is now quite pointless. 11...B-K2 would have been relatively better.

12 ....   B-Q2
13 QN-Q2   QR-B1

Black no longer has any good moves!

14 K-K2!!   ....

An extraordinarily deep move. He sees through Black's plans, and in addition he prepares a particularly powerful continuation of his over-protection strategy.

14 ....   N-N5

Just what White was waiting for.

15 N-K1!!   ....

This was the point of his previous move! Black is now forced to exchange off the attacking bishop at Q3. But in that event White's king knight enters the fray with fearful effect at Q3, while the square KB3 becomes available to the queen knight. Surely a grandiose piece of strategy. The fact is that I'm a marvelous player, even if the whole chess world bursts with envy.

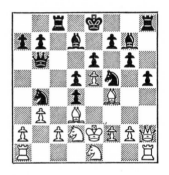

15 ....   NxB
16 NxN!   ....

Naturally not 16 PxN? which would have been quite inconsistent. The pawn on QB2 is unimportant, and Black only wastes precious time by capturing it.

16 ....   RxP
17 QR-K1!! ....

White continues his overprotection without much ado.

17 ....   P-R4

This counterattack has no punch. Black would naturally like to get a passed pawn plus a rook on the seventh, but it is too late for that.

18 K-Q1! ....

Now the menaced rook must scurry back, for capture on R7 would be much too dangerous.

18 .... R-B3!!

At last Black gets the right idea: overprotecting his pawn at K3. But it is already too late.

19 R-K2 K-K2

Introduced into tournament play by me. See the note to White's 14th move. The king overprotects K3.

20 KR-K1 R-K1!
21 N-B3! ....

Completing the overprotection of K5 and thus deciding the fate of the game. Black has no defense. Note the esthetic effect created by White's position.

21 .... B-KB1

Now Black threatens to complete the overprotection of K3 by playing ...N-N2. But White has prepared a brilliant combination.

22 P-KN4!! ....

Much stronger than the obvious B-N5ch etc.

22 .... PxP
23 Q-R7!! ....

Now one clearly realizes the masterly understanding of position which went into White's eighth move (Q-R2!!).

23 .... PxN

Had Black continued overprotecting by 23...N-N2 there would have followed 24 B-N5ch, P-B3; 25 BxPch, K-B2; 26 N-N5 mate. Black's basic error was that he started overprotecting much too late.

24 B-N5 mate

One of my best games! I am proud of it if only because Herr Sistemsson is one of the strongest Scandinavian players. The game made an overwhelming impression on the players and spectators as well as on my opponent. The game has become famous in Denmark as "the immortal overprotection game!"

Chess Review, 1951.

MANNERISMS OF THE MASTERS
By Paul Hugo Little

Much more goes into a game of chess than the mere moves that appear in the score. A complete listing of the peculiarities of chessplayers would probably be longer than Modern Chess Openings. *The following observations were made during the great international tournament at Nottingham in 1936 and the U. S. open tournament in 1937.*

To the eyes of the uninitiated, chessplayers appear to be a queer sort. Not dangerous, mind you, merely queer. Certainly a man who stares unceasingly at a board with bits of wood on it, and emits heart-rending groans and sighs from time to time, does unnerve a spectator unacquainted with chess and chessplayers. But to the true chess enthusiast, these sounds are an integral part of the game.

Now, not all masters groan and sigh. Not all masters play alike, so why should it be expected that they will react alike? It isn't; and they don't.

In the heat of the fray, under the strain of an oncoming sacrificial combination or a winning rook and pawn ending, the master may express his grief, chagrin, joy, hope or despair according to his temperament and his position. This is a helpful clue to the spectators, because often they can glance over a tournament room and tell just whose game is in the last throes.

And yet sometimes no one can tell whether the master is expressing joy or sadness. Winter, the English master, will sit stooped over the board with one hand on his hip and the other propping up his chin.

Then, without warning, he will nervously search for a cigarette, abandon his search in the middle of it (wise, since English cigarettes are bad), and seize his head in his two hands, twisting it from side to side and lowering his head near the board so that he can have a convenient receptacle if ever his head does come off. Numerous bets are made at every B.C.F. congress that Winter's head *will* come off.

And of course Alekhine still twists. However, he contents himself with a wisp of hair, not wishing to go the whole hog (or head). He coughs in staccato fashion during the progress of a game, and usually not because of a cold in the thoracic region. At Nottingham [1936] it was easy to explain the cough when one regarded the cigarette stubs left by the Doctor after a game. (And English cigarette stubs to boot.)

C. H. "O'Death" Alexander, who made the best score of all the English players at Stockholm [1937], rocks back and forth on his chair, humming tunelessly as he rocks. The tune is probably not "Britannia Rules the Waves" because C. H. O'D. has good Irish blood in his veins. There is another little thing about him which cannot be overlooked. He is to date the only man ever to play in a B.C.F. congress wearing shorts. (C. H. O'D., not the B.C.F. congress!)

Bogolyubov sits complacently in his chair, his legs widely spread apart, and contemplates the board benignly, occasionally darting a humorous glance at his opponent. This gives him the aspect of a benevolent Buddha, an aspect heightened by the Buddha-like paunch which he has developed through his cultivation of beer in its relation to the human throat.

Capablanca purses his lips philosophically, and slides out of his chair with a lithe grace which belies his forty-odd years as he walks from board to board to see how his colleagues are faring.

Euwe bends over the board intently, folding his hands in his lap and flexing his arms from time to time. A wisp of hair falls over his temple as he bends, and sometimes he brushes it back quickly. He, too, walks rapidly from board to board, since walking is part of his general training.

Flohr frowns so anxiously that one almost fears that he will burst into tears. But when he has reached a position bound to yield him good prospects, he looks up at all around him with a boyish, infectious smile.

Fine and Reshevsky indulge in a moderate amount of swaying, and both are very intent, although Reshevsky usually manages to look more serious. Fine does little flourishes with his knuckles, and sometimes wields a pencil in geometric designs in the air. Kashdan manages the most reverentially pensive look yet seen on the face of a master, and sometimes blinks rapidly to make sure that he has two bishops and not two *knights* on the board.

Botvinnik has no real mannerisms, except for his studious gaze, enhanced by his large spectacles which give him a professorial appearance. He smiles hesitantly and is extremely modest. He appears to be the most normal of the lot.

Tartakover is versatile, in keeping with his scholastic accomplishments. He sways, takes off his glasses repeatedly and rubs his eyes, looks fixedly ahead to make sure of the move his opponent has made before he finally writes it on his score sheet, purses his lips, puts a finger to his brows to support his chain of thought (a motion used by Capablanca, also), and often reprimands himself silently, shaking his head and moving his lips. In defeat he is jocular, satirical over his misfortune.

Lasker shoots out the fierce glance of a lion, whose prototype he is over the chessboard. As he smokes his cigars, he holds on to them cautiously. He does not smoke with the spendthrift ease of a man who has no cares; rather, he cherishes the cigar.

Miss Menchik is undoubtedly the most placid of all the masters. She sits stolidly, surveying the scene and shunning the spectators. She is imperturbable, unless some unlucky onlooker whispers a bit too audibly. Then she will turn slowly around, regard the culprit, and emit a loud "Sssshhhh!!!" Her rival, Sonia Graf, is her exact opposite, being extremely masculine in action as well as in dress. She rocks sideways, taps nervously with a pencil or a cigarette, glances hastily from side to side.

The American masters, coming from a country where people are always up and doing, have introduced motion into mannerism. Harold

Morton sits sideways, one leg crossed over the other, and kicks the top leg to and fro. Then suddenly he will untangle himself and seek to plunge himself into the board, raising and lowering his head in one-two, one-two tempo to see how his opponent is reacting. Whether his opponent reacts or not, Harold remains mercurial.

Jaffe glowers at his opponent from lowered eyelids and beats out a Morse code with a pencil or cigarette. However, he taps the cigarette a bit more lovingly than he does the pencil.

Mugridge is a head-holder and chin-nurser par excellence. Being of a more restful nature than Winter, he does not seek to find out whether his head can be screwed on or off. Cohen waggles his foot, the while contemplating the board benignly. But unlike Bogolyubov, his benign look is tinged with a mild expectancy, as if he were waiting for his opponent to overlook mate in two. Sometimes the opponent does, and then Cohen is benign no more, but rather the man of action.

Treysman folds his arms across his chest and lowers his head as if he had just heard his death sentence read. He, too, is a foot-waggler. But he waggles up and down where others waggle from side to side.

Of course there are others. Their number is legion. There are head-scratchers, nose-twitchers, ear-pullers, lip-biters. And they can all be found, not in the State Hospital for the mentally unsound, but at the chessboard in a tournament room.

Chess Review, 1937.

WHAT IS A BRILLIANCY?

By I. A. Horowitz

As Horowitz puts it, this question "has stumped the sages of the ages." Few subjects have aroused such heated controversies in the chess world.

What constitutes a brilliancy? A rollicking queen sacrifice? Or masterly maneuvers? The question has stumped the sages of the ages.

Brilliancy awards of the past have been full of error and argument.

Schlechter's brilliancy against Salve at St. Petersburg, 1909, was extinguished by cool analysis long after the honorarium had vanished.* Torre's brilliancy against Gruenfeld at Marienbad, 1925, was discredited by incompetent judges who challenged its soundness. They acknowledged their error after the prize had been given to another player. Reti purloined the brilliancy prize at New York, 1924—according to John Barry. Marshall's game against Bogolyubov was his choice. There it was a question of peaceful positional play versus bombastic sacrifices, culminating in an announced mate in five.

In order to standardize judgment in such matters, the French author Le Lionnais set up a yardstick of his own. The brilliancy should be correct, ingenious, and economical. A glittering brilliancy in five moves is less attractive in a game than a commonplace crusher in four. The brilliancy should be perilous, exciting, spectacular, original, rich in depth, and containing diverse combinations. The actual combinations which occur over the board, should be implemented with concealed combinations which occur only in the notes. The loser should have put up a goodly measure of resistance, and a logical coherence should predominate over the whole game. These are the qualities which make for acceptable brilliancy.

Chess Review, 1949.

THE MYTH OF THE BRILLIANCY PRIZE
By Dr. Savielly Tartakover

As a man who "has been around" for almost fifty years of international play, Tartakover knows whereof he speaks when he tells some of the strange stories behind the awarding of brilliancy prizes. We are apt to assume that such prizes are awarded with the strictest impartiality, but sometimes, alas! the judges are human, all too human. Maybe the term "brilliancy prize" ought to be replaced by "consolation prize."

* According to Tartakover, the committee *knew* the brilliancy was unsound, but awarded Schlechter the prize because he had done badly in the tournament! See his article, "The Myth of the Brilliancy Prize," in *Chess Review*, March, 1951.—F. R.

Alexander Alekhine (see 11, page 305).

A Chess Game with Living Pieces (see 12, page 305).

... At the international tournament at Teplitz-Schoenau, 1922, the supreme judge of brilliancy was the late lamented Viktor Tietz. And there the mighty Akiba Rubinstein—despite one of his less mighty moments—fell heir to a windfall of no less than four out of seven brilliancy prizes! Tietz rescued Rubinstein from ignominy by bailing him out with brilliancy prizes on the ground that any Rubinstein victory is a classic example of profundity and logic.

The term "brilliancy" parades under fundamentally diverse conceptions. In the masters' tournament of Nurnberg, 1906, for example, prize judge Amos Burn awarded the top honor to the game Duras-Wolf. Not only did this *partie* lack the effulgent luster, but also the winner managed to snag a pawn and the exchange.

"This game, after all, did not contain a sacrifice," a bystander complained.

"So what?" was Burn's placid reply.

Teplitz-Schoenau, 1922, provided another amusing incident. There I received the third brilliancy prize for the rook sacrifice in my game with Maroczy.

TARTAKOVER

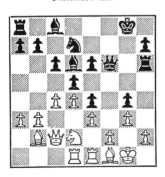

MAROCZY

Black played 17 ... RxP! and, after many vicissitudes, won in 36 moves. Immediately afterwards, I submitted a precise analysis of all the variations to the prize committee, in which I not only demonstrated the soundness of the sacrifice, but also its urgency. For on the preparatory move 17.. N-B1 (with the idea of ... N-N3, ... B-Q2, and ... R-KB1), White consolidates with an equally good series of defensive moves, beginning with 18 B-N2.

Despite this, thought one of the judges, the game did not rate a prize. "The sacrifice of the heavy piece," he said, "could not have been made with all the ensuing ramifications in mind."

According to this authority, the awarding of the brilliancy prize for hazardous play contradicts the very essence of a brilliant game!

Who knows? Possibly in the future, the American lie detector or some similar apparatus will reconstruct the true calculations of the chessmaster.

Chess Review, 1951.

TIME WITHOUT END
By Edward Krisch

Modern tournament and match chess is unthinkable without the use of time clocks, yet many of us do not know how this indispensable gadget came into general use. Krisch tells the story with a wealth of fascinating and amusing detail.

Today, the phrases, "in serious time trouble" and "overstepped the time limit," have become bywords in tournament books and in game annotations. Today, "prepared opening variations" are the order of the day to seriously handicap the unwary opponent by compelling him to consume precious time in unraveling the strange maze. The important role that time has played in tournament and match games has never been clearly depicted.

The events that ultimately convinced the chess world of the necessity for a practical time limit form a heartrending story.

In George Walker we have a reliable witness to prove the extreme slowness of play: in the Labourdonnais-McDonnell, 1834 match "Many of the games last long, long hours." *

And again the Staunton-St. Amant, 1843 match was regarded by impartial contemporary players as a test of physical endurance rather than a chess match. We will not tax the reader with a dry recital of statistics and would bring but one incident among many to his attention: the 21st match game, the 66 moves of which occupied 14½ hours!

Certain critics frankly admitted themselves puzzled and raised the question "To what avail this purposeless prolongation?"

Others pointed out that the prolongation was far from purposeless, but rather a deliberate attempt to fatigue and wear out the opponent. According to a post-match statement issued by Staunton's umpire, H. Wilson, St. Amant consumed three-fourths of the total time on his own moves. The famed French player, Deschapelles, severely criticized both contestants and suggested a maximum playing time limit in the event of a return match. In letters addressed to the German astronomer, Schumacher, Deschapelles vented his indignation:

"The average games lasted nine hours, that is, nine times longer than the games of the great masters. The contestants were slow at every move—they labored under an exhaustion hardly mental but rather physical—an exhaustion that compelled them to adjourn play in search of air and refreshments."

In the following decade, the chess world's attention was forcibly focused on the great London, 1851 tournament. Once again the incredible slowness of play roused a torrent of criticism:

"... Consumes hours over moves when minutes might suffice, and depends not upon outmaneuvering, but out-sitting his antagonist; patience ceases to be a virtue, and one cannot help expressing deep regret that there is not some legal or moral force which may be brought to bear upon the offender."

Our jeremiad of slow play is epitomized in the following plea: "Time is the capital of our country, and only a degree less valuable than credit with our banker. Juries, ere now, have convicted men, and judges have

---

* Regarding McDonnell's slowness, see p. 74.—F. R.

hanged them, to save time. Railway companies at the present day break our legs, and sometimes our necks, to save time. Our chessplayers are the only men in this busy country who disregard it and are insensible to its value. If this sin could be laid to the charge of match players alone, I'm not sure that I should be at the trouble of complaining, for I am not one of them; but it is the besetting sin of the fraternity."

To whom we and succeeding generations owe gratitude we will never know. We know him only as an anonymous contributor who signed himself as *"A Cantab"*:

"Let each player have a three-hour sandglass at his elbow, and a friend on either side to turn it. While the player is thinking the sand must be allowed to run; while his opponent is thinking his glass will be laid horizontally on the table and the running suspended." This method proposed in 1852 merited the energetic backing of H. Staunton and found almost universal acceptance in the English-speaking countries.

How extremely fortunate that the very first timing proposal considered gauging an entire *cycle of moves* rather than imposing a maximum time limit upon *any one move!* The original suggestion has been carried over into modern tournament play by universal acceptance with minor improvements only as to the timing method and the length of the playing cycle.

But not without many a struggle!

A second proposal sponsored by von der Lasa considered using two watches and noting the time consumed on each move by each opponent. This laborious move-by-move computation gained a strong following in continental Europe, probably because of the widely announced disadvantages of the sandglass:

1. Temperature and humidity effect upon the sand!

2. The great danger that a flustered player might turn up the wrong end of the glass!

Another matter that plagued our forbears was the penalty to be invoked in such cases wherein one contestant overstepped the time limit. The Paris international tourney, 1867, sought a solution by the following rule: "A fine of five francs payable to the tourney committee (!) to be imposed for every 15 minutes' infraction over and above the regulation time limit of 10 moves per hour." The first-prize winner, Kolisch, seriously overstepped the time limit in his games vs. G. R. Neumann and Czarnowski. Critics were not slow to point out that under the above rule it was no longer a question of chess ability but rather of finances! This mistake was not again repeated in any major tournament. Outright forfeiture was henceforth the accepted penalty for any time limit violation.

By 1883 a truly mechanical timing device—the ingenious tumbling chess clock—made its debut as the invention of T. B. Wilson of Manchester at the London international tournament with astounding success.

By 1900 our present day push-button chess clock was perfected by Veenhoff of Groningen.

In 1933-34 an ultra-modern chess clock devised by Curtis R. Wilson of Oakland, Calif., utilizing but one clock movement made its appearance.

Chess Review, 1946.

THE TIME MACHINE
By Fred Reinfeld

The colorful story of the time clock, which has added fun, excitement—and sometimes heartbreak—to tournament chess.

Many players never become fully reconciled to the chess clock. Their initial nervousness never quite wears off. What can be more nerve-racking than to hear the seconds ticking away at a galloping pace as one struggles to master an intricate position? What is more upsetting than having to make ten moves or so in a matter of two minutes?

But whatever the drawbacks of the time clock may be, they are heavily outweighed by its advantages. The good points are two in number, one negative and the other positive. The privilege of unlimited time in the early nineteenth-century tournaments and matches was so cruelly abused that some means had to be devised to limit the amount of time at the players' disposal. Think of poor Paul Morphy, so badgered by Paulsen's interminable sitting that he actually burst into tears!

The positive advantage of the time clock is that it has added to chess a sporting element which is not present in the game itself. By speeding up the play, the time clock made chess a spectator sport. By compelling the chessplayer to struggle with the clock as well as with his opponent, a new, thrilling, three-cornered struggle was made possible. How big a difference the clock makes, is seen in the fact that a game as played over the board is quite different from the same game as it appears in print. It may be said that knowledge of the time consumed is necessary to complete understanding of a game. You don't believe it?! Well, consider some of the stories (or perhaps legends) that have been woven about the use of the time clock.

Sammy Reshevsky is notorious as the world's worst sufferer from time pressure or the most dexterous player in situations where time is short. Sammy generally meditates so profoundly during the opening stage that having to make fifteen or twenty moves in the last five minutes is quite a common occurrence to him. It is curious that the laboriously considered moves are often surprisingly inconclusive, while the rapid transit moves, played at lightning pace, are generally incisive and to the point.

The time pressure scrambles do not always turn out so happily. Sometimes a player oversteps the time limit—that is, he fails to make the stipulated number of moves within a specified period of time. It is then the Tournament Director's melancholy but unavoidable duty to declare the game forfeited by the player who has failed to keep up with the time limit. On such occasions tempers run high, evidence is contradictory, decisions sometimes arbitrary. The mechanisms of the clocks often function with something less than machinelike accuracy, and this has been especially true since 1941; shortages of labor and materials have made it impossible to manufacture time clocks during the past five years.

Probably the most remarkable instance of an important time pressure decision took place several years ago in the United States Champion-

ship. In an exciting game between the leaders, one of the players overstepped the time limit. The Tournament Director walked over to the
table, seized the clock from the rear, turned it around and ... forfeited
the wrong player!! When informed of his mistake, he replied ma-
jestically: "Does Kenesaw Mountain Landis reverse himself?" And
there the matter rested.

So great is the tension of time pressure that many little tragicomedies
are unwittingly enacted by the players. There was the time Reuben
Fine spilled a cup of coffee over himself in his hurry to smack the clock.
There is the famous instance of a player, who shall be nameless, who
found himself in such severe time pressure that he never noticed the
fearful havoc caused to the seat of his pants by a lit cigarette which
had been placed on his chair. There are countless stories of players in
time pressure whose moves were being taken by a friend who expos-
tulated: "Don't move so fast, I can't write so rapidly!"

Games are generally lost on time pressure toward the end of the
first sitting, but there have been exceptions. For example, during the
Carlsbad tournament of 1929, poor Maroczy held out for fourteen
hours against Saemisch, only to overstep the time limit on the 109th
move! Picture his exasperation!

TABLE OF TIME-CLOCK PROGRESS

Year	Event	Cycle	Method
1861	Anderssen-Kolisch ....24 moves in 2 hours		Sandglass
1865	Dublin ....20 " " 2 "		"
1866	Anderssen-Steinitz ....20 " " 2 "		Clocks
1866	Steinitz-DeVere ....24 " " 2 "		Sandglass
1867	Dundee ....30 " " 2 "		"
1867	Paris ....10 " " 1 hour		"
1870	Baden-Baden ....20 " " 1 "		Clocks
1870	Mackenzie-Congdon ....24 " " 2 hours		Sandglass
1871	Cleveland ....10 " " 1 hour		"
1872	Steinitz-Zukertort ....15 " " 1 "		Clocks
1873	Vienna ....20 " " 1 "		"
1875	Philadelphia ....15 " " 1 "		Sandglass
1883	London ....15 " " 1 "		Tumbling clocks

Edward Krisch prepared this table to summarize the changes in time clock technique during the
early years when the "time machine" was still a novelty.

Undoubtedly the most successful case of coping with time pressure occurred in a match between City College and Columbia in 1931. Sidney Bernstein, unaware of the stipulated starting time for the game, made his appearance at the Marshall Chess Club one hour and 59 minutes after his clock had been started! The time limit required 40 moves to be played in the first two hours. Bernstein took half a minute to toss off his coat, sit down at the table, and start moving. He played 38 moves in less than the remaining half-minute, and the game ended in a draw. In international tournament play there is generally a provision that a player who fails to show up after his clock has been running for an hour is automatically forfeited. In this instance, Bernstein benefited by the absence of such a rule.

Many a famous game has been decided under time pressure conditions. That was the case, for example, in the game which Herman Steiner drew in the Prague international team tournament in 1931. Steiner's was the last American game still going in the final round. If he won or drew, the American team would be first; if he lost, the team would fall down several places in the standing. Steiner had had an uphill game all the way; toward the end, the combination of a bad position plus hair-raising time pressure got to be too much for the other American players: the situation was so tense that they had to leave the playing room. A few minutes later, they were being showered with congratulations! Steiner's opponent had blundered, and rather than risk loss, which would harm the position of his team, he had offered Steiner a draw. It was the only way out of the time pressure, and it assured victory for the U. S. A.

The scientists promise us a mechanical chessplayer one of these days. He will feed on machine oil and play perfect chess. No mistakes, no time pressure! It will be the end of an era.

Chess Review, 1946.

PREMATURE CELEBRATION
By Edward Lasker

At the completion of the next to the last round in the international tournament at Scheveningen in 1913, Alekhine had made mathematically certain of the first prize, and Edward Lasker had a good chance to win the third prize. The following excerpt from Lasker's Chess Secrets *tells of the resulting celebration and its aftermath.*

... After winning this game I was certainly in high spirits, and when Alekhine, in equally high spirits, proposed to take everybody to a night club who wanted to help him celebrate his victory, I did not hesitate accepting, feeling certain that I would win my last round game and that I would have no difficulty in drawing my adjourned game with te Kolsté. He, like Janowski, Olland, and Yates, wisely refrained from joining the party.

But the gods who had made Janowski lose to Yates and thus freed Alekhine from all care, willed otherwise. Alekhine ordered champagne for everyone, including a number of French hostesses who saw to it that the bottles were emptied fast and replenished without delay. As the night wore on, Alekhine became happily intoxicated, and he refused to let us go home. The strange thing I noticed was that he insisted upon dancing exclusively with a woman about twice his age and twice his circumference, although there were plenty of young girls around. At about four in the morning Mieses, who was the only one left outside of Alekhine and myself, sneaked quietly away. It was after seven when they finally closed the club, and Alekhine and I staggered home in deplorable shape. At nine o'clock the inevitable happened. I sat down to play my adjourned game and ruined it within a few moves. Goodbye, third prize. The only good thing about the speed with which I lost the game was that it left me with a few hours in which to sleep before starting the last game in the afternoon. Otherwise, I might have dropped lower yet. I won the game, but Dr. Olland and Yates also won, and so I had to be satisfied with fifth place. Even at that I felt elated at the result as it gained for me official recognition as International Master. Nevertheless, I swore I would never again drink and look at the girls during a tournament.

Alekhine appeared late for his game, and his mind seemed still to be in the night club. Janowski made short work of him, thereby accomplishing no more, to be sure, than narrowing the difference between their scores down to half a point; but the result of this game once more convinced M. Nardus that Janowski could beat any master in the world if he only half tried. And so Janowski could continue to bank on a fair-sized check from Nardus on the first of every month. He could have lived quite comfortably on this stipend, but on the third of the month he was usually cleaned out again, due to the unreasonable behavior of the roulette wheels at the various gambling resorts within easy reach from Paris.

Alekhine, Janowski, Nardus, and I decided to stay another week in Scheveningen to recover on its sunny beach from the strain of the tournament. But a couple of days later only Nardus and I were left. Alekhine suddenly declared he had to go to Paris on an urgent mission, the nature of which we could not imagine. And Janowski seemed to have inexplicably forgotten that he had promised to see a friend in Ostend right after the tournament. In his case it was easier to surmise the cause of his departure. Next to Monte Carlo, Ostend had the most famous casino of Europe. For Janowski, his pockets bulging with the second prize, to be within a stone's throw of Ostend and not to challenge its roulette tables, was as improbable as to see Naples and then not to die.

I had hardly been back in England for a week, when I received a cable from Alekhine to the effect that he had been robbed in Paris and that he would like to borrow fifty pounds. At the same time he informed me that he had made arrangements with the chess clubs of the Hotel Continental and the Café de la Régence to sponsor a short match of three games with me the following month. I sent him the money, though I felt a bit mystified by the robbery story. When I got to Paris to play the match, I asked Janowski what he knew about the matter and he told me Alekhine had appeared in Paris with that rotund girl he had met in the night club in Scheveningen, but that after a week's time she had no longer been seen in his company.

Our conclusion was that, robbery or not, the girl had the money, and what became known later about Alekhine's amatory inclinations, adduced circumstantial evidence in favor of our conclusion.

Whatever his weaknesses or aberrations from the norm in sex matters, Alekhine had become a tower of strength in chess. I lost all three games of the match.

Chess Secrets.

RECOLLECTIONS OF ALEKHINE
By H. Golombek

While the consensus of opinion marks Alekhine as anything but lovable, he was without question a man of attractive personality, interesting even to those who disliked him. Golombek seems almost uniquely qualified to sum up the man's good and bad points in a disinterested spirit; his evaluation was specially prepared for this volume.

While of no great chessmaster can it be said that "his name was writ in water," since his games must live after him and so keep his memory fresh and indeed immortal as long as chess itself survives, still there is a great danger that the personality of the master, his colorful whims, his defects and his virtues, his very physical appearance may become dim and eventually forgotten as his contemporaries die out.

For this reason reminiscences of the great chessmaster, while these are still green in our memories, are both valuable and interesting; and, just as no player left behind a greater (or even as great) wealth of beautiful games as did Alekhine, so none I ever met in the chess world had a more colorful or striking personality. Tall, of commanding presence with handsome features—though when seen close up, his nose had a curiously hammer-blunt appearance—at first glance it was apparent that this was a man of genius.

He had, too, a deceptively piercing gaze. Three times I sat opposite him in tournaments and struggled valiantly against his formidable play. The only concrete result I obtained was later to become a line in *Modern Chess Openings,* which, later still, I disproved to my own satisfaction, if not to that of my unfortunate opponent who had put his trust in *MCO.* Anyway, on every occasion that I played him I felt that his eyes were boring through me and discovering my most secret thoughts—and while this may be all very well on a visit to a psychiatrist it is the reverse of helpful in over-the-board play. It was only after the third game that I learned that in reality Alekhine was extremely short-sighted!

I knew Alekhine during the period 1930 to 1939; that is, during the time when he was at the height of his powers and also during a period of decline in his chess strength. The Alekhine of the early Thirties was undoubtedly the most varied chess genius the world has ever seen and his performances at San Remo and Bled were extraordinarily impressive. But as success followed success, there came ominous isolated incidents which showed that all was not well. The surprise generally felt at his loss of the world championship to Dr. Euwe in 1935 was not shared by those who knew how heavily he had been drinking. This was a besetting weakness which he never really shook off; though to his credit it must be said that he temporarily, at any rate, abstained from heavy drinking for a period before his return match in 1937. It must be said, too, that even when drunk he could see a great deal further over the board than most chessplayers sober. I remember that at the Warsaw international team tournament of 1935 I was showing a game I had won that day to the fellow members of my team. Alekhine came up, recognized the game and complimented me on it in mellow if somewhat thickly intoxicated tones, and in a flash indicated a vital winning variation we all had missed.

Like practically all great chessmasters he was an egoist whose activities were prompted by the two great driving forces of vanity and ambition. He was prepared to work hard, dreadfully hard, in his desire to reach the highest place in the chess world, and he entered every tournament and match with a vast amount of specially prepared theory.

But he markedly differed from some (notably Capablanca) in that he was passionately attached to chess at any and every moment of the day. When his tournament game was finished it was not his practice (like Capablanca and, later on, Botvinnik) to leave the room at once, but he would sit around engaged in deep analysis and enjoying every moment of it.

In a way this was a great tribute to the powerful fascination of the game. For many of the world's great masters have been interested intensely in chess solely because their other interests were limited and weak. Outside chess their intelligence and culture have not been great and there are a number of grandmasters alive today of whom this is most true. But Alekhine was a man of great intelligence—and that not only at chess. Witness his doctorate in law at the Sorbonne in Paris, a degree not lightly earned and certainly not to be gained by an unintelligent man. Witness, too, his writings on the game which must rank with the best the chess world has produced. The number of young players whose imagination has been stirred and for whom fresh vistas have been opened by his *My Best Games of Chess, 1908-1923* must be legion.

It is true, however, that in writing this book and others he owed much to other masters and was not always frank in acknowledging the debt. In his collections of games, for example, he owed a great deal to the French masters, Renaud and Kahn. There was, too, one curious case in which Alekhine owed an unconscious debt for which of course he could not be censured. I was the editor of the book he wrote on his return match against Dr. Euwe in 1937. He sent me the manuscript by airmail from South America, but an accident happened to the mail and the manuscript eventually reached me with six sheets missing. The publishers were anxious to send the copy to press as soon as possible so as not to lose the topical value of the book, and Alekhine was on tour in South America with no fixed address. Had I written to him for the missing annotations it might be anything up to six months before I heard from him. So I set to, and, imitating his style as best I could, annotated a game and a half myself. Alekhine never discovered what had happened and in fact reproduced my notes as his own in his second collection of games, *My Best Games of Chess, 1924-1937*. Needless to say, I am quite proud of this assimilation of my work with Alekhine's and, looking back now, it is clear to me that I learned a great deal when editing the match book in question.

When the book was published, it had a number of inferior rivals in the shape of works on the same subject by would-be masters and self-styled experts. I remember seeing Alekhine give a simultaneous display in England at which he was asked to award a book to a player who had done well against him. Unfortunately he was handed one of these rival publications on his own match. To make matters worse, it was by a notoriously incompetent writer. Alekhine's snort of indignation and his denunciation of the work are still vivid in my memory. "This," he said, "is a very bad book; mine is the best." He firmly refused to have anything to do with such an inferior production and the organizers were obliged to send for a copy of Alekhine's own book before he would make the award.

Researches by Dr. Buschke have shown that Alekhine's retrospective notes are not always to be trusted, to put it mildly, and there was a case in point in the Margate international tournament of 1938 in which I competed. It was in this tournament that Alekhine won a really wonderful game against the Finnish master, Book. Some of my readers will know the game—the remainder can find it in Alexander's *Alekhine's Best Games of Chess, 1938-1945*. The chief feature of the game is the remarkably intuitive nature of the sacrifices involved. Immediately after it was finished, Alekhine, Book, and myself engaged in a post-mortem dealing with the fascinating variations that might have—but had not—occurred in the game. We came to a key point on which the whole validity of the sacrifice depended. The main alternative to what Book had actually played was fairly obvious, but Alekhine produced a brilliant variation that he had intended playing in the event of Book's choosing this line. Dazzled by its sparkle, we assented to the soundness of the sacrifice.

But Book is one of the most thorough and exhaustive of all present-day masters and he spent the free day that followed in analyzing the position. He discovered, not only a fatal flaw in the line Alekhine had given as his intended reply, but also the correct winning line, of which neither player had had the remotest idea during the course of the game. This was duly shown to Alekhine in my presence later on in the tournament and he had to agree to its validity. Judge of my surprise, and still more so that of Book, when a couple of months later Alekhine published the game with elaborate annotations in which he gave the very line that poor Book had worked out after the expenditure of much labor on his free day as his own intended reply *during* the game. It is a sad comment on human vanity that Alekhine did not realize that he was all the greater player for having made a purely intuitive sacrifice, and that he should stoop to make a dishonest retrospective change in order to stake a claim to be a perfect calculating machine.

In one matter of calculation he was indeed remarkably weak. Unlike Emanuel Lasker and Capablanca who were both experts at the game, he was a very poor bridge player. This was all the more peculiar in that he was a most enthusiastic devotee of the game. Perhaps the explanation is that at heart he was such a keen chessplayer that his mind could never be put seriously to card problems, or perhaps he was not blessed or cursed with card sense. Whatever the reason, I, who am far from being a good bridge player, well remember winning rubber after rubber from him during the Montevideo tournament of 1939. In the actual chess tournament Alekhine won every game and I was second; but the opposition was not very strong and left us much free time for other diversions. Alekhine always played in partnership with his wife and she once plaintively remarked, after he had gone several tricks down when doubled in an atrocious six no trump contract, that if they continued playing they would have to stake and lose their château in France.

Mention of Capablanca reminds me of the great controversy that raged over and between these two during their lives. There was indeed a profound antipathy between these two great figures both in character and in style of play. On the rare occasions when they could be persuaded to play in the same event, incidents were sure to arise, either through jealously by one of the other's "extra" privileges, or through the fact that neither could be got to speak to the other, which made for great difficulties when games were adjourned. Their progress through such an event chiefly consisted in attempts to score off each other and usually Capablanca won in the contest of wits since he had the cooler head.

An example of this came in the final ceremonies of the Buenos Aires, 1939 team tournament. Here the notables such as local mayors, officials, and guests of honor were seated on the raised platform at one end of the hall, whereas in the main part were placed the lesser fry including members of the teams. Capablanca, whose native language was Spanish, had seen to it that he was given a place of honor on the platform. But Alekhine, though he spoke some·Spanish, was naturally nowhere nearly so fluent as his rival and found himself consigned to the main part of the hall with the rest of us. I was seated very near him and can still see in my mind's eye the baleful glare he fixed on Capablanca when he saw him enshrined aloft. How he fumed with rage at the numerous flowery compliments to Capa that interlarded the official speeches!

Various attempts were made to bring them together; but all in vain, and this was clearly a case where two stars could not move in one firmament.

From what I have written above, the reader will deduce that Alekhine was far from perfect. But I hope I have not given a wrong impression of the man and his personality. With all his faults he was very likable. He was not at all aloof from, or condescending to, the ordinary master. He did a great deal for chess and the chess world by taking part in almost innumerable chess events and finally he left the chess world a heritage of such a collection of magnificent games as we are not likely to see produced again by one man.

Chess Review, 1950.

ALEKHINE PAYS A DEBT
By B. H. Wood

My first approach to Alekhine came when I asked him, as world champion, for a series of articles in a chess magazine which I was founding. He named a staggering figure, from which he would not bate one halfpenny; I accepted. Within three months he had (by common knowledge) drunk away his title, and these expensive articles were no longer from the pen of a world champion. His fall was a terrible shock to him; worse than the defeat even, was the attitude of the world of chess. Never greatly liked, he had made enemies everywhere and, restrained hitherto by his renown, they now emerged like rats from their holes to revile and belittle him. He retired like a wounded lion to his château in France, and for weeks I could not get a word out of him. Finally, I had to issue my magazine without the article from his pen that had been promised. The time came to send off his monthly check. What to do? I deliberated a while, then sent it off as usual. I was sorry for him. Within a few days came two such articles as I have never printed before or since.

Of his relations with Capablanca I could write pages. The urbane, sarcastic Cuban was his complete opposite, in almost every way except genius for chess; and the two came to loathe each other.

Illustrated London News, 1949.

SIDELIGHTS ON ALEKHINE
By Thomas Olsen

In 1940 Alekhine told some intimates that he would not mind losing his title to a master of the younger generation—Keres, Botvinnik—but he did not want to lose it to a player of his own generation. "I dominate them all!"

In tournaments Alekhine analyzed his adjourned games for hours and hours: during his meals, in bed or on a pocket set, and mentally while he was walking.

Alekhine unlike Lasker and Capablanca really loved chess. He read everything which appeared on the game and was *au courant* with the smallest analysis ever written by a tyro in some unknown periodical.

Alekhine was no church-goer. But he believed profoundly in the immortality of the soul—especially of his own. "I cannot conceive that nothing should be left of me after my death...."

Alekhine's culture and intelligence were extraordinary. He was an exceptionally well-read man and had really fluent command of about ten different languages.

Alekhine's partiality for alcohol caused his downfall. After his blindfold displays he would drink brandy in ordinary tumblerfuls. It is no secret that he played through some team tournaments in a glaring state of intoxication and he would agree to a draw, before playing, against all dangerous opponents in these events.

Alekhine was admired by all for his marvelous genius, but his character was unfortunately not up to his intelligence. He had innumerable acquaintances all over the world but few real friends. His selfishness and his oblivion of services rendered stunted all sympathy.

Chess, 1946.

AN AMERICAN CHAMPION
By Fred Reinfeld

Marshall was as likable as a man as he was great as a master. Over a period of 15 years, covering some hundreds of meetings, I saw no reason to modify the first favorable impression. Of how many people can this be said?!

For Marshall, chess was fun. No matter how hard the game or how powerful the opposition, he was always irresistibly attracted by sacrificial combinations, tempting attacks, nebulous complications. He played by instinct rather than calculation; where others analyzed painstakingly, he intuitively sensed hidden possibilities. His method, or lack of it, brought him many fine wins, as well as disastrous losses.

Marshall was beloved throughout the chess world, not only as a player but as a man. Away from the chessboard, all his sharpness disappeared. It was my good fortune to know Marshall for about 15 years toward the end of his career, and I never ceased to marvel at the delightful contrast between his remarkable qualities as a fighter, and his gentle, always good-humored, tranquil character when he was not playing a serious game. There was no more delightful companion with whom to analyze newly played games as they appeared in newspaper or magazine. When playing over a modern game, he would grumble at the newfangled opening moves; but this mood would not last long.

Soon he would begin pointing out the most extraordinary tactical finessess—effortlessly, without thought as it were. The very game itself would often dissolve into absorbing daydreams of variations that had never happened.

Chess Review, 1946.

A DAY WITH DR. EUWE
By T. Liket

Only a man with the enormous energy, determination, and ability of Dr. Euwe could have managed the triple career of teacher, chessmaster, and journalist and attained high distinction in each field. And the result?—successes which are not appreciated, failures which are condemned without mercy....

At Noordwijk [1938], Euwe had to be content with fourth place—rather a disappointment for us Hollanders. But when the circumstances are taken into account, we must conclude that we ought to be more than satisfied! It is simply incomprehensible how anyone can stand the strain that Euwe is subjected to.

8:00 A. M.: Off to school.

12:15 P. M.: Home for lunch. The telephone rings: "Please, Dr. Euwe, we had a team match yesterday and six games are adjourned; could you adjudicate these today, because it is so annoying waiting until we know the final score. Shall I give you the positions?"

12:35 P. M.: The telephone rings: "Dr. Euwe, this is Mr. Jansen speaking. I'd like to ask a question. Yesterday I played a match game and started off with 1 P-K4, my opponent answering with the Sicilian Defense. After 19 moves, he left your book and I got a lost game. What should I really have played?"

12:45 P.M.: The telephone rings: "Hello, this is Liket [editor of the *Schaakwereld*]. How about your column for number 51?" "I think I'll have it ready to mail to you tomorrow night." "But that will be too late. I must have the galleys tomorrow, otherwise we can't go to press in time." "All right then. I'll prepare the column tonight, after I return from Noordwijk."

12:55 P. M.: The telephone rings: "Dr. Euwe, I played over your game with Pirc from the paper and studied it very carefully. If you had played B-B4 instead of P-KB4, he would have had to play N-N3 and I don't see what he could do after that." "Yes, you're quite right; but if he plays Q-Q5 instead of N-N3, I lose my bishop—which I naturally want to avoid."

1:12 P. M.: The telephone rings: "Oh, Mrs. Euwe, can I talk to Dr. Euwe? I've found a winning continuation in his adjourned game with Spielmann." "No, sir, impossible; he's running down the stairs at this very moment, on his way back to school—I don't even know whether he can make it in time." "Oh, what a pity! But I'll call again after school, otherwise it may be too late; he has to play off the game tomorrow."

4:10 P. M.: Back from school. A man sits waiting for him with the winning continuation.

4:15 P. M.: He greets his daughters. "Hello, Father, are you going away again? You know you promised to play that new game with us. When will we get around to it?" "As soon as Noordwijk is over; goodbye." He rushes off in the car.

5:15 P. M.: Entrance of the Rembrandt Hotel at Noordwijk. An elderly gentleman approaches him triumphantly: "Hello, Dr. Euwe, don't you recognize me? My name is Pieterse. Don't you recall that in 1934 I played against you in your exhibition in Oudegeest? The game ended in a draw; the ending was very cute—would you like to see it?" "I would, but it will have to be some other time; Kmoch, the tournament director, has just told me that it is time to start play."

10:30 P. M.: The game is adjourned. Dinner at last.

11:15 P. M.: The car dashes off.

12:15 A. M.: Home. He finishes the column for the *Schaakwereld*.

1:15 A. M.: Goes to bed, intending to get up somewhat earlier in order to have time to analyze the adjourned game.

8:00 A. M.: Off to school, etc., etc.

9:00 A. M.: On the trolley. A man is reading his paper on the rear seat.

Conductor: "How did Euwe make out yesterday? Did he lose?"

Passenger: "No, the game was adjourned, but I think he has a bad game."

Conductor: "I'm afraid he's beginning to decline. Everyone passes his peak sooner or later."

Passenger: "It does seem to be rather tiring for him!"

Conductor: "Tiring? What do you mean tiring?! Do you know what's tiring?—when you have to stand up all day on the trolley, selling tickets and giving the correct change—that's physical and mental labor. But a chessplayer...he just sits in his chair till the game is over...."

Chess Review, 1938.

1937: CHAMPION AND CHALLENGER
By Paul Hugo Little

When the 1937 match for the world championship took place, Euwe was 36 and Alekhine was 45. Two years earlier, Alekhine had lost his title to Euwe in an exciting match which had kept the whole chess world agog as it took its astounding course. In 1935 it had been pretty general knowledge that Alekhine's heavy drinking was playing hob with his phenomenal skill. As the 1937 match started, both players were unknown quantities.

Euwe is tall, slim, and dark, with spectacles. A wisp of hair falls on his forehead as he bends his head to scrutinize the board before him. He is very serious as he contemplates a combination, but after he has made his move, he glances quickly about him; and if he sees a friend among the kibitzers, he smiles spontaneously and warmly. During play he sometimes drinks tea and indulges in a bit of Edam cheese or perhaps some chocolate.

His preparation for a tournament or a match consists of long walks, bicycling, plenty of sleep and showers. He watches his diet carefully, and this care for his physical condition has had much to do with his success. For the mental tribulations that every chessplayer must undergo are less fatiguing if the body can respond with good health and energy to the demands put upon it by the mind.

Euwe is serious and careful, although not to the extent of his earlier overcautiousness. Calmly he plans his maneuvers. As he moves the pieces in execution of his plan, a certain care and grace characterize the movement of his body.

Alekhine is emotional; tensely and vibrantly emotional. He is blond, of impressive build. Erect and alert, he gives the impression of being a statesman. He, too, wears spectacles. During play he will sit sideways at the board, supporting his chin with one hand while the other rests on the table or on his leg. Then, presently, he will fidget about for a cigarette. He smokes incessantly, using a full package during an average game.

He drinks coffee and tea, eats chocolate. He can sit for a long time in silence, but when he is away from the board he will confer with one of his fellow masters and burst out excitedly into the most voluble conversation, gesticulating energetically to emphasize his points.

Alekhine, the bold, the attacking, flings caution to the winds. He will sit almost broodingly for a few moments to decide upon his move. Having decided, he makes the move with a nervous gesture of his hand. Sometimes he twists a wisp of hair while he ponders.

Chess Review, 1937.

WORLD CHAMPIONSHIP: A LAYMAN'S VIEW

The light touch in chess is apt to be fearfully heavy-handed. Not so this editorial in the London Times on the 1937 match for the world championship. Urbane, whimsical humor is nicely blended with a keen understanding of the players' styles and personalities. At the time this editorial appeared, I contrasted it with the niggardly treatment of such events in the American press, which gave the match "less space than a spelling bee in Hackensack, a marbles championship on the East Side, or a boy scout jamboree in Oscawana."

Chess is said to be becoming more esoteric. If it is true some of the blame must be laid at the door of the present champion of the world [Euwe]—not because of his play, for there never was a great player who made the game appear so deceptively simple, but because of his name. A section of the lay world has always derived a fearful joy from the nomenclature of chessplayers. They swallowed glutinous polysyllables greedily and asked for more. Morphy, Blackburne, Bird, Burn, Marshall, and the like never seemed to them quite the real thing; the inner essence of the game resided in names like Dus-Chotimirsky, Bogolyubov, Przepiorka. With these they delighted to wrestle, and felt in mastering a new sesquipedalian the same exaltation that comes to a new master when he announces mate in three. But that is not their Waterloo. There was something to stand up against in Znosko-Borovsky, Ilyin-Zhenevsky, and Abramavicius, but to grapple with such a name as Euwe * is like fighting with shadows, with a disembodied spirit or a puff of smoke.

Chess above all other games lends itself to the postmortem. It is

---

* Euwe's name (pronounced "Ayweh") once inspired this limerick by H. D'O. Bernard:

> A Dutchman exclaimed with some fervor:
> "When writing to our Doctor Euwe,
>   Kindly say it's untrue we
>   Pronounce it as Youwe:
> It's rather more Yerver than Erver."
>   —F. R.

not even necessary to have seen the pieces moved to be able to lay down exactly what the pundits have done wrong. Moreover, the critic is unhampered by the "touch-and-move" rule and the ruthless ticking of the chess clock, and is quite likely to be right. So in clubs and cafés where these peculiar people foregather there is a frantic brandishing of pocket boards, dog-eared newspaper cuttings are thumbed again and again, and neglected eggs congeal in their own poached blood as passionate partisans proclaim, "He should have fianchettoed his bishop," to be answered with, "If he had, White would have opened the rook file and established his passed pawn." For every move there is eager canvassing of a dozen positions that might have been, but were not, evolved; and after the storm and stress of debate has subsided, the "scores" will at last be laid up in the reference books together with a wealth of minute comment more elaborate than is bestowed on any other text except Holy Writ.

In contrast with all this acrimony, the two combatants in Holland, though surrounded with eminent players from every part of the globe—all furious doctrinaires—sit over the board in a palsied stillness. There is in progress not only a conflict of personalities but a conflict of styles. Dr. Euwe is a schoolmaster, and in his play gives constantly the impression of trying to reduce this involved business of knights and pawns to a logical simplicity such as any schoolboy ought to understand. But as fast as he disentangles the threads Dr. Alekhine, the lawyer, with his passion for intricacy and complication, proceeds to tie them up again. There is a place for every piece, and Dr. Euwe has an all but infallible precision in getting every piece tidily into its place; it is proof against everything except Dr. Alekhine's genius for knocking other people's pieces out of position. Dr. Euwe, always absolutely true to form; Dr. Alekhine, notoriously addicted on his "off days" to almost elementary lapses, balances them on other days with flashes of amazing brilliance, scarcely explicable except by inspiration or black magic. Only six games have been played so far, but already it is apparent that the apprehensions of Señor Capablanca ten years ago, that chess had reached a deadlock, are entirely baseless. Both players have been throwing their opening strategy into the melting pot. The spirit of enterprise has so taken hold of them that there are even signs of something very like a revival of gambits. Of six games played, four had definite results and the two draws have been due to no lack of pugnacity but to the success of a player exercising his utmost ingenuity to stave off threatening defeat.

London *Times*, 1937.

THE SCORE DOESN'T TELL
By Hans Kmoch

A player's score in an important match or tournament doesn't tell you everything about what happened. The score takes no account of the severe nervous strain, the worry, the anguish, the fierce competitive fervor, that goes into every game. In this connection, what Kmoch has to say about Najdorf's superb victory in the great Amsterdam tournament of 1950 is very enlightening.

Najdorf had his chance and stole the show, playing better, or more steadily at least, than ever before. He surpassed Reshevsky and, indeed, excelled Botvinnik's score at Groningen. Like Reshevsky, he didn't lose a game. Unlike Reshevsky, he never had a losing position. And he turned in some very fine games, two, at least, of eternal beauty. His combination against Haje Kramer will stand as the marvel of the tournament; his 100-mph attack versus Tartakover as a monument to Najdorf's zeal. For all his ingenuity and numerous successes of late, Najdorf had never before scored so impressive a triumph.

According to Najdorf's own statements, however, he was lost in every game. No sooner had he made a certain number of moves than he would storm into the pressroom—almost with the punctuality of a clock—to announce wildly that he was going to lose because of some oversight, some grave risk, or some surprising move by an opponent. For all that these announcements were repeated with all the dramatic intensity of which Najdorf is capable, none ever came through. That dreadful atack of Reshevsky's—it came to a standstill. That careless sacrifice against Gudmundsson—it proved to be sound. That surprise move of Pilnik's—it worked as a boomerang.

Like many of his colleagues past and present, Alekhine included, Najdorf plays really well only if pricked to the utmost alertness by the spur of fear. He is unique, however, in freely admitting so with complete disregard for "face." As he commented on one such occasion: "I just have the urge to undress myself in public."

Chess Review, 1951.

SAMMY, THE CHESS WONDER CHILD
By Edward Lasker

Contrary to the popular notion, there have been very few child prodigies in chess. Prodigies who succeed in later life—Morphy, Capablanca, Reshevsky—are even rarer. In Sammy's case, we are lucky to have a good deal of authentication which is as reliable as it is interesting.

In 1920 American chessplayers were stirred by the appearance of the child prodigy, Sammy Reshevsky, who toured the country, giving exhibitions of simultaneous chess. In spite of the glowing reports which the papers had printed of the child's exploits in Europe, chessplayers here remained skeptical until Sammy came to New York and actually played twenty games simultaneously against opponents some of whom belonged in class A in their clubs.

When we read about this performance in Chicago, we concluded that Sammy was probably quite a little older than advertised. A few days later I received a letter from Sammy's "manager," asking whether I could arrange some chess exhibitions for the boy wonder in Chicago and nearby Milwaukee, and I gladly agreed. I raised about $1600 for a week's visit during which Sammy was to give four exhibitions, one in Milwaukee, and three in Chicago....

My first meeting with him has remained an unforgettable memory. I was waiting for his arrival on the platform of La Salle Street Station.

When the train disgorged its passengers I carefully scanned the young boys among them, and I soon noticed one in the company of a foreign-looking man who glanced around hesitantly and who I thought could very well be Sammy's manager. But somehow I could not believe that the boy was Sammy. True enough, the papers had proclaimed that he was only eight years old, but I was fully prepared to meet a boy of ten or twelve. The child which this man had by his hand could not be a day older than six. Nevertheless, he turned out to be Sammy. I was completely stunned. I refused to believe that this baby could play chess, to say nothing of playing it masterfully.

Besides, he did not look at all like a child who liked to study, or pore over a chessboard. With his rosy cheeks, blond hair, and sparkling blue eyes, a picture of health, one would rather have expected him to be neglecting mental activities in favor of physical exercise.

To make my speechless astonishment complete, the boy asked me, as we were boarding a taxi, whether I could play blindfold chess. When I suggested we might play a game after arriving at the hotel, and on the way I would point out to him some of the Chicago sights, he refused. We had to start the game then and there. He did not evince the slightest interest in the big hotel in which I had reserved a room for him. He walked through the lobby as if in a trance, thinking of his next move. After entering his room, he immediately threw himself on the bed and told his manager not to disturb us while we were finishing our game.

The incredible thing to me was that he actually played a strong blindfold game, never making the slightest mistake regarding the position of the pieces. It was not until the endgame was reached that I succeeded in getting the upper hand. Then a very amusing thing happened. Sammy, who until then had not permitted anything to distract him from the game, suddenly jumped from the bed and said: "I am hungry now. Let's go out and find a restaurant where I can eat."

It turned out that he was considerably encumbered by a strictly orthodox Jewish education. He would eat nothing but kosher food, and while eating he wore his hat. Fearing that he would suffer embarrassment if he were to cling to orthodox habits which seemed strange in this country, I said to him: "Look Sammy: you know that God has made people everywhere with different habits. It would not be right for you to think that the habits where you come from are better than those in other countries. If God did not like the way people eat here, he would not let them prosper, would he? So, why don't you adopt the American customs?"

He listened intently, and for a minute he thought hard about what I had said. But then he looked up to me, and with a wonderful smile which seemed to express the appreciation of a joke as well as reprobation for saying something very foolish, he replied, in what appeared to be one of the favorite English phrases he had picked up, "What are you talking about!" That ended the argument. Probably he had been sufficiently used to the way people looked at him in surprise when he put on his hat in a restaurant, not to feel any embarrassment.

The day after his arrival I took him out to Sears, to meet Julius Rosenwald, and we were invited to stay for luncheon. A number of the top executives of the firm ate at the same table with Mr. Rosenwald, and Sammy certainly furnished entertainment for them, quite apart from the amusing picture he made, sitting with his hat on, and spurning the dishes which the others ate. He whispered into my ear telling me that all he would eat was a couple of boiled eggs. Then he launched an attack upon Mr. Rosenwald which he had apparently conceived as soon as he noticed that he was in the presence of an important personage. He asked: "What kind of a car have you?" Mr. Rosenwald, somewhat surprised at the question, said: "A Pierce Arrow." Sammy: "I want to drive it." Mr. Rosenwald: "I am sorry, Sammy, my chauffeur isn't here at the moment. But if you'll wait, I'll be glad to phone him and he will take you for a ride." Sammy: "I don't want your chauffeur. I want to drive the car myself!" Mr. Rosenwald: "No, Sammy, my car is much too big. You couldn't possibly drive it." Sammy: "What are you talking about! Your car isn't bigger than a Locomobile! In New York I drove nothing but Locomobiles!" Loud laughter from all the men at the table greeted this information, and Sammy seemed hurt. To console him, I said: "Never mind, Sammy, I will let you drive my car." His face lit up. He got up from the table and said: "Good-bye, Mr. Rosenwald. I am going to drive Mr. Lasker's car." That ended the luncheon party.

Then the fun began. I had to take him to my home immediately, to get the car out. He insisted on taking the wheel, although he had to stretch his neck to get his eyes barely level with the windshield to see where he was going. It was all right as long as we were in the residential district where there was hardly any traffic. But I had to think of some forceful argument to make sure that he would relinquish the wheel when we approached the business section. I told him there was a strict police law forbidding boys under fifteen to drive cars, and if a policeman saw him he would be arrested. That stratagem worked. He seemed to have a holy respect for the police. He said: "All right, when you see a policeman, you drive."

Everything went well for a while, when suddenly he ducked down to the floor, letting the wheel go. Terrified, I grasped it and said: "For Heaven's sake, Sammy, what are you doing? Do you want to get us killed?" He answered: "I had to. Didn't you see the policeman?"

He was so scared that he let me drive all the way into town, to the hotel. He had to leave for Milwaukee that afternoon, where his manager wanted him to have a good night's rest before giving his first exhibition in the Middle West. Sammy had grown very fond of me, and he asked me to come with them to Milwaukee. I explained that I had some work to do but that I would go there the next day, in time to see him play.

When I got to the hotel where the exhibition took place, I found the play room crowded to the last square inch with hundreds of spectators, around the twenty tables which had been roped off for the players. I waited in the hall for Sammy to appear. After a few minutes he came, led by his manager. Across his chest Sammy wore a wide red sash on which medals were pinned like orders on the chest of a foreign diplomat.

Sammy seemed a little nervous, not knowing whether he had to meet very strong players. When he saw me, he ran from his manager, grasped my hand, and whispered into my ear: "Stay with me. You must walk with me inside the ring. Don't leave me!"

The effect he had on the crowd was indescribable. They could not believe their eyes when they saw Sammy's size. For once, the newspapers had not exaggerated. Sammy's eyes were only about five or six inches above the tables. The thunderous applause which had greeted him changed into dead silence as soon as he began to play. I walked from table to table in back of him, and after every few steps he looked around to make sure that I was still there to give him courage. He played the first four or five rounds very cautiously. Then one of the players made a very bad move. Sammy turned to me, all smiles, obviously relieved, and he whispered something to the effect of "Look who thinks he can play chess."

From then on he was visibly at ease. If I remember correctly, he won nineteen games and drew one.

The exhibition at the Illinois Athletic Club in Chicago, which took place two days later, was the most impressive of the kind I have ever witnessed. A crowd of fifteen hundred people had to be accommodated. The club rose to the occasion by emptying its huge swimming pool, placing the tables of the twenty players in it, and opening to the onlookers five stories of galleries which surrounded the open shaft of the pool. In this exhibition Sammy actually defeated one of the strongest players of Chicago, who had not considered it beneath his dignity to be one of the twenty opponents lined up against the child wonder....

Chess Secrets.

INTERVIEWING A CHILD PRODIGY
By Thomas B. Sweeney

He was a little devil, just about the average height for eight years of age. When I entered his Taft Hotel room in New Haven his father and mother who were present, stood in the background. I walked over to him, told him that I was a representative of the *News*. He seemed to understand my words and grasped the whole situation right away. I forget precisely what we talked about, though I wrote it up as an interview in the *News* some time in the fall of 1923. I do remember, however, that he referred to his recent match against 21 selected players from the U. S. Army in which he had beaten 20 and tied one—playing them all simultaneously.

He began describing the position on the board of the pieces at a given situation in the course of one of the games, and showed how he had come not to win it. It was plain that he could remember every game that he had ever played, and it was, of course, impossible for me to follow his mental analysis of the positions in the various games that he was describing to me without any board before him. To me, however, the most amusing part of the whole incident was that after showing this phenomenal mental agility, as soon as the interview was closed, and as I was going out of the door, he got up on the bed and started jumping up and down—throwing a pillow at the ceiling and catching it as he would bounce to his feet again, even as you and I.

Chess Review, 1941.

BALLAD OF CHESS
By Paul Hugo Little

I am not one to hail with praise
The wondrous bleatings of a seer,
However mystifying his ways;
But recent acts have made it clear
That one should not forever jeer
Lest, at some time now unforeseen,
With vengeance subtle and severe
The jinns of fate give vent to spleen.

So I had cast incredulous gaze
On the Great Zo-Zo in strange gear.
"Nonsense," I cried. "This is a craze.
You say a woman will interfere
In my affairs and cause me fear,
And that she's bound to come between?"
"Beware," he answered with a leer,
The jinns of fate will give vent to spleen!"

I cleared my mind of mental haze
And sought my chess club to find cheer.
And found a friend of former days.
We both began to persevere

DR. MAX EUWE

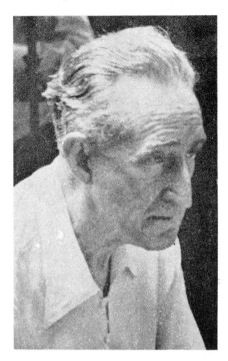

FRANK J. MARSHALL

Three Grandmasters (see 13, page 305).

HARRY NELSON PILLSBURY

U. S. Championship, 1942 (see 14, page 306).

When suddenly the world grew drear;
I gasped in terror as his queen
Gave check, ending my rook's career.
(The jinns of fate gave vent to spleen!)

ENVOY

An oversight had cost me dear,
Yet more than rooks may lose their sheen
When chessplayers will not give ear
And jinns of *mate* give vent to spleen!

Chess Review, 1933.

AN OLD QUESTION
By Richard Reti

Du Mont refers somewhere to Modern Ideas in Chess *as a "lovable book." The adjective comes as a surprise, but then I am reminded of the breathless eagerness with which I read Reti's masterpiece as a schoolboy. The greatness of Reti's achievement lies in this: his book not only gives us pleasure; it teaches us how to enjoy other books, other games. These modern ideas will always be modern.*

What is chess? A game to which the most serious men have devoted their whole lives and about which bulky volumes have been written. The question is, would you call it a game or a science? If we trace the history of chess we shall find that the game was in vogue mostly in those countries that played a leading part in the matter of culture. In the declining Middle Ages the Arabs, at that time the greatest leaders in culture in the world, introduced chess into Europe. The oldest European authors on chess we find lived about the year 1500 in Spain and Portugal, the countries which in the age of material and intellectual discoveries were the leaders. In the Renaissance period in Italy the names of Polerio and Greco stand out. In the eighteenth century and in the Napoleonic era France led Europe, both in politics and taste. That was the time of the activity of Philidor and Labourdonnais, when Napoleon himself devoted his leisure hours to the game.

In the nineteenth century the countries where chess was generally in vogue were England and, later on, Germany, Russia, and America. After the World War [1914-1918], chess and the revival of chess tournaments have made a bridge for intercourse between erstwhile hostile nations and have thus done their part toward international reconciliation more quickly than art or science could do.

If we seek an explanation of the value of a game which was played with preference by people of the highest degree of culture, we shall probably find it in the following considerations: chess is a fighting game and Lasker has already pointed out that every human being has the instinctive need for a fighting game, be it of a sporting kind, such as cards, or a board game. It is the desire to test one's strength, no matter how, and to seek victory as a compensation for our being, in modern times, mostly harnessed up in a framework of machinery, and as a consequence being bound to maintain throughout an even pace. People of the highest culture are not satisfied with just any game. In the long run neither games that depend on physical skill nor games of chance content them. But in chess we get a fighting game which is purely intellectual and excludes chance. It depends in chess upon the fighting capacity of our intellect whether we win or go under, and it is just that which gives to the game the depth contained in it.

We fight differently when we are in a happy state of mind than when we are sad—and it is not only the momentary disposition, but also character that shows itself in chess. The extra-cautious, the petty, the tricky, and the reserved, variable opportunist—these are easily recognizable and cannot in the long run wrest success from the straightforward opponent, who always seeks quite unconsciously the right paths through all difficulties. The above considerations may afford us instances of the possibilities of expression that bring chess so near to art.

Is it possible, we ask ourselves, that a game can at the same time be an art? Well, we can partly answer that by saying that games and art do not differ from each other as much as we think. They have much in common.

Then again, in a materialistic sense, both are absolutely objectless and further, the player of games, equally with the artist, builds up his own world and flies from the sameness of the everyday one to the kingdom he has set up for himself. And lastly every art was once a game and a pastime. The wall pictures of the prehistoric man, the songs of the ancient Greek shepherds or their masked comedies were not very far remote from art. As soon, however, as the luckless lover began to pour out his woes upon his lute then came the dawn of art. The essence of art consists in the ability of the artist to sink his soul in his work.

A hundred years ago chess was no doubt only a game, but he who has felt, for example, the deep sense of devotion that pervades Rubinstein's games knows that we find there a new and ever progressing art.

Modern Ideas in Chess.

THIRTEEN CENTURIES OF CHESS
By C. J. S. Purdy

For years I have been proclaiming that the Australian Purdy is the world's outstanding writer on chess. His work is alive with ideas, crackling with wit and good humor, and notable for its originality and clarity. His predigested history of chess is not quite representative, for it gives no hint of his superb gifts as an annotator and theoretician. Nevertheless, he shows to advantage in his masterly organization of a maddeningly ramified subject, and in his ability to highlight important details. I do not know of any other article on chess history which presents so much information with such delightful informality.

1. CHESS AND ITS PAST

What would chess be without its history? The question is unanswerable because its history is a very part of the game. Chess links us with the past—its dignity and its repose. For me chess conjures up a bewildering pageant. Caliphs of Baghdad, Icelandic warriors, medieval knights and their ladies, wandering minstrels—with chessboards as part of their equipment, monks diligently copying chess manuscripts, soldiers, kings, and courtiers of all ages, Robert Louis Stevenson playing on a voyage to Sydney—one could go on and on.

Chess rivals in strangeness and splendor the reputed Seven Wonders of the World, and the way of an eagle in the air. For it has bridged East and West, and it has kept untarnished its original lure through thirteen centuries. That a game should merely remain in existence so long is remarkable enough—amid changing fashions. Yet chess has remained always the king of games. In the twentieth century it has actually gained: there have been more international contests in chess than in any other sport, and on a sixth of the earth's surface the game has gathered many millions of new adherents during the regime of the Soviets.

Over a thousand years ago, chess was already inspiring men to devote their whole lives to playing it and writing of it. Ancient Baghdad had its Steinitz, its Lasker, and its Nimzovich, who developed the science of the opening and the endgame; it had its experts who played several games simultaneously blindfold, and its ardent problem composers and solvers.

Our Authority

As a schoolboy of fifteen, shortly after learning the moves, I was fortunate enough to gain temporary access to Murray's monumental *History of Chess*. Some of its 900 pages—those dealing with various Asiatic offshoots of the original Indian game—I skipped, but the rest was enthralling. I made copious notes, some of which I hashed up into an article which was published in the Sydney *Sun*. Perhaps that article induced many *Sun* readers to take up chess, just as Murray's book redoubled my own interest in the game.

To my mind, Murray's *History of Chess* is the most important book on chess ever written, and the English-speaking chess world owes more to Professor H. J. R. Murray, of Oxford, than to any other man—for his book is the fruit of many years of research of a most scientific and scholarly kind. There are other histories of chess, but no single work to compare with Murray's. One by Forbes, the best known to English-speaking readers, was shown by Van der Linde to be inaccurate and misleading. Murray acknowledges his debt to Van der Linde.

The Tutankhamen Fallacy

Nearly every reader has heard that "chessmen" have been found in ancient Egyptian tombs, including Tutankhamen's. Actually, the pieces found have never been proved to be chessmen. Indeed, it is almost certain they were used for board games quite unrelated to chess.

Consequently, there is no foundation for the frequently made assertion that chess—or some direct forerunner of chess—was played "thousands of years ago." Murray quotes Professor D. W. Fiske, using italics: *Before the seventh century of our era, the existence of chess in any land is not demonstrable by a single shred of contemporary or trustworthy documentary evidence.... Down to that date it is all impenetrable darkness.*

Murray's book appeared in 1913, but some years ago he reiterated the statement in the *British Chess Magazine*.

So if you are told in some "Literary Digest" or "Quiz" or "Believe It or Not" column, or any other journalistic slobberings of this decadent era, that chess is 2000, or 3000, or 5000 years old, retain a healthy skepticism on the point.

Sanskrit Allusions

After about A.D. 600, various references to chess occur in Sanskrit literature. The game was undoubtedly invented in India, and the evidence points to Northwest India or the upper basin of the Ganges. As this district was then a stronghold of Buddhism, it is not unlikely that the game was invented by Buddhist monks. The Melbourne veteran, F. K. Esling, a keen student of chess history, is a supporter of this view. His speculation is that the game was deliberately invented as a bloodless substitute for war, in the hope that men's minds might be turned from the lure of actual fighting—the taking of life being abhorrent to the Buddhist religion.

War Game

Chess was certainly invented as a war game. The pieces, apart from the central king and counselor, originally represented the four parts of an ancient Indian army: elephants, cavalry, war chariots and infantry. The two pieces representing cavalry were placed and moved exactly like our knights, and the war chariots moved like our rooks, while the eight foot-soldiers had the pawn's move but without the option of the two-square debut. The elephants, however, were much weaker than our bishops; they moved diagonally but only two squares, neither more nor less. The counselor, on Q1, also moved diagonally, and only one square, but later on its power was increased in parts of India to that of a modern bishop.

How this piece became a queen after many centuries, and gained its present great power, belongs to a future section of this series.

2. WESTWARD

From India, chess went rapidly to Persia, thence, later on, to the Arabs; thence—through the Moors—to Spain, and thence to all Europe except Russia. Chess went to Russia from India direct.

That, in a nutshell, is the history of Indo-European chess up to the early Middle Ages. Before taking up the thread where we left it, let us glance briefly at the Far Eastern varieties of chess.

Chinese Chess

China certainly got chess from India, but possibly not till after the Mohammedan penetration of India began, about 700. This is suggested by the Chinese enlarged board. For some of the Arabs experimented with various kinds of enlarged board and extra pieces, only to revert ultimately to the old Indian 8x8.

The Chinese made a radical change by placing the men not on the squares, but on the intersections of the lines. This seems fantastic to us because we use a checquered board, but all over Asia the board is simply a set of criss-cross lines. The intersections scheme is highly economical, e.g., a board of 64 squares has 81 points. In Chinese chess, with 72 (9x8) squares, there are 90 points.

The Chinese have always tended to pile quaint complications on to their games. Thus, in chess they later introduced a "river" across the middle of the board. The horses, chariots and foot soldiers—note the retention of the old Indian names—can cross the river, but the elephants cannot. Moreover, three pieces are limited to a home base of nine points. They are the general (king), governor (same move as the general), and the counselor.

There are four pieces with the chariot's (rook's) move, but two are called cannons, and cannot capture an enemy unless some other piece (called a "screen") is in the way! This is complexity for complexity's sake.

But there was a sound reason for changing the name king to "general." Report has it that the Emperor Wen-ti (589-605) visited an inn and saw some foreigners playing some pre-chess game called *t'shu-p'u*. One of the pieces was called *I pai ti* (white emperor). Wen-ti remarked, "Dashed sacrilegious, what! Bad show, chaps," and had them all executed instantly. This got around.

The elaborate ivory sets often seen are not for Chinese chess; they are carved by Chinese for Europeans. The Chinese use flat chips bearing the pieces' names, as in mah-jongg.

Chess has long been so popular in China that it is unfashionable, and it is left mainly to the masses.

Shogi (Japanese Chess)

The Japanese unanimously admit that chess came to them from China. It may have come very early indeed, before the introduction of the intersections idea, for the Japanese play on the squares as we do. They have no river. Their board is 9x9.

However, the Japanese introduced the most radical change of all. So radical that while playing chess we need never be haunted by the thought that millions of Japanese are doing the same thing. In shogi a captured piece becomes part of the capturer's army! Also, other units besides the pawns obtain promotion.

Some educated Japanese learn Western chess. As a boy I had some games with a Japanese doctor whose play was well above average.

The Chinese general, governor, and counselor appear in shogi as the jeweled general, gold general, and silver general. The horse becomes the honorable or laurel horse. Our rook is the fragrant chariot or spearman. As in China the game is unfashionable among the aristocracy, pseudo-aristocracy, plutocracy, intelligentsia, and pseudo-intelligentsia. It is left to the impoverished masses. But it is highly organized. Shogi players are said to number five million, and there are many professionals. That's enough about shogi.

Malayan Chess

Chess is very popular in the Malay lands, particularly Sumatra, Java, and Borneo.

The Malays got the game from India, but their rules were subsequently much influenced by Moslem chess and, later on, European chess. In fact, Portuguese and other European contact in the sixteenth century brought about exactly the same chess revolution that had occurred in Europe. The counselor and the elephant, formerly feeble pieces, acquired the powers of the modern queen and bishop. Also, the pawns gained the right to move two squares initially.

The Bataks of Sumatra are chess fiends. Almost every male Batak is a player. They play usually for stakes, and so violent are the passions aroused that the village headman sometimes bans chess for a whole season.

Burmese Chess

Burmese chess has the same board and men as Indian chess. Its radical difference is that the players select their own layout for the pieces at the beginning.

When two Burmese play chess, the winner gives the loser a dab on the cheek with powdered lime. And why does he have powdered lime so handy? Because he keeps it to pepare his betel nut for chewing. Thus the score is kept for a series of skittles. Some players, when there is a glut of powdered lime, give a dab for every check to the opponent's king. This enables a Burmese who comes home with powder all over his face to offer his spouse the watertight explanation that he forgot to castle.

3. DICE IN CHESS

Some think that chess started as a four-handed game; others that the four-handed game was an offshoot. The board was the same. Each player had four pieces: king, elephant, horse, chariot (no counselor), and four foot-soldiers, and a throw of the dice decided what was to be moved, though the player could exercise skill in deciding where to move it. This game never "took on" outside of dice-mad India.

Some of those who say the two-handed game was first still think chess was first played with dice. Others, especially supporters of the Buddhist invention theory, say the dice game was a corruption. Anyway, the two-handed dice game certainly flourished in India alongside the game of pure skill.

We have to thank the Mohammedan religion for thrusting the dice game into obscurity. All religions have opposed gambling, but only one effectively.

In Europe the dice game reappeared. Even as late as the thirteenth century we have a reference to it in the French romance, *Huon of Bordeaux*. The hero is about to play chess with Ivoryn's daughter.

" 'Lady,' said Huon, 'which game will you play? Will you play it with moves or with dice?' 'Let it be with moves,' said the lady, with clear voice."

The long life of the dice variety of chess accounts for the otherwise puzzling denunciations by the clergy in the Middle Ages, of "dicing and chess." The two would not have been so often mentioned together if chess had never been associated with dice.

In the end, the dice game simply died of inferiority.

Chess Comes to Persia

Chess reached Persia from India before the seventh century. It rapidly obtained such status that a poet of the time mentioned it among the essential accomplishments of a national hero.

Then (638-651) came the conquest of Persia by the Arabs in the sacred name of Mohammed, who had died in 632. Persian culture was assimilated by the conquerors, who found chess much to their liking.

Was Chess Legal?

But during the centuries that followed, chess caused Mohammedan jurists a perpetual headache: just how did chess stand with the late Mohammed? Mohammedan law is incredibly wide in its scope. It covers every possible action a human being can perform.

Mohammed himself was born about the time chess is first mentioned, but his own conquests did not carry him into India or Persia where the game was played.

The only passage in the Koran that gave a basis for dealing with chess was this:

"O true believers, surely wine and lots and images and divining arrows are an abomination of the works of Satan, therefore avoid ye them that ye may prosper."

"Lots" covered all gambling and games of chance. Dice-chess was thus forbidden to all true believers. So also was playing straight chess for stakes. An Arab writer described with pious horror the gambling at chess that went on in India.

But it didn't end there. Chess pieces, if carved to look like elephants, horses, chariots etc., were images and therefore Satanic, at least according to the Sunnite branch of the religion. As it happened, ordinary players had never gone in for such chessmen. The average Oriental is a very poor man, and was even in those days. He used—and still uses—an extremely simple pattern of chessmen, requiring a minimum of workmanship, and quite unrecognizable, unless you were told what they were. For instance, the elephant was reduced to a couple of ears, represented by a lump of wood with a piece cut out of the top—the two side parts left were the ears. The use of these pieces avoided any argument as to whether chess came under the "images" ban.

Richly carved pieces were not unknown, however, and probably anyone wealthy enough to buy them was wealthy enough to use them and get away with it.

Jumbo, Bishop, or Fool?

Lovers of paradox may note that Christianity is represented among the chess pieces partly through the influence of Mohammedanism! It came about thus.

When chess came to Europe, the split lump of wood was not recognized as an elephant nor was it generally known that the name *al fil* meant "the elephant." The piece became, in different places, an old man, a count, a bishop, and a fool. Undoubtedly the split piece of wood suggested both a bishop's mitre and a jester's cap. The piece remained a bishop in two countries, England and Iceland. And because England was the first country to introduce chess diagrams in printing, other countries still use a bishop's mitre in diagrams just as we do. For instance, the Russians diagram their *slon* (elephant) and the Germans their *Laufer* (runner) as a mitre. The French, however, diagram their *fou* as a cap and bells, evidently because it would be rude to call a piece a fool and show him as a bishop.

Horses, Bows, Wives

Some Mohammedan jurists still condemned chess because of the tradition that Mohammed had disapproved of all recreations except three: the Prophet had declared that a man should limit his amusements to his horse, his bow, and his wife or wives.

The jurist ash-Shafii got round this by claiming that chess was not necessarily only a recreation; it might be played as a mental exercise for the solution of military tactics. Ash-Shafii himself played chess. His legal opinion was quoted by Mohammedan writers for centuries.

These legal controversies went on and on. In the eighth century (the second century by the Mohammedan calendar) chess was a popular game throughout Islam, ie., the Moslem world, right from Spain to the Indus.

4. Caliphs and Chess

Chess anecdotes are related about nearly all the Caliphs. The Caliph, of course, was the supreme ruler of the Moslem world in succession to Mohammed himself. Some of these anecdotes follow, all in chronological order:

One of the first Caliphs was Omar b. al-Khattab, father-in-law of Mohammed. He died in 643. He was asked if chess were lawful. His wisecrack was, "There is nothing wrong in it; it has to do with war."

The Caliph Abdalmalik b. Marwan (died 705) was a keen player. He was asked by a dignitary named ash-Shabi whether he was not ashamed of playing. The Caliph asked him if chess were *haram, maisir,* or *ansab.* That is, was it punishable by law, was it gambling, or was it "images"?

On ash-Shabi admitting that it was none of the three, the Caliph just went on playing. By the way, this man ash-Shabi must have been a man of colossal nerve, for he himself was an inveterate chessplayer. He was known to have played chess for a stake and to have forgotten the hour of prayer in his absorption; and also to have played chess in the street, a practice laid down as definitely unworthy of a true believer; he covered his head so that his identity should not be discovered, for he was a big shot.

A later Caliph was playing chess when a Syrian visitor was announced. The Caliph ordered a slave to cover the board before the visitor entered. He then proceeded by tactful questions to find out how far the Syrian was instructed in the Mohammedan religion. On finding that he was quite unlearned in it, he had the board uncovered and resumed his game, saying, "There is nothing forbidden to the uneducated."

The Caliph al-Mahdi (died 785) wrote a letter to the people of Mecca, saying that he had heard things about them which he "condemned and abominated"—including "the assembly of fools for dicing, archery, chess, and all vanities which lead astray from the remembrance of God." Yet chess was played in the Caliph's own court. The poet Abu Hafs, who habituated the court, played blindfold, and was named ash-Shatranji (the chessplayer), so well were his skill and enthusiasm known. A writer credited the Caliph himself—probably falsely—with the composition of a chess problem!

The most famous of all the Caliphs, Harun-al-Rashid (died 809) of Arabian Nights fame, was not only a chessplayer himself but a chess patron. He granted pensions to strong players. The latter would probably have subscribed to Tennyson's theory that

> In sooth it was a goodly time
> For it was in the golden prime
> Of good Haroun Alraschid.

He is said to have bought for 10,000 dinars a slave girl who was famed for her chess skill. Trying conclusions with her, he lost three games in succession. Asked to choose her reward, she begged forgiveness for some friend of hers who had incurred the Caliph's wrath.

Harun's eldest son, the Caliph al-Amin (died 813) was playing chess in Baghdad when the city was under siege. A messenger was sent to inform him that the situation was most critical. The Caliph waved him aside, saying, "Patience, my friend, I see that in a few moves I shall give Kauthar checkmate." This beats Drake by about 800 years.

Al-Amin's brother, al-Ma'mun (died 833), was the next Caliph. He seems to have been a good enough player to realize his weakness, for he is quoted as saying, "Strange that I who rule the world from the Indus in the East to Andalus in the West cannot manage 32 chessmen in a space of two cubits by two."

Al-Ma'mun also said that chess was more than a game; that it was an excellent training for the mind.

He always insisted on his adversary playing his best. One day he perceived that his opponent, a courtier, was "pulling his punches." The Commander of the Faithful upset the board in his wrath and said to all present, "Bear witness to the vow which I now make that I will never play chess with this person again."

During al-Ma'mun's reign there lived four players who were ranked as "aliyat" or chess grandees—masters to use the modern term.

The Caliph al-Mu'tazz (died 869) was playing chess when a messenger arrived with news of the death of the Caliph's predecessor and rival, al-Musta'in. The messenger proudly presented the former Caliph's head. Al-Mu'tazz, deep in his game, merely muttered, "Righto! put it down there, you'll find some beer in the ice chest," or words to that effect, and went on playing.

This Caliph's son, b. Mu'tazz, who met an untimely end, wrote a much quoted poem on chess. I have seen an enormous quantity of verse written on chess; and the less said about most of it the better. Even the famous stanza in the *Rubaiyat* is bloodless and wooden. To my mind, this simple little poem, written over a thousand years ago, has never been equaled.

The first and last couplets express some sort of unhappiness in the life of this poet prince, who found a needed refuge in chess.

> O thou whose cynic sneers express
> The censure of our favorite chess,
> Know that its skill is science's self,
> Its play distraction from distress.
> It soothes the anxious lover's care,
> It weans the drunkard from excess;
> It counsels warriors in their art,
> When dangers threat, and perils press;
> And yields us, when we need them most,
> Companions in our loneliness.

5. THE GOLDEN AGE OF MOSLEM CHESS

I have mentioned four players ranking as masters, who flourished in the beginning of the ninth century. They were succeeded by al-Adli, who was supreme for most of the second quarter of the century. Near the end of his life, he was at last defeated in a match played in the presence of the Caliph al-Mutawakkil (died 847). The new champion was ar-Razi.

Like modern world champions, both al-Adli and ar-Razi were chess writers. Little of ar-Razi's work has survived, but the great as-Suli, of whom we shall hear shortly, had a much higher opinion of him than of al-Adli, whose writings he criticized at great length.

To digress for a moment, I mention that not only the Caliphs but other wealthy and powerful people made a practice of keeping strong chessplayers in their households. About 870, a certain b. Darraj gate-crashed into the house of Ahmad b. Mudabbir, Collector of Taxes in Palestine. On discovering the uninvited guest, the host remarked:

"A parasite may be pardoned his intrusion upon other people's society whereby he disturbs the charm of their intimacy and discovers their secrets, but only on condition that he is endowed with certain talents, as a knowledge of chess or the ability to play the lute or guitar."

The parasite said, "That goes, big boy, I'm a wiz." So the host ordered a page to play him at chess as a test. The parasite asked, "How much if I clean up?" He was promised 1000 dirhems if he proved himself superior to the whole company in all the accomplishments mentioned. He said this would suit him but that he would like the money placed beside him on the table—just to inspire him. It was. He beat the page, but the doorkeeper who had let the parasite in and who saw trouble coming if the fellow got away with a grand, produced another page who duly defeated the stranger, thus keeping the money in the family.

It is not known when ar-Razi died, but he had no immediate successor. It is during the reign of the Caliph al-Muktafi (902-908) that we next hear of a master. This was al-Mawardi, who gained the Caliph's high favor and settled down at court.

But now there came stories of the extraordinary chess brilliance of a certain Abu-Bakr Muhammed b. Yahya as-Suli, descendant of a Turkish prince. The Caliph was not disposed to believe that anyone could defeat his favorite, and a match was arranged in his presence. The Caliph openly "barracked" for al-Mawardi. This embarrassed as-Suli, but he soon recovered his nerve, and completely overwhelmed his adversary. Thus convinced, the Commander of the Faithful turned to al-Mawardi and, wishing to convey to him delicately that he was no longer his white-haired boy, said poetically, "Your rose water has turned to urine."

As-Suli was a historian of note, and also a ready versifier and a convivial and entertaining companion, but it was chess that made him immortal. His reputation as the greatest player of all time remained unchallenged in Arabic chess circles for at least six centuries, and the highest praise that anyone could give a move was to say, "It is worthy of as-Suli himself!"

As-Suli remained a favorite at court during the reigns of three Caliphs. The third was ar-Radi (died 940). One day ar-Radi was walking in the gardens of his country seat, when his courtiers vied with each other in praising the beauty of the lawns and flowers and comparing them with the wonders of the world. "Stop!" cried the Caliph, "As-Suli's chess charms me far more than these flowers, and more than all that you have mentioned."

With this Caliph's death, as-Suli at last fell out of favor. He fled from Baghdad and went into hiding at Basra, where he died in poverty* in 946.

As-Suli far outshone his predecessors both as a player and a writer. "We see him criticizing them," says Murray, "not unkindly, but with the touch of superior knowledge. We have his favorite openings, founded no longer on mere caprice but on definite principles. We have endgames which happened to him in play over the board and in blindfold play.... We see him as the first player to try to enunciate the underlying principles of play."

As-Suli had a grateful and able pupil named al-Lajilaj (meaning the stammerer). Al-Lajilaj became the great historic figure among the Persians, the Turks, and the Mogul Hindus, just as as-Suli did among the Arabs themselves. He, too, was a chess writer, and in his manuscripts he paid homage to as-Suli in much the same way that Lasker did to Steinitz nearly a thousand years later. But little is known of his life.

The golden age of Moslem chess may be said to end about here. In Murray's words, "the light of the Eastern caliphate was flickering out, and the center of Moslem life was moving elsewhere."

So we must now leave Baghdad, and wander more at random over the face of the earth. Chess was already firmly established in Europe.

---

* The circumstances of as-Suli's death stamp him as a true champion.—F. R.

6. Blindfold Chess in Olden Days

Reuben Fine writes in *Chess Review:*

"If we wish to discover how far chess has advanced in 150 years, blindfold play is one of the most convincing answers. In Philidor's day three games was a miracle; today the record is forty.* Blindfold chess is an index of the chessplaying ability of the human mind."

If Fine is right, the standard of play was higher among the Moslems many centuries ago than it was in Europe 150 years ago.

Nearly every chessplayer thinks, like Fine, that Philidor was the first exponent of simultaneous blindfold chess. In Philidor's day there was no one to contradict. Indeed, the promoters of Philidor's display feared that posterity would refuse to believe that a man had played three games of chess blindfold simultaneously, and they engaged an attorney to draw up a document for witnesses of the display to sign—an excellent publicity stunt, incidentally.

Yet, centuries before, such exhibitions had been common among the Moslems, and the evidence indicates that a higher number than three was reached—possibly ten.

First of all, there are the recorded words of one Abu'l-Abbas b. Juraij (1139-1232):

"I was contemporary with as-Saquali (the Sicilian), al-Yahudi (the Jew), and b. an-Nu'man, all of whom played blindfold."

As Safadi (died in 1363) writes in his *Sharh Lamiyat al'Ajam* of a soldier in Egypt named 'Ala'addin, who was blind, and yet "used to play chess with the nobles and beat them utterly." And in 1331 he saw in Damascus a man named an-Nizam al-Ajami, who played two games blindfold and one over the board at the same time, winning all three. He could call the positions at any time.**

The Mogul emperor, Timur (died 1405), was a chessplayer and patron. The most skilled player in his domain was 'Ala'ddin at-Tabrizi,

---

* Written in 1945. Since then Najdorf has established a new record of 45 simultaneous blindfold games!—F. R.

** What is curious about all these accounts is the lack of reference to chess notation, without which blindfold chess is almost unthinkable.—F. R.

a lawyer. The emperor used to say to him, "You have no rival in the kingdom of chess, just as I have none in government."

This at-Tabrizi seems to have been the Tarrasch of those days (Tarrasch was the man who said, "There are now two chessmasters, the other is Lasker"). Anyway, at-Tabrizi wrote as follows:

"I have passed my life since the age of 15 years among all the masters of chess living in my time; and since that period till now when I have arrived at middle age, I have traveled through 'Iraq-'Arabi, and 'Iraq-'ajami, and Khurasan, and the regions of Mawara'n-nahr (Transoxiana) and I have met there with many a master in this art, and I have played with all of them, and through the favor of him who is Adorable and Most High I have come off victorious.

"Likewise, in playing blindfold, I have overcome most opponents, nor had they the power to cope with me. I have frequently played with one opponent over the board, and at the same time I have carried on four different games with as many adversaries without seeing the board, while I conversed freely with my friends all along, and through the Divine favor I conquered them all."

There is also a Persian translation (dated 1612) of a much earlier Arabic work on chess by Muhammed b. Omar Kajina, in which the last chapter deals with blindfold play. The author states that there have been players who could conduct four or five games simultaneously blindfold, and goes on to say:

"I have seen it written in a book, that a certain person played in this manner at ten boards at once, and gained all the games, and even corrected his adversaries when a mistake was made."

Bland, a chess historian, records that about 1567 a player in Constantinople played ten games blindfold simultaneously, winning them all. This may be the player referred to in the manuscript.

The part about the expert correcting his adversaries gives the story the stamp of truth. Blindfold players all do this without much additional effort, and yet to the uninitiated it sounds impossible. Had the story been an invention, the narrator would not have thrown in such an apparently fantastic detail. Actually the blindfold player has to visualize the board so clearly that he quickly "sees" the impossibility or ambiguity of any move called.

Cossack horsemen of olden days often played each other at chess without board or men while riding. This reminds me to mention that while the playing of several games at once is of no practical use, the ability to conduct a game without board or men can be at times exceedingly valuable. As a preliminary, learn to visualize the color of every square so well that if anyone calls, for example, "White's QB5," or "Black's KR4," you can answer instantaneously, "Black!" or "White!" as the case may be. This enables you to visualize a move the more readily.

7. A LETTER FROM H. J. R. MURRAY

The title of this series induced several correspondents to send us old newspaper cuttings, claiming discoveries of chessmen in ancient Egyptian tombs. If admitted, these "discoveries" would make chess thousands of years old. At the time of the Tutankhamen excavations, newspapers all over the world published such claims.

Knowing the claims to be baseless, but needing corroboration, I wrote a few months ago to the world authority, Mr. H. J. R. Murray, asking him to smash the claims. His reply follows:

Dear Mr. Purdy,

Your letter reached me today, and I am very glad to be able to write to you on the antiquity of chess. My article in the *British Chess Magazine* to which you refer appeared in December, 1936 with the title "How Old is Chess?" It made no reference to the Egyptian game-boards that have often been found in tombs there, because nobody who has seen the boards or studied the question now thinks that these boards have any relationship to chess.

[Mr. Murray describes the boards in detail; they were nothing like chessboards and all the men were alike. He traces the whole history of the game right up to its present form, backgammon.—C. J. S. P.]

In my *B.C.M.* article I said:

The earliest contemporary mention of chess occurs in a Persian romance written about the year 600 A.D. . . . Among the accomplishments of the hero of this romance chess is mentioned by its Persian name of Chatrang.

In the course of the next 50 years (600-650) we have two references to chess in Sanskrit writers who lived in the Ganges Valley about 65 miles northwest of Cawnpore. The earlier of these references is somewhat obscure, the latter is perfectly clear. In it Bana describes the good order prevailing in the kingdom of Kanauj under its Rajah, Harsha (600-648), and says, "Only chessboards teach the positions of the army." [Presumably meaning that the army never had to be called up.—C. J. S. P.] The word "chaturanga" is used, meaning (1) army, (2) chess. The "chatrang" of the Persian word is simply an adoption of the Sanskrit name, and shows that the Persians obtained the game from India.

As a result of the Arabic conquest of Persia (640-650) the Moslem world learned chess, and started one of the most brilliant periods in the history of the game. We meet with the first Arabic literary mention soon after 700; we hear of blindfold players and women players before 750; the Caliphs, including Harun-al-Rashid, became players; from 800, players are classified according to their skill, and matches to settle the right to be in the master class were played in the presence of Caliphs . . . ; problems were composed and recorded from about 800 onwards; al-'Adli wrote the first book on chess about 850, including openings, problems, derived games, knight's tours, and a valuable chapter on the differences in his day between Persian and Indian rules.

The Moors carried chess into Spain, 713-750. . . . The Eastern Empire in Constantinople learned chess before 800.

Between 650 and 750 a second Persian work was written which tells the story of the introduction of chess into Persia in the reign of Khusru I (531-578). It describes the game as one of pure skill [important as favoring those who think the skill game preceded the dice game.—C. J. S. P.] and gives the names of the chessmen. The introduction of chess in Khusru's reign is confirmed by independent historical works.

We have accordingly satisfactory evidence for the existence of chess in the Ganges Valley and in Persia by 600 A.D. How much older may the game be? As a general rule it is found that where a country has a literature, literary mention of chess appears within 50 years of the introduction of the game, or any notable changes in its rules.

The Persian story of the introduction of chess tells how an Indian ambassador brought the game to Khusru and challenged him to explain the game or pay tribute. It seems likely that the Indian would use a recently invented game for this purpose.

More cogent is the fact that from 450 to 550 Northern India was devastated by successive waves of Hun invasion, which shook Northern Indian society to its foundations and severed the chain of tradition.... All three considerations point to an invention of chess round about 570 A.D., and explain how the Chinese traveler Fa-hien, who was in India just before the Hun invasions began and wrote a detailed account of his travels, makes no mention of chess.

So much for my article. Some people would dismiss the Persian story of the introduction of chess on the grounds that it is incredible that the Persians could have solved the riddle proposed by the Indian ambassador. But Khusru had already sent his physician, Barzoi, to Kanauj secretly to obtain a copy of the Fables of Pilpay. It is not impossible that Barzoi had seen chess played in India and brought back information as to the game.

Most board games fall into three classes: (1) race games, played with dice or similar instruments; (2) war games; (3) hunt games. The old Egyptian games fall into class (1); our representatives are backgammon, snakes and ladders, ludo etc. In class (3), Fox and Geese. The Egyptian games cannot be ancestors of chess since they belong to a different class of games.

Yours sincerely,

H. J. R. Murray

Check!, 1945.

ON CHANGING THE RULES OF THE GAME
By Barnie F. Winkelman

There is much good sense in this review of some of the suggested successors to chess. Viewed cold-bloodedly from the perspective of thousands of years, chess will eventually require some alteration—as did the Oriental and medieval varieties. But the game as we know it today has provided us with so many pleasurable hours that it would be a minor form of suicide to discard chess in its present-day form.

A recent contributor suggests a fundamental change in the game of chess by varying the promotion of the pawns. The project is advanced in all seriousness by a strong player, and hence is all the more inexplicable to this commentator.

There is indeed no hardier perennial in the literature of chess than the recurrent proposal to alter the rules—the so-called "invention" of a new game. Each suggestion of this kind is put forth with great enthusiasm by its sponsor and with a high claim to originality. Not infrequently there is a rousing whoop of joy by the proponent over the child of his brain; at the very least a smug sense of achievement, and at all times a naive belief that something in the line of progress or reform has been accomplished.

Many years ago in the October, 1898 issue of the *American Chess Magazine* which featured a new and intricate variation of the Rice Gambit, a simple soul inserted the following advertisement:

CHANCELLOR CHESS

An opportunity is now offered to the public to secure a copy of Ben R. Foster's ingenious work entitled *Chancellor Chess* or the new game of chess. A new piece is added to the game, having the power of rook and knight combined, and the chessboard is enlarged to nine squares. When it was first introduced it created a furor in the chess world heretofore unknown. Price only 50 cts. postpaid.

The present generation of chessplayers knows little of the Rice Gambit, whose intricacies were not fully explored by the researches of hundreds of experts, and is not even aware that chancellor chess ever existed, let alone created a furor.

In spite of all this, the recurrent cry that chess is too simple and that a new and better game has been conjured up, re-echoes through the years.

In the July-August issue (1928) of the *American Chess Bulletin,* a misguided enthusiast takes up the lament of Capablanca that the game has become exhausted. He suggests the name of "Blanchess" for Capa's proposed modified form of the game, and is enthralled by the thought that his own mind has been functioning in harmony with the great Cuban. He writes to Capablanca (who has no one but himself to blame if he has unloosed a storm of crank letters):

"In adopting the names Duke and Templar I did so.... It is very curious that you should have quite independently thought of Duke for the Rook-Knight piece."

And this is the finale:

"I have introduced the game to more players and found them most enthusiastic over it. I am certain it has come to stay, even if many old chessplayers do not care to try it. I shall always like the old game, but shall, I think, always prefer the new, and the majority of those who try it will do likewise...."

In the same issue there is reference to Capa's 100-square board, and, alas! a letter on the same general subject by the late C. S. Howell. He deems the suggestion a bit too radical, but submits his own innovation, ending his letter with the curious sentence: "This proposal is made seriously."

In the *British Chess Magazine* (January, 1929), we find a nightmarish proposal for "Double Chess" submitted by one who hides under the name "Craigelachie." Three valuable pages are devoted to an explanation of the new game, its advantages over the old, and the fond faith of its godfather in its bright future.

Double chess! With two sets of men, with a board of 192 squares, "to allow much larger scope for the display of individual subtlety or strategy." And the same issue contains an interesting game between Capablanca and Kmoch, and the diagramed position after the 27th move. Here Kmoch overlooked a winning line, and the real possibilities of the position (that White should simply have played Q-Q1 and Q-K2) have never been pointed out.

The most entrancing addendum of the "Double Chess" proposal occurs at the end of the article. It states:

"This game was Entered at Stationers Hall, April, 1927, and Copyright obtained in the U.S.A. the same year by Julian S. Grant Hayward."

Recently the newspapers announced that certain members of the teaching staff at Princeton had found chess too simple for their superminds, and had perfected a new game known as "Three-Dimensional Chess." The reports did full justice to the intellectual prowess of the "professors," but a rival claimant immediately declared that the new game was his own invention. In fact he not only had formulated the new game, but he sought mental relaxation playing it after he had mastered the old game of chess and found no further stimulation in it.

At all times chess enthusiasts with a flair for the novel and the picturesque have been diverted by the mysteries of "Fairy Chess." On the Continent, "Cylinder Chess" and other intricate forms of chess have had wide vogue. The game of Kriegspiel can be viewed as one of the most popular of such innovations.

The justification for all such efforts to add sparkle and variety to chess is certainly debatable. Usually they are urged by weaker players whose repertoire is limited to one or two openings, who might do well to plough more deeply in the old furrows. Even the greatest of the masters—with a few notable exceptions—have found chess not only inexhaustible, but exhausting, and a single lifetime all too short to grapple with its limitless problems. In spite of years of study the most talented experts can only scratch the surface of midgame positions, and many types of endings baffle all analysis over the board. Recently a group of the leading American players found itself completely at a loss in an ending of only five pieces (king and two pawns versus king and rook), which was set up for their study by an able analyst from the Midwest.

On a less notable plane are these many proposals for changing, adding or eliminating, put forth from time to time by those who know little or nothing of chess. This eagerness of the novice to improve the game, even before he has acquired the rudiments of its technique, is peculiar to chess. Rarely do we meet the suggestion that baseball ought to be played on a hexagon or a pentagon instead of a diamond, or that another fielder (in or out) should be added, or that five strikes instead of three be allowed the batter. The rules of our national pastime, dating back less than a single century, are treated with due deference. Nor is the outcry for altering the rules of golf or tennis particularly noticeable.

In none of these games is change as fundamental and far-reaching as it is in chess. Though we alter the size of the ball in golf, impose new penalties and restrictions in football, or set up new regulations in billiards...the essential art remains. But the slightest rearrangement of the chess pieces—not to mention the addition of a new piece or of new squares—is like a change in the keyboard of the piano, or a re-alignment of the strings of the violin.

Usually these plans emanate from folks who are never content to play the game. They must perforce also draw up the rules. Nor will they take the time or trouble to learn from the past. They must give us a new game—*their* game—even before they have grasped the essentials.

However, the urge for "reform" often springs from nothing more solid than an insatiable desire for novelty, an itch for the new, a recoil from anything that is old. There is here a curious combination of vanity, a perverted inventiveness, and the misdirected zeal of creative but undisciplined minds that has its counterparts in every sphere of human activity.

Finally we have the "democratic" ideal as the motivating force behind many of the proposals for new rules. We will restore equality in chess! Years of study and experience have given the master great advantages over those who now take up the game. Not for us to follow in his footsteps by a program of study and hard work. We will simply transpose the knight and bishop, and at a single stroke all "book" is rendered obsolete. Private property has been abolished in Caissa! Master and tyro can start afresh and on an equal footing.

The proponents of these little communistic innovations do not even envisage any possible objections. They are so overwhelmed by their visions of a chess utopia that they are astounded that the chess world does not immediately forsake its outmoded pastime and take the new contraption to its bosom. It never occurs to these gentry that chess devotees who have spent years of research and exploration do not relish an overnight dictum that relegates all this to limbo.

Nor can such zealots appreciate that the chief appeal of the game, and its challenge to struggle with its purely artificial intricacies, are its century-old traditions, the immutability of its laws, and its present vogue in nearly the same form all over the world.

Overlooked too is the consideration that *chess has a great literature,* an evolution of theory over a thousand years, a maturing philosophy. We play over the games of Philidor or Greco, we compare the styles of Anderssen and Morphy, of Pillsbury and Capablanca. We follow the development of chess knowledge and skill as each generation adds its quota to our understanding of the depths of opening and midgame strategy.

A double error of the advocates of change resides in this. They completely misinterpret the mind of the average chess enthusiast. They feel that he, like themselves, is attracted by something novel—a new thrill, the delight of a child with a new toy. Whereas in fact the lover of chess has come to the game as a refuge from all the new fads, the changing fashions, the vapid frivolities of a careless world. He does not play chess because it is the smart thing to do, or because the moneyed people are doing it, or because it's all the rage, or the very latest thing. Or even because he expects to get a new thrill, or to grasp all its beauties and pleasures in an instant. He wishes a game that has withstood the test of time, and, with much effort and cooperation on his own part, in due time he looks forward to enjoying some of the delights a real art offers to the artist.

Strangest of all is the triumphant shout of those who—lacking all historical or other understanding of chess—proclaim the miracle of their discovery. The silly innovation with which they would ruin a noble game, strikes them as a grand invention. They patent it, copyright it: spend money on it—believe they will grow rich on royalties—when in fact, it is nothing—nothing at all.

Now let us appraise the present status of chess. We have with us players who have forsaken all else—family, friends, profession—and who after 30 years are still well below the master class.

Of the openings our own Napier wrote: "It is remarkable how much hot water a master can wade into in the first ten moves, after a half century of opening exploration."

And in the complex midgame the best experts flounder about helplessly. Once the thread of the game has passed from our hands, we see nothing—or nearly—or less than nothing at this stage. Here our blindfold performers and our simultaneous experts become afflicted with time trouble, and overlook what is startlingly clear after it is pointed out. . . .

As for the endgame—far from being a mere matter of mathematics, we have only scratched the surface of possible maneuvers at this point. How welcome are adjournments and how great the task of analyzing the average ending! Under a time limit—at all stages—we merely play by intuition, and how much we missed is later revealed by analysis.

Let us learn to play chess first: thereafter we can consider a new game.

Chess Review, 1937.

CHESS: TO BE OR NOT TO BE

By B. H. Wood

Writing in a more dispassionate frame of mind about proposed variants of chess, Wood manages to impart a good deal of most interesting information.

The struggle between tradition and innovation is as incessant in chess as elsewhere. Following the boxing maxim: "The bigger he is, the harder he falls," iconoclasts innumerable have delighted to assault chess, the game of all games sanctified by the centuries, and, by suggestions sometimes wild, sometimes quite scatterbrained, but very seldom of any use, attempted to win a little fame in the history of its development.

The best ideas of the past have, of course, been absorbed. A couple of friends of mine recently gave a genuine trial to the chess of centuries ago, moving pawns one square only, restricting the queen's move likewise to one square only in any direction, etc. They found it intolerably slow. To *some* iconoclasts of the past, we owe much today.

Of recent suggestions, Capablanca's received far the most publicity: that the board be increased by two squares all round; *i.e.,* from 64 squares to 100; and that two new pieces be introduced on each side. His ostensible motive was that "the game had become too easy." His defeat by Alekhine shook the supporters of his "New Chess" profoundly.

F. V. Morley, in his book, *My One Contribution to Chess,* proposed extending by sixteen squares—eight each side—the part of the board empty at the start of the game. On this idea as a pendant, he dangled some of the most inconsequentially delightful drivel I have read for some time.

One strong offshoot of chess, the four-handed game, has never progressed in favor much since its introduction about 1850, but never showed the least inclination to die out. Four sets of chessmen, colored respectively black, white, yellow, and red, become involved in a wild *mêlée* on an enlarged board. The four contestants, partnering in pairs as at whist or bridge, sit round like generals attempting to control the course of a campaign with troops somewhat unamenable to discipline. I have only once played four-handed chess; as we started about 1 A.M. and ended about 5 A.M., and the occasion was a farewell party to me in the Faroe Islands, the wildness of the *mêlée* may perhaps be exaggerated in my recollection.

As soon as sea warfare came to our general attention, somebody hit on the idea of "mining" certain squares of the board beforehand, unbeknown to your opponent. When he plays a piece on to one of these squares, you say "bang!" and remove it. As a refinement of tension, you may let one of his pawns visit—and survive its visit to—that square, thus deluding him into thinking it is safe. Then, when his queen goes there—"Bang!" To his protests, you complacently reply that the pawn was of too shallow draft to set off the mine, or it was a wooden vessel and the mine was a magnetic one.

King Abdullah of Jordan is said to have invented an atomic bomb piece which in given circumstances can destroy the whole opposing army at a go. While I salute him for his topicality, I cannot but deplore —especially from a son of the patient East—this sullying of chess with a sudden death as bad as a double bezique.

Some leading London players are experimenting, in their more *fin de demi-siècle* mood, with a distortion of chess which can call for deep cogitation and produce excellent games. White makes one move, Black answers by making two, then White makes three, and so on. Check may be given only on the last move of such a series. After a few turns, a player's composite move may consist of a pawn's starting on its initial square and wending its way through to queen and the new queen's wiping off several enemy pieces before the quota of moves is exhausted. The most extraordinary thing about this game, to my mind, apart from the excellent contests it can provide, is that even masters, tackling the problem quite seriously, have not been able to make up their minds whether it is an advantage to have the first move or not.

Illustrated London News, 1951.

THE STALEMATE FALLACY
By T. H. Tylor

When Tylor wrote his attack on the stalemate rule, he released about his unhappy head a swarm of peevish maledictions which are still buzzing. One incensed critic went so far as to call him a naughty boy— surely a quaint epithet as applied to an Oxford don! Despite all the hullaballoo, I doubt that the last has been heard of Tylor's suggestion.

In civilization as in nature, destruction and progress walk hand in hand, hence the epoch of war has always been that of evolution. This is equally true of the arts and sciences. The suspension of many normal activities and vested interests makes this time singularly appropriate for a critical inquiry into the present stage of evolution attained by the royal game of chess.

The most general criticism is that the high standard of play is tending to an increasing number of drawn games. This has gone far to lessen interest in draughts, and, in chess, after the Great War, many suggestions were made by Capablanca, Alekhine, and others aimed at a reduction of draws by increasing complexity and like means. These suggestions involved an almost complete revision of the game and received little support. It is proposed here to examine the thesis that stalemate is without historical foundation and irrational, and primarily responsible for a vast percentage of draws, and hence should be abolished.

From a perusal of Murray's immortal work on the history of chess, it appears that no rule has received so varied a treatment. The chess codes of Japan, the Mongols, and Hindus declare stalemate illegal. The old Indian rule was that stalemate was a win to the side suffering therefrom. This rule, characterized as illogical by Murray, is attributed to an attempt to reconcile the finite bounds of the chessboard with the limitless possibilities of real war. It had much vogue in Asia and was introduced into this country about the year 1600 by merchants, impressed with the great playing strength of Russian opponents they encountered at the big continental fairs. It is even recorded that adjourned positions were entrusted to a notary public for certification, to be continued at the next fair. This version of the rule is mentioned in A. Saul's *Famous Game of Chesse-play,* published in London in 1614, and justified on the ground (considered puerile by Murray) that the player who has staled his opponent "hath disturbed the course of the game, which can only end with the grand checkmate."

The rule that stalemate is a draw was introduced here from the Franco-Italian school by Sarratt in 1808 and generally adopted by the leading clubs under his influence in 1820. The older French rule was that the king was imprisoned but on his release all the pieces resumed their activity, rather as in four-handed chess.

Coupled with the fact that both Chinese and Moslem chess treat stalemate as a win for the player inflicting it, it is submitted that this brief historical sketch shows the rule to have no solid historical foundation.

In logic, it is even more wanting. Once the principle of alternative moves be established, no ground exists for the insistence that I must not only show that I capture your king whatever move you make, but that he was also in check or *en prise* when it was your turn to move. In effect, I am compelled to move twice consecutively. If this terminology is not acceptable and it be argued that it is illegal for you to move into check, the answer is that if I have reduced you to legal immobility, that should suffice as in draughts. The derivation of "checkmate" supports this. "Check" is from the Persian *Shah,* a monarch, and "mate" from the Persian *mât* meaning "at a loss," "helpless," or "defeated"— from *mandan,* "to remain." I have found no argument, other than those described as illogical or puerile above, in support of the present rule beyond a certain naive humor which it reflects.

A comparison of its practical advantages and disadvantages likewise demands its abolition. In not more than a dozen famous instances, it has involved sparkling combinations in important games. It is the theme of innumerable artificial endings, but this field of art would be far more enhanced by the extreme nicety of wins were it abolished. In the vast majority of cases, it merely operates to increase the margin of superiority necessary to enable the better player to consummate the win in the finite limits of a game. Glaring instances are provided by king and two knights versus king; king, bishop, and wrong-colored rook pawn versus king; and innumerable piece, mixed, and pawn endings which have to be abandoned because nothing more than a stalemate is possible. To all this must be added the countless games in which chances of bringing about a superiority sufficient to enforce stalemate have to be deliberately rejected in the hope that more inferior play by one's opponent may occur in time for a win to be realized under the present rule. The naked fact emerges that the present rule has little to commend it, whereas its indirect effect is to necessitate a far higher degree of inequality between the contestants than expediency demands, at a grave sacrifice of logic; and that, with the examples of Chinese and Moslem chess as historical precedents, the rule should be changed.

It is further submitted that the present rule would never have received the countenance it has but for the widespread adoption of the Moslem rule that to bare your opponent's king of all defense was a win without proceeding further. Both stalemate and bare king were wins in Aragon. It is the absence of either that leads to so many draws here.

In conclusion it is submitted that this proposed change would cause a minimum disturbance in chess theory and practice except in the end-game, in which keener powers of perception and greater precision in calculation would be required, with a beneficial enrichment as the inevitable result.

British Chess Magazine, 1940.

THIS MADE CHESS HISTORY

By Kenneth Harkness and Jack Straley Battell

The Chess Review *series on von Kempelen's famous Automaton Chess-player is to my way of thinking the finest piece of historical chess writing extant. The articles are a masterly combination of careful research and exceptionally clear exposition. As originally published in* Chess

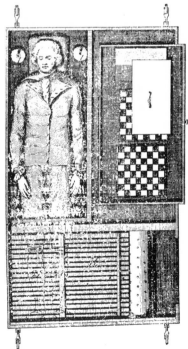

The Automaton Chessplayer
(*see 15, page 306*).

The Automaton Chess-player (see 16, page 306).

Review, *this fascinating series ran to nine articles, of which the first three, posing and solving the problem of the Automaton, are reprinted here. The authors claim, by the way, that "for the first time in history, a complete, accurate, illustrated explanation is given here of the secret workings of the Automaton Chessplayer."*

1. THE AUTOMATON CHESSPLAYER'S DEBUT

There was a buzz of conversation among the courtiers and honored guests at the Royal Palace in Vienna. What was the strange new device the Baron von Kempelen was going to display? Was it true that he had promised the Empress Maria Theresa to build a machine that would astonish everyone by its power?

Apparently it was to be a scientific exhibition of some kind, judging by the large number of scholars and scientists in attendance. It was said that the Empress had commanded the presence of these intellectuals because von Kempelen had promised to show something they would be unable to explain. Of course, everyone knew that this was probably an exaggeration. After all, this was the year 1770. What was there left for science to discover? What new power could baffle the intellects of these advanced thinkers?

An announcement silenced the conversation in the court: Baron Wolfgang von Kempelen, Aulic Counselor on Mechanics to the Royal Chamber, celebrated for his mechanical genius and many notable inventions, would now exhibit, for the first time in history, his amazing new Automaton Chessplayer!

The nobles and guests exchanged derisive glances and whispered to each other. A machine that played chess? A machine that could think? Apparently the good Baron was about to perpetrate a hoax.

As the audience watched with amused interest, the Baron's new invention was wheeled into the room by an attendant. The spectators saw a life-size figure seated behind a chest about four feet long, two feet wide, and three feet high, mounted on castors. A chessboard was screwed to the top surface of the cabinet. The mustachioed "Turk" was

dressed in Oriental costume and wore a turban on his head. The left
hand held a long Turkish pipe.

Polite applause greeted the appearance of this impressive-looking
machine. At least this exhibition promised to be amusing. And who
could tell? The Baron was a serious fellow, a famous inventor. Was it
possible that he had really devised a machine that could calculate? But
no, that was absurd.

Baron von Kempelen was given a more enthusiastic round of applause as he stepped forward to explain his invention.

It gave him great pleasure, the Hungarian declared, to be able to
fulfill a promise he had made to Her Majesty about six months before,
during an exhibition of magnetic experiments at the Royal Court. At
that time he had promised the Empress to build a machine that would
have a much more surprising effect than any of the magnetic games
displayed by M. Pelletier.

Now he had completed his machine, which they saw before them—
the Automaton Chessplayer. Entirely unaided by himself, the Automaton would not only play chess but would probably defeat any member of the audience who cared to test its powers. All he would do, the
inventor explained, was to wind up the clockwork of the machine from
time to time. The Automaton would do the rest.

And now, if someone would volunteer to come forward and play a
game of chess with the Automaton. . . .

But the audience was skeptical. They were in no mood to be hoaxed
by a so-called Automaton Chessplayer when it was quite obvious that
a small man or boy could easily be concealed in the cabinet or inside
the figure. Some of the spectators voiced aloud their skepticism, asked
if they were not to be permitted to look inside the machine.

Von Kempelen had been waiting for this. But of course they could
look inside. He had intended to show them the interior later—but if
they would rather see it now he would be glad to oblige.

Whereupon the exhibitor unlocked and opened the left door of the
cabinet, exposing to view a conglomeration of wheels, levers, cylinders,
and other pieces of clockwork. Then he started to unlock the remaining doors but suddenly straightened up and called to an attendant for

a lighted candle. He explained to the audience that there was a great deal of machinery in the cabinet and that a light was needed to demonstrate that there was no one hiding behind this machinery.

When the attendant returned with the lighted candle, von Kempelen went to the rear of the cabinet and opened a door directly behind the clockwork mechanism already exposed to the audience. Holding the candle so that the audience could see the light shining through the maze of machinery, von Kempelen demonstrated, to the satisfaction of all, that no human being was concealed in this small compartment.

Shutting the rear door, the inventor returned to the front and opened the long drawer at the bottom of the cabinet, showed that it contained only chessmen and other properties.

Then von Kempelen opened wide the two front doors of the larger right-hand compartment of the cabinet. *Now all three front doors were open and the drawer was fully exposed!*

In the large compartment, the audience could see wheels, spring barrels and a couple of horizontal quadrants. Resting on the floor of the compartment were an oblong casket, a cushion, and a lettered tablet.

A glance inside the large compartment showed that no person was concealed in it. However, to dispel any suspicion that the compartment had a false back, the inventor again went to the rear, opened a small door, held the lighted candle in the aperture. The spectators looked through and saw the light in the rear, just as they had looked through the small left-hand compartment.

Without closing anything, von Kempelen wheeled the Automaton around until the Turk's back was to the audience. Lifting the Oriental's robe, he exposed the structure of the figure, opened doors in the trunk and thigh. Now the audience could look inside the figure and see that it was full of wheels and levers, with no possible space in which to hide a person.

Still without closing anything, and with the Turk's draperies over his head, the Automaton was rolled around the room. The spectators were permitted to peer inside to their hearts' content!

One member of the audience, Karl Gottlieb von Windisch, declared later in a published letter that he had not been backward in his scrutiny of the interior. "I searched into its darkest corners," wrote Windisch, "but found no possibility of its concealing any object of even the size of my hat."

Another eyewitness, named Dutens, wrote: "It was suspected that a child was hidden in the machine. I examined with attention all parts of the table and figure and assured myself that this imputation did not have the least foundation."

The inspection over, the Automaton was wheeled into an enclosure behind a balustrade. Here von Kempelen removed the various properties from the drawer and cabinet, made some adjustments of the mechanism inside the figure, then closed all the doors, covered the Turk with his robe.

In further preparation for the exhibition, the inventor removed the pipe from the Turk's hand, placed the cushion under his elbow, set up the red and white ivory chessmen on the board. Then he took a large key from his pocket and "wound up" the machine—while the audience heard the familiar clicking sounds of a clockwork ratchet-wheel.

Finally, von Kempelen faced the assembly, holding aloft the oblong casket he had removed from the cabinet. This casket, he declared, held the secret of the Automaton's power. As the audience would see presently, the left arm of the Automaton would move chessmen from square to square. The *mechanical* power for this movement, he explained, was provided by a source of energy well-known to everyone. But the secret of the force which *controlled* the arm of the Automaton and caused it to place the chessmen on the proper squares was contained in this casket. He was sorry, but he was not at liberty at present to explain this power. He could not divulge the contents of the casket, nor permit anyone to look inside.

So saying, the Baron placed the casket gently on a little table near the Automaton. With remarkable skill and ingenuity, this mechanical genius and great showman had dispelled all suspicion that a human being was inside the Automaton. Instead, he had planted the idea in the minds of the witnesses that the machine was run by the clockwork mechanism they had seen with their own eyes.

Von Kempelen was ready for the next and most important test of his illusion.

History does not record the name of the first person to play the Automaton. Presumably the unknown hero who volunteered to test the powers of this strange machine was one of the scientific witnesses whose presence had been commanded by the Empress.

Standing in front of the Automaton, the nervous volunteer heard the whirring noise of machinery in motion, then saw the Turk's head move from side to side, as though scanning the board with his eyes. After a few moments of seeming meditation, the left arm raised slowly, hovered over a pawn, then grasped it firmly with the fingers and placed it two squares forward.

The entire audience looked at this astonishing spectacle in amazement. One old lady got up from her chair, crossing herself, and retired hurriedly to a curtained window recess. She would have nothing more to do with such black sorcery.

No doubt the Turk's opponent was also ready to flee from the balustraded enclosure. But after all, this wooden dummy had done nothing supernatural as yet. Summoning up his courage, he made his reply to the first move.

Again the whirring sound was heard, the Turk's arm rose, the second move was made. A legal chess move and—more important—a logical move.

The learned scientists in the audience moved to get a closer view of these uncanny proceedings. The others remained rooted to their chairs, half-amused, half-frightened.

Move by move, the weirdest game in the history of chess continued. There was no doubt about it. The Automaton was playing chess—strong, logical chess! With no visible aid from any person, this clockwork machine was performing the functions of a human mind. It was out-thinking its bewildered opponent.

It was obvious that there was no means of communication between von Kempelen and his machine. Except to wind up the Automaton, an operation which he performed every ten or twelve moves, the exhibitor remained at a distance, frequently turned his back to the Turk and conversed with spectators. At intervals he peered into the casket which was supposed to contain the secret of the Automaton's power, as though checking up to see that everything was in working order.

The Turk made all his moves with great dignity and composure. To warn the opponent that his queen was threatened, the Turk's head bowed twice. To announce check, he bowed three times. At one stage of the game, the flustered opponent made an illegal move. The Turk shook his head, replaced the offending piece, exacted a penalty by moving a piece of his own. (This special penalty was imposed for any infringement of the rules of chess.)

At the conclusion of the game (the result is not recorded but the Turk probably won), von Kempelen again opened the doors of the cabinet and uncovered the figure, thereby demonstrating that no one had climbed in after the first inspection.

Thus ended the debut of the astonishing Automaton Chessplayer. The credulous were willing to believe that von Kempelen had invented some new power which operated in an unknown manner through the mysterious casket. The scientists were completely baffled, could offer no explanation. The exhibition had been an unqualified success.

Von Kempelen had created one of the greatest illusions of all time. During the following *seventy years,* the fabulous Turk performed before thousands upon thousands of people in public exhibitions throughout Europe and the United States. As in the first exhibition, the audiences were permitted to inspect the interior before and after each showing. Yet in all that time, *no one fully discovered the secret of the Automaton by observation alone!*

2. The Secret of the Automaton

During its long life (1770-1854) von Kempelen's Automaton Chessplayer was exhibited before countless thousands of persons in Europe and America.

Many attempts were made to expose the illusion. Scores of books and articles were written on the subject, over a period of fifty years, but none of these solutions was entirely accurate. Most of them were sheer nonsense.

The more intelligent observers believed, correctly, that an operator was hidden in the cabinet. They went to great lengths to prove that a wooden figure could not possibly play chess without human aid. So much so, it is apparent that many credulous spectators believed that it was a miraculous clockwork machine endowed by its inventor with the ability to play chess.

However, it is one thing to declare that a person must be hidden in the cabinet, but quite another to explain how he was concealed from view during the inspection of the interior by the audience. Where was the operator when the drawer and doors of the cabinet were opened?

It must be remembered that most spectators were under the impression that they saw all of the cabinet's interior displayed at once. For instance, Karl G. von Windisch, eyewitness of the Automaton's debut, declared that "the entire Automaton is seen at the same time uncovered; the garments being also turned up and the drawer opened, as well as all the doors of the chest."

As chronicler George Walker expressed it, "thousands of individuals have seen its performance who would have had no scruples about taking their oaths that they had viewed the whole of the interior of the engine at once. In this respect, the ingenuity displayed by its original constructor is above praise. Man loves so to be duped!"

Most of the early pamphlets and articles made no serious attempt to explain the manner in which the player was hidden—or else they suggested absurd theories, inconsistent with the facts.

One of the most amusing was a 20-page pamphlet entitled *The Automaton Chessplayer, Exposed and Detected* by Philip Thicknesse, published in London, 1784. The author, according to George Walker, "appears to have been one of those true old English grumblers who find fault with everything and therefore are certain now and then to be in the right, *by chance.*"

Thicknesse believed that a child was hidden in the cabinet and his main cause for complaint was the high price of admission (five shillings) to see this piece of imposture. He commented shrewdly that the

Automaton was exhibited only one hour daily "because the invisible player could not bear a longer confinement; for if he could, it cannot be supposed that they would refuse to receive crowns for admittance from 12 o'clock to 4, instead of only from 1 to 2."

Thicknesse set forth his qualifications as an exposer of frauds in these words:

"Forty years since I found three hundred people assembled to see, at a shilling each, a coach go without horses.... The Duke of Athol, and many persons present, were angry with me for saying it was trod round by a man within the hinder wheel; but a small paper of snuff put into the wheel soon convinced all around that it could not only move, but sneeze too, like a Christian."

Fortunately, Mr. Thicknesse was not given the opportunity to prove that the chessplaying Turk could also sneeze like a Christian.

Another pamphleteer claimed that a dwarf, hidden under the Turk's drapery, thrust his legs into "two hollow cylinders" (nonexistent) in the small compartment of the box. After the exhibitor had demonstrated that this compartment was empty, the dwarf was supposed to have climbed inside.

But these and similar "exposures" had no effect on the popularity of the Automaton, being unaccompanied by any detailed proof. Much later, however, Robert Willis, of the University of Cambridge, was astute enough to analyze, by observation, the *positions* of the hidden operator during the inspection of the interior.

The article by Willis, with supporting diagrams, was first published in *The Edinburgh Philosophical Journal,* 1821. The Automaton was then 51 years old and had been on public exhibition for 38 years! By that time, the novelty had worn off and it was shortly after this (in 1825) that the Turk was brought to America, to take a new lease on life.

But Willis had discovered only part of the secret—and that imperfectly. His explanation of how the operator viewed the chessboard and moved the pieces was entirely wrong. Willis imagined that the concealed player saw the board by looking through the robe of the figure, so that his head was separated from the spectators by only a thin veil.

He also believed that the operator moved the pieces by inserting his arm inside the Turk's.

Although the theory offered was incorrect, it was accepted by many "authorities" as the correct explanation. For instance, Edgar Allen Poe, in his famous exposure of the Automaton in *The Southern Literary Messenger,* April 1836, advanced substantially the same theory as his own solution, after having seen the article by Willis.

Strange as it may seem, a true exposure of the most important part of the Automaton's mechanism was published in 1789, just a few years after the Turk began his public career! The explanation appeared in a book by Freiherr Joseph Friederich von Racknitz, entitled *Ueber den Schachspieler des Herrn von Kempelen und dessen Nachbildung. Leipzig und Dresden, 1789.*

The author built an Automaton of his own, patterned after the original Turk, to demonstrate that such a machine could be operated by a hidden player. The book describes and illustrates, with colored plates, this second Automaton.

Von Racknitz used exactly the same method as von Kempelen to acquaint the operator with the moves being made on the board above him. Both Automatons were equipped with mechanism to enable the operator to move the head, arm and fingers of the figure.

The similarity was so marked that some historians believe that a confederate must have revealed the secret to von Racknitz. However, we find this difficult to accept because it seems clear that the confederate would also have revealed how the player was hidden in the cabinet. Yet the Automaton built by von Racknitz was entirely different in this respect, and much less ingenious.

Von Racknitz concealed his player by making him lie full length behind the drawer. Only a boy or very short man (less than four feet tall) could have been hidden in this manner.

Nevertheless, the career of von Kempelen's Automaton would probably have been cut short and the cause of chess would have suffered if von Racknitz' explanation of the important controlling mechanism had been publicized. Fortunately, his book was either misunderstood or not believed!

In England and America, the critics interested in the subject were apparently unable to read German, the language in which the book was printed! So far as we know, it was never translated into English. However, this does not explain why the book had no effect on the popularity of the Automaton's exhibitions in Germany and other countries.

A possible explanation is that the subject was complex and could only be understood by a person who would take the trouble to study von Racknitz' description and diagrams in detail. That they were misunderstood is clear from Poe's references to the book.

Poe calls the author *Mr. Freyhere* and refers to the book by Freiherr (Baron) von Racknitz in these words:

"In 1789 a book was published at Dresden by M. I. F. Freyhere (*sic*) in which another endeavor was made to unravel the mystery. Mr. Freyhere's book was a pretty large one, and copiously illustrated by colored engravings. His supposition was that 'a well taught boy, very thin and tall of his age (sufficiently so that he could be concealed in a drawer almost immediately under the chessboard)' played the game of chess and effected all the evolutions of the Automaton. This idea, although even more silly than that of the Parisian author, met with a better reception and was in some measure believed to be the true solution of the wonder, until the inventor put an end to the discussion by suffering a close examination of the top of the box."

This is an absurd misinterpretation of von Racknitz' description and illustrations. Moreover, Poe makes no reference to the real subject-matter of the von Racknitz treatise—the method of communicating the moves and controlling the Turk's arm.

It is possible, of course, that Poe did not actually see the book. As so often happens, he may have been repeating the errors made by other writers, without giving credit to the intermediary source. If he had the book before him as he wrote, then he had the solution under his nose and could not understand it!

Whatever the reason may be, the von Racknitz book made no impression on the history of the Automaton. The later explanation by Willis was much easier to understand, even though incorrect. Hence, it was accepted by Poe and many others before him.

The illustrations in the von Racknitz book succeeded in achieving only one fantastic result. Being freely misinterpreted, they gave currency to the rumor that a legless man occupied the interior of the cabinet!

3. THE AUTOMATON'S SECRET REVEALED

The first authentic revelation of the Automaton's secret was published in the *Magazin Pittoresque* for 1834. A brief article in this French periodical described, in a general manner, how the player was hidden, explained how he was able to "see" the moves of the game and control the Automaton's arm. The material for this article was furnished by Mouret, the "Director" of the Automaton from about 1819 to 1824.

"This very skillful player," writes historian George Allen in *The Book of the First American Chess Congress*, "... sank into habits of intemperance and died in 1837. He was, therefore, in the lowest stage of his degradation when he betrayed the secret of his old employer." The old employer was Johann N. Maelzel (1772-1838), who exhibited the Automaton in Europe and America from 1805 to 1837.

In 1836, the magazine *Palamède* republished Mouret's disclosures, with some additional details, in an article by de Tournay. The *Palamède,* earliest chess magazine in history, was the highest possible authority in the chess world. Its publication of the de Tournay article gave the stamp of authenticity to the earlier revelations in the *Magazin Pittoresque.*

A third description of the Turk is given in *The Chess Monthly,* New York, for 1857. This magazine published an explanation of how the Automaton was operated, based on the testimony of Dr. John Kearsley Mitchell, co-owner of the Automaton in 1840.

Although his memory was faulty, Dr. Mitchell had first-hand knowledge of the Turk's anatomy, having examined it thoroughly and having operated the machine. He supplies many details of the construction which appear in no other records.

When he departs from facts personally known to him, Dr. Mitchell's account is erroneous in many respects. For instance, he was under the impression that the Automaton's structure had been changed, but this was not the case. He also gives a false description of the routine followed by exhibitors when exposing the interior of the cabinet. But these and other errors are unimportant, the true facts being obtainable elsewhere.

There are scores of books and articles on the Automaton, describing in full detail the outward appearance of the Turk, explaining how the exhibitions were conducted, offering various solutions. So far as we know, however, the disclosures by Mouret and the description by Dr. Mitchell are the only authentic revelations of the Automaton's secret.

Unfortunately, neither Mouret nor Dr. Mitchell supplied illustrations. In fact, no genuine illustrations of the construction of von Kempelen's machine have ever been published. The illustrations that have come down to us show only the outside of the machine, one with the doors open and the other with the doors closed. If mechanical drawings were made, they have not been preserved.

From the scanty records available, we have pieced together the following explanation of the Automaton's well-kept secret. This description is not entirely complete, for no record was made of important mechanical details. However, the facts are accurate and are sufficient to provide an understanding of the Turk's operation.

The Automaton was operated by a strong player hidden inside the cabinet. This much was taken for granted by many observers in the past. But how was the player hidden when the interior was exposed to view?

To enable us to answer this question we must first examine the interior of the cabinet, as illustrated in the accompanying sketches.*

As we have seen before, the cabinet was divided into two compart-

---

For a full appreciation of the Automaton's mechanism, the reader should study the illustrations between pp. 276 and 277 and note 17 on p. 306.—F. R.

ments by a partition. On the spectator's left was a small compartment, filled with machinery. On the right was a much larger compartment—about twice the size of the small one. Beneath both these compartments was a long drawer, extending the full width of the cabinet.

When the drawer was opened, the spectators could see that it was deep enough to go all the way to the back of the cabinet. Remember, the drawer was pulled out to its fullest extent. If the drawer had been only half the depth of the cabinet, the audience would have been suspicious. (Willis and others thought it was this type of drawer, but it is clear from corroborated accounts that the drawer *seemed* to be as deep as the cabinet when it was pulled out. This is confirmed by Dr. Mitchell.)

But the drawer was deceptive. It was a *telescopic* drawer. The sides were the same depth as the cabinet and went all the way to the rear, but the back of the drawer was on wheels and stopped half way when the drawer was pushed in. The back part of the drawer, with the exception of the sides, telescoped into the front part. When the drawer was pulled out, the movable back was caught by the sides and drawn forward.

This is our interpretation of the description given by Dr. Mitchell. The ingenious construction is not fully explained. However, the effect is clear. When pulled out, the drawer gave the appearance of being as deep as the cabinet. When closed, there was an unoccupied space *behind* the drawer. This space extended the full width of the cabinet (about 4 feet) and half the depth (slightly more than 12 inches).

On the floor of this trough behind the drawer was fixed an iron railroad, about 3 feet long. A low seat, with iron runners, was placed on the rails. The operator sat on this stool and was able to slide backwards and forwards on the greased runners. He occupied this seat throughout the entire exhibition.

The floor of the large compartment was also deceptive. As shown in sketch No. 1, the rear half of this floor was hinged in two places. When the operator slid forwards, flexing his knees, this section of the floor lifted up and formed a table in front of him. When he slid back, as in sketch 2, the hinged door dropped and covered his legs.

The partition dividing the cabinet into two compartments was another important part of the illusion. This partition appeared to be solid wood but was actually made in three pieces. The piece in front was solid, but in the rear the partition was composed of two hinged doors. Each door was half the thickness of the solid part of the partition. When the doors were in contact with each other (as in sketch No. 1, immediately behind the operator), they seemed to form part of the entire partition, the surfaces being smooth and uniform on both sides. But one door could be swung into the large compartment, the other into the small compartment.

The two doors of the partition are visible in sketch No. 2. One door faces the operator, closing off the large compartment. The other door has been swung into the small compartment and is at the operator's right. In this position, the door divides the small compartment into two sections. When the operator is sitting in the rear section, his head and trunk are hidden by the two doors.

To conceal the divisions in the floor and partition, and to cover up other secret parts of the machine, the floor, ceiling, sides, and back of the large compartment were all lined with dark cloth.

In the starting position of sketch No. 1, the operator had turned back some of the floor covering (not shown) to permit the hinged floor to rise.

With the constructional details known to us, we can appreciate how the illusion was created, how the operator was hidden while the interior of the cabinet was shown to the audience.

Let us go through the routine invariably followed by von Kempelen and his successors:

When the show began, the drawer and all the doors of the cabinet were closed and locked. *The operator was in the position of sketch No. 1.* His entire body was in the large compartment. Behind him, the two doors of the partition were in contact with each other, so that the whole partition seemed to be one solid piece of wood. (Of course, the audience could never see the top of this partition, but a bulge on either side might have been noticed.)

The exhibitor first opened the door of the left hand compartment and the audience could see the machinery. This "machinery" was actually made of thin brass and could be compressed into a very small space whenever the operator so desired. To the audience, however, it looked like the real thing.

Leaving the front door open, the exhibitor then went to the rear of the cabinet, raised the Turk's drapery, and opened a small door directly behind the exposed machinery. Holding a lighted candle at this door, he permitted the spectators to look through the machinery and satisfy themselves that no person was hidden in this small compartment. Which was true! The operator was in the other compartment.

The exhibitor then *closed the rear door* and allowed the Turk's draperies to fall over it. We can be sure that he closed this door quietly and unostentatiously. The success of the illusion depended upon the audience forgetting about this door. So far, it did not seem important to the spectators. They had been shown that the small compartment was "full of machinery."

As soon as the operator inside the cabinet heard the door being closed, he slid back, as quickly as possible, into the position of sketch No. 2. To do this, he turned his body and pulled towards him the first door of the partition. Then he pushed the second door away from him, compressiong part of the collapsible machinery in the small compartment. Sliding back into the rear of the small compartment, the floor of the large compartment dropped down and concealed his legs. Then he leaned forward and covered the floor with its cloth, smoothing it out carefully. Finally, he pulled the partition door towards him, thereby sealing off the large compartment. He had to perform all these operations quietly and quickly.

While the operator changed positions, the exhibitor returned to the front of the cabinet, opened the drawer and showed the contents to the audience. The act must have been timed carefully to prevent any appearance of delay on the part of the exhibitor and yet allow the operator sufficient time to change positions.

When the front doors of the large compartment were opened, *the operator was in the position of sketch No. 2.* The audience could look in the large compartment and see no trace of him. He was completely out of sight, his head and trunk being hidden in the rear of the small compartment, his legs under the floor of the large compartment.

The exhibitor then opened a small door in the rear of the large compartment and shone a light through it, to demonstrate that there was no false back. Then he lifted the Turk's robe over the figure's head, so that the draperies hung down and helped to cover the closed door at the back of the small compartment.

The Automaton was turned around, so that its back faced the audience and two doors in the figure were opened—one in the loins and a smaller one in the left thigh. Looking in, the audience could see more wheels and levers.

With all open doors swinging, the machine was turned back to its original position. Now the spectators were fully convinced that they were being shown the entire interior of the cabinet and figure—*and that they were seeing everything at the same time!* The three front doors, the drawer, the door in the back of the large compartment, and the two doors in the figure *were all open* and the spectators could peer inside. But the little door behind the small compartment was closed and hidden by the Turk's hanging draperies.

There was no danger of the spectators being able to discover the partitions hiding the operator in the small compartment. The front door was open, but only machinery could be seen. The entire compartment, including the partition door, was lined with dark cloth. The maze of fake machinery in front of the partition was an effective screen. If a skeptical member of the audience peered into the small compartment, his vision would not penetrate far enough to see the partition. It would seem to him that the compartment was full of machinery from front to back. This had already been suggested to his mind when the exhibitor illuminated this compartment by holding a candle at the rear door.

The illusion designed by von Kempelen was extremely clever—in timing and arrangement. The method of showing the interior completely bewildered the spectators. There seemed to be no possible crevice in which a man could be hidden. As von Windisch put it, there seemed to be "no possibility of its concealing any object of even the size of my hat."

After the inspection of the interior, the exhibitor prepared the Automaton for play. He removed various properties from the drawer and cabinet, closed all the doors, shut the drawer, covered the Turk with his robe.

From the drawer he had taken a set of red and white ivory chessmen. These he set up on the Turk's board, the white pieces on the Turk's side—for the Automaton always had the first move.

The pipe was removed from the Turk's hand and a cushion placed under his left elbow. Then the exhibitor "wound up" the machine.

The exhibitor's preparations took some time but seemed perfectly natural. It was during this time that the player inside the box was making his own preparations for playing the game. The first thing he did, as soon as the doors were closed, was to make room for himself. All the interior furnishings were movable. He swung the partitions and "machinery" against the outer doors and walls of the cabinet, making the inside one large compartment, with no subdivisions.

Then the operator removed the cloth lining from the floor, back and ceiling of the cabinet. In the back of the cabinet there was an opening and behind this opening was a compartment in the Turk's body (see sketch No. 4). A lamp or candle had been concealed in this compartment. The operator removed the light and placed it on the table in front of him. Originally part of the floor, the table became the operator's workbench. It was undoubtedly provided with the necessary catches to hold it rigid.

A peg-in chessboard, about 8 inches square, was attached to the table. There is good reason to believe that this board was permanently fixed in position. Poe refers to a "small protuberance about eight inches square" which he could see on the floor of the compartment when the inside of the cabinet was shown. At that time, it was covered with cloth. Poe thought it was the operator's seat!

Each square of the peg-in board was numbered and each square was provided with *two* holes. In one set of holes, the player inserted red and white chessmen, lining them up in the starting position of a chess game and with the white pieces on his own side of the board.

Finally, the player attached a lever to the lower end of an upright rod in the body of the Turk. The lever extended into the cabinet. At the end of the lever was a handle with a sharp point. The player was ready to begin the game.

The manner in which the game was conducted is the most interesting part of the Automaton's secret. The exact details of the mechanism are lacking, but the purpose and operation are clear.

It was necessary for the operator to know what moves were made on the board above him by the opponent. This was accomplished by the use of magnetism. The opponent's chessmen (the red pieces) were magnetized. Under each square of the Turk's chessboard hung an iron disk with a spring counterpoise. Inside the cabinet, each square was excavated to make the chessboard thin and allow the magnets to act upon the iron disks. When the magnetized chessmen were placed on top, the disks were attracted and swung up into the square excavations. Under vacant squares, or squares occupied by the Turk's men, the iron disks hung down in their normal positions.

Sketch No. 3 illustrates the principle employed to communicate the opponent's moves to the player in the cabinet. Here two of the magnetized chessmen are standing on squares. Underneath, the iron disks have been attracted upwards by the magnets. Under the vacant square, the iron disk hangs down in its normal position.

This sketch does not illustrate the *exact* method used by von Kempelen to suspend the iron disks under the squares. We have thought it better to illustrate a simplified version of the system because the available descriptions of von Kempelen's "little levers" are not clear.

For the sake of the record, we quote the following from Dr. Mitchell's account in *The Chess Monthly:*

"Under each (square) hung a little lever, well balanced, to which was attached a small disk of iron. These disks, when attracted by magnets placed on top of the box, swung up into the excavations and remained there quietly until liberated by the removal of the magnets, when they vibrated for some seconds like a well-hung bell.

"The means by which the disks of steel were balanced were curiously ingenious. A thin piece of copper wire, coiled into a flat spiral, served to counterpoise the disk. Any disturbance in the equilibrium of these little levers could then be instantly corrected by the concealed operator, who had merely to coil up or uncoil the wire, in order to effect the desired adjustment."

The writers of the articles published in the *Magazin Pittoresque* and the *Palamède* called these indicators *"les petites bascules en fer"* which can be translated as "little iron rockers."

The exact design of these little levers with their counterpoises is not known to us. A possible design could be worked out, but it might not correspond to the original. Hence the simplified version of sketch No. 3.

In any case, the purpose of the magnetic indicators is clear. The operator inside the box could look up at the chessboard over his head and "see" where the opponent's pieces were located. When the opponent made a move, one of the disks dropped down, showing that a piece had left this square. Then the disk under another square swung upwards, indicating the square to which the piece had been moved. The squares of the overhead chessboard were numbered from 1 to 64, corresponding exactly with the numbers on the peg-in board. Each time the opponent made a move, the operator duplicated it on his own board.

To make the Turk's moves on the board above him, the operator was provided with apparatus which controlled the arm and fingers of the Automaton. Of necessity, this was a highly complicated piece of mechanism. Von Kempelen solved all the difficult problems and made it possible for the hidden player without seeing the board, to move the Turk's pieces as he desired.

When the operator decided to make a move for the Turk, he first made the move on his peg-in board. Then he grasped a lever, as illustrated in sketch No. 4. The pointer of this lever was resting in a hole in the table, at the left side of the chessboard.

The operator raised the lever—and the Turk's arm rose from the cushion. Then he moved the lever sideways or in an angular direction until the pointer was over the desired square on his peg-in board—the square from which he had just moved a piece. As he moved the lever in this fashion, the Turk's arm made the same movements and the Turk's hand hovered over the corresponding square on the board above. Then the operator lowered the lever and pressed the point into a hole in the square. As he did so, the Turk's arm descended until the hand was just over the piece to be moved. The operator twisted the handle of the lever and the Turk's fingers grasped the piece.

To move the piece, the operator raised his lever, guided it to the second square, lowered the point of the lever into the peg-in board, untwisted the handle. Up above, the Turk's arm followed the same motions, carried the piece to the correct square, released it when the operator untwisted the lever's handle.

The move made, the operator guided the Turk's arm back to the cushion by moving the lever away from the peg-in board and inserting the point into the hole from which it started.

Readers with mechanical knowledge will realize that this apparatus was a form of *pantograph*. The Turk's arm followed all the movements of the lever below but magnified these movements. The fingers were controlled by springs, operated by cords attached to the pantograph lever. Each square of the peg-in board had two holes—one for a chess piece, the other for the pantograph pointer. Sketch No. 4 illustrates the general idea of the system.

The pantograph and the magnetic chessboard were the main features of the Automaton's mechanism. There were, however, some other embellishments:

The movements of the Turk's head were accomplished by a special lever. When the lever was turned from side to side, the Turk shook his head. When the lever was raised up and down, the Turk nodded.

The "whirring noise" heard by the audience when the Turk's arm was in motion was produced, of course, by the operator.

Ventilation for the player was provided by spaces between the overhanging cabinet top and the sides of the chest.

Thus explained, the Automaton's secret may "resemble a comedy," as de Tournay expressed it, but it was a brilliant comedy, a masterpiece of illusion which mystified the populace of Europe and America for nearly seventy years.

Chess Review, 1947.

THESE FUELISH THINGS
By Desperdan

Some time ago I wrote in Relax with Chess—*under the seductive title,* "8,372,849,743 x 6,247,623,822": *"When Professor Weiner of the Massachusetts Institute of Technology invented a calculating machine which requires only one ten-thousandth of a second for the most complicated computations, he was quoted as saying, 'I defy you to describe a capacity of the human brain which I cannot duplicate with electronic devices.'*

"Up to the time these lines were written, the Professor had apparently not yet perfected an electronic device capable of making such moves as Tartakover's 20th in the following game. The day may yet come, however, when we shall see such books as Robot's 1000 Best Games, *or when chess tournaments will have to be postponed because of a steel shortage."*

Professor Weiner should be interested in the work being done by Desperdan in this field.

This is the tale of A. J. Cain,
Who made a Chess Electric Brain,
And after long experiment,
Found to his great delight, it went.

Connected by a common plug
To two small holes above his lug,
And fed with a current from the main,
It made a champ of A. J. Cain,
A man whose play had been so poor,
He'd never won a game before.
Sometimes he ran it in reverse,

To see if it could make him worse;
But found it didn't—as you see,
One can't be worse than lower Z.
Aggrieved opponents would declare
This apparatus most unfair;
But A. J., beaming, would explain
It was the product of his brain;
And though they used their brains direct,
That didn't mean they could expect
That he, too, should so cerebrate:
Its use was quite legitimate.

So, though some said his methods stank,
He soon reached England's foremost rank,
And up to Blackpool made the trip,
To play there in the Championship.
He squared the chap who ran the joint
To plug him to a nearby point;
And one by one, the chess elite
He grimly battered to defeat
(Negotiating horrid jams
Against ingenious Abrahams).

At last, upon the final day,
Cain had the Champion to play.
Now each of them had scored a run
Of wins, and beaten everyone;
Which meant this last round must decide
Which finished first (unless they tied).
Cain and Brain had White; and soon,
Attacking hard, they called the tune:
With subtle and aggressive chess
They had the Champion in distress.

But suddenly there came a hitch:
For Cain ('twas his move) turned the switch,

But no electric impulse came
To show the next step in the game.
He said, perturbed: "Now, what the deuce—?"
The truth then dawned: They'd cut the juice!
For in his little plan to win—well,
He hadn't thought of Mr. Shinwell.

Cain tried anon (but tried in vain)
With GAS to work the Electric Brain;
But found it would not come to terms
With things like cubic feet and therms:
It ran only on volt and watt,
And watts were what he hadn't got.
He sought to have the game adjourned.
His application though was spurned.
Officials said: "This cannot be.
There is no reason we can see;
So back you go. Tick-tock! tick-tock!
The time is running on your clock."

His own unaided brain was quite
Inadequate to make a fight,
For he had never understood
The plans the Brain had proved so good.
Cain moved—so badly, t'other chap
Thought long, suspecting some deep trap;
But moved at last, with cheerful mind,
Singing: "Let joy be unconfined."
The game went on, the juice stayed off,
And lookers-on began to scoff:
"This game's the worst we've ever seen—
Can Cain move nothing but his queen?"
(Not without reason, for A. J.
Was playing in his Z class way.)

At last the power came on again:
Too late to save him, though; the Brain
Signaled: "I can't resuscitate
A game within two moves of mate!"

And so Great Britain's chance was gone
To be the first to gaze upon...
An all-Electric Champion.

But A. J. Cain is working now,
Beneath the flickering light of candles,
On a knotty problem: HOW
TO WORK THE BRAIN WITH HANDLES.

Chess, 1947.

BOOKS ABOUT CHESS
By B. H. Wood

A chessplayer without a chess library, his own or borrowed, is unthinkable. How to cope with a literature consisting of some 20,000 titles is a problem which has both its attractive and its exasperating facets.

More books have certainly been written about chess than about every other game put together. Caxton's *Game and Playe of the Chesse* (about 1475) was one of the first books ever printed in English, and the stream has been in flood ever since. It is an aspect of chess which the layman can find almost frightening.

About ten years ago, I started to build up a chess library for reference purposes. From the first I rejected more books than I chose; for instance, though chess problems fascinated me in my youth, and I composed several, I felt that I must draw the line somewhere: I possess a bare half-dozen books on Problem Chess or Fairy Chess at most. Then, the motive of my collection was utility; as chess has progressed steadily, decade by decade, the weaknesses in old methods and openings being revealed and new resources evolved, the countless chess books dated earlier than 1900 were rejected almost *en bloc,* though not always without a wistful backward glance.

An Oklahoma Professor of English [Dr. Kester Svendsen]* is busy collecting fiction in which chess has a place in the plot. Starting from *Through the Looking Glass,* the library list takes in some scores of detective novels and, wandering through the whole range of world literature, such classics as Shakespeare's *Tempest.* I left my Oklahoma friend alone in his task.

Another field which might interest a psychologist is the collection of books written by world-famous chessplayers on subjects outside chess, such as Philidor's works on music, Staunton's three-volume commentary on Shakespeare, or, in modern times, Gerald Abrahams' novels and political pamphlets on war guilt, etc. Sanity again decreed only one course—rejection.

Thus I set drastic limitations—yet within them my library has rapidly expanded to some 1600 volumes, and continues to grow by at least 150 more yearly.

On the French Defense alone, the opening 1 P-K4, P-K3, I can consult no fewer than five specialized works: by Mieses (Leipzig), Le Lionnais (Paris), Maroczy (Budapest), Czerniak (Buenos Aires) and Stalda (Milan), apart from detailed surveys in each of the 130-odd books on the chess openings as a whole, and more or less useful references in scores of general textbooks.

Every month, well over a hundred different chess magazines are issued in various parts of the world; eight in England, about as many in Germany, five in the U.S.A....one in New Zealand. Each goes into my library, bound, at the end of the year.

Of tournament books, I have some 400, though there are still many gaps to fill. These are books published after important tournaments, giving the scores of all the games played, usually with comments on the play and often with photographs of the contestants. Since the day hardly ever dawns when no such tournament is in progress somewhere,

---

* Dr. Svendsen's bibliography, comprising 553 items, was published in the *Southwestern Journal,* Volume 5, Number 4.—F. R.

there is a constant flow of new additions to this section. It is the one I find myself most often consulting; the games, averaging perhaps eighty per book, provide a bottomless reservoir of study of every type of stratagem in opening, middle game, or ending.

Illustrated London News, 1949.

Chess Celebrities

ROUSSEAU CONFESSES

I possessed an equally solid expedient in chess, to which I regularly devoted my afternoons at the Café Maugis, on the days when I did not go to the theatre. I there made the acquaintance of M. de Légal, M. Husson, Philidor, and all the great chessplayers of the day, without making any progress myself. However, I had no doubt that in the end I should become a better player than any of them; and this, in my opinion, was enough for my support. Whenever I became infatuated with any fresh folly, I always reasoned about it in the same manner. I said to myself, "Anyone who excels in something, is always sure of being sought after. Let me, therefore, excel in something, no matter what: I shall be sought after; opportunities will present themselves, and my own merits will do the rest." This childishness was not the sophism of my reason, but of my indolence. Frightened at the great and rapid efforts which would have been necessary to make me exert myself, I endeavored to flatter my idleness, and concealed its disgrace from myself by arguments worthy of it.

The Confessions.

CELEBRITIES AT THE CAFÉ DE LA RÉGENCE
By George Walker

During the period 1770-1800 the Café de la Régence was the Stork Club of the eighteenth century. Among the famous men to be seen there were Voltaire, Diderot, Rousseau, Robespierre, and Napoleon.

And the attraction that brought them and held them there was—of all things—chess! George Walker brings them all to life in this brilliant evocation of a bygone age.

Jean Jacques Rousseau was wont to play daily in the Régence, attired (poor creature!) in a fur cap and flowing Armenian robe; and we read in Grimm's *Letters* that the crowd at last so eagerly pressed around to get a peep at the author of *Émile* that it was feared the glass of the front would be driven in; the nuisance being only averted by a guard of the city police mounted at the spot matitudinally.

During the next generation, the café was for a time nearly deserted, in consequence of its having become a favored resort of Robespierre. The lair of the tiger is dangerous, even while he sleeps. Robespierre was passionately fond of chess; and once, it is reported, granted the life of a young French officer to a beautiful girl who came to the Régence attired in man's clothes to gain an opportunity of presenting her petition to the tyrant. She checkmated Robespierre, and then frankly revealed her sex and demanded the life of her lover. She left her chair with a written order for his immediate release, and a passport, by virtue of which the joyful pair passed the French frontier in safety.

What names, what reputations, are identified with chess! And can we blame the enthusiast who loves that which embodies so many historical groupings of the great, emblazoned panoramically upon the mind's perception? Why, as I sit this very evening in the old café, I can picture to myself the shades of the departed called from their rest, and joyfully once more doing battle in chess around me. I can fancy that grand pioneer of the French Revolution, the brilliant but infidel Voltaire, sparkling with fancy-flights and ready repartee; pouring forth exultingly the most exuberant conceits, and unbending, over the chessboard, that intellect at which kings and cloisters quailed and trembled. Voltaire's was the good old coffee-house day of life; when scented perukes, amber vinaigrettes, silver-hilted swords, and clouded canes made up part of the stock in trade of the professional and literary beaux. Voltaire played a match at chess with Frederick of Prussia, and calculated many of his moves in the room where I now ponder. Is that nothing? I can believe I hear the ringing of the courier's spurs as he receives his despatch, and mounts yonder at the door, to ride post to Berlin.

Voltaire was strong in chess, since we know a first-rate player could give him but the knight; while Rousseau was decidedly inferior in skill. Fancy the two playing together; the witty lord of Ferney confounding his brother sophist with the ingenuity of his "coups," and sending forth St. Preux sulky and checkmated, to write a fresh chapter on the persecutions of the strong. Around are Holbach, Diderot, Grimm, and d'Alembert, taking a rise out of the unsophisticated Swiss; while old Légal, Philidor's chessmaster, looks down upon the group with the supreme indifference of a mere one-idea'd, first-rate chess professor. What cares Légal for the Encyclopedists?—his soul is in the heaven of MATE, and all beside to him is vanity. "Philosophers as you are," mutters Légal, "I should like to play you all together—a crown the game."

And we are presented in a twinkling with a fresh group—the children of the first generation. Citizen Robespierre, in the powder and ruffles he so closely clung to, is playing chess with Fouché,* now poor, and of mean repute. Fouché was so wedded to chess that he is said to have bestowed a place in the customs upon Deschapelles in return for teaching and practice. In the tableau before us, Citizen Fouché is all smiles and compliments before the great dictator; while the sly, catlike eye of Robespierre sweeps at each glance both board and hall, to see if the latter hold any one of the denounced—any heads which are due to Madame la Republique—any job of work for neighbor Samson. "Friends depart"; while the lingerers around subdue their voices, and strain for a smile. Fouché himself shivers in his shoes, and his fingers shake as they move the pieces. One youth alone meets Robespierre's glance, and quails not. Napoleon, the young lieutenant, is there among the spectators, and like carvings of bronze are his impassive features. Bonaparte at one time played chess in the Régence daily; while waiting, like the sailor whistling for a wind, to get employment from the

---

* Joseph Fouché (1763-1820), later Napoleon's minister of police and head of his spy systems.—F. R.

Directory. The sun of Montebello was yet to rise. I can fairly see Napoleon before me now; here, seated at the adjoining table, calling, like a soldier of fortune, for his demi-tasse, but yet giving the order as one having authority, in a tone of voice like trumpets sounding.

Napoleon was a great advocate for chess, which he practiced constantly. He was even wont to say that he frequently struck out new features relative to a campaign, first suggested by the occurrence of certain positions of the pieces on the chessboard. He played chess all his life. In his youth, at college, in manhood, on shipboard, in camp, *en bivouac*. He solaced himself with chess in Egypt, in Russia, in Elba; and lastly, on that darksome rock which yet contains his bones. It was while captive in St. Helena that the magnificent chess equipage sent to Napoleon as a grateful offering for personal favors was refused free passage because the pieces bore the imperial arms of France. History blushes while she records the disgusting details of this jackass-kick at the dethroned lion. A chessboard on which Bonaparte constantly played at St. Helena is in possession of the officers of the 91st Regiment there in garrison.

As might be anticipated, Napoleon as a chessplayer was not really of great force. His soul demanded a larger field for the expression of its faculties. His chess was that of Marengo, of Austerlitz, of Jena. Upon our mosaic of 64 squares, I could have given him the rook; upon his own board he could afford the odds to Julius Caesar. Bonaparte had no time to make chess a study. He played the openings badly, and was impatient if his adversary dwelt too long upon his move. Every minute of the clock was life to a mind so energetic. In the middle stage of the game, when the skirmish was really complicated of aspect, Napoleon frequently struck out a brilliant *coup*. Under defeat at chess, the great soldier was sore and irritable; although it was presumed that those favorites with whom he played were doubtless far too courtly to carry victory unpleasantly far. Had the scene of battle been the humble, forgotten Régence, and the time twenty years back, the chief might have won fewer games than he did at the Tuileries.

In the thousand and one tomes of memoirs printed relative to the modern Charlemagne—Bourrienne, Marchand, and others have recorded several anecdotes connecting Napoleon with chess. I shall here introduce one, hitherto unedited, which comes to me direct from M. Labourdonnais; who received it, and other curious details upon the subject, verbally, from the Duc de Bassano, Count Merlin, and M. Amédée Jaubert. It is well known that in Egypt Bonaparte constantly played chess with M. Jaubert; his chief opponents, that way, during the Polish and Russian campaigns, as well as during the armistice of Vienna, previously, in 1809, having been Murat, Berthier, and the Duc de Bassano. It is a fact that the majority of Napoleon's marshals were chessplayers. Eugène de Beauharnais patronized the art; and Murat many times kept the Duc de Bassano planted at the chessboard the greater part of the night. But now for my Napoleon anecdote, in almost the very words of Labourdonnais.

While about to enter upon the famous Polish campaign, the emperor was one day playing chess in the Tuileries with Marshal Berthier, when the Persian ambassador was announced, as requesting an audience. The game was at an interesting crisis, and Napoleon would no more permit it to be suspended than would Charles of Sweden leave his chessboard when the Turks commenced battering down his house in Bender. Bonaparte ordered the ambassador to be shown in, and M. Jaubert was commanded to the presence as interpreter. The emperor continued his game with Berthier, overwhelming the astounded Persian with questions all the while in his usual rapid mode of asking to gain information. The Mussulman found it difficult to plant his replies suitably, the various topics being Turkey, Persia, Mohammed, and the Koran; Eastern harems, wives in sacks, the military discipline, and ten thousand other matters. The Persian, however, steered his way like the truly skilled diplomatist he really was. He exalted Persian institutions to the seventh heaven, or a little higher, and dwelt especially upon the horse soldiers of Ispahan as being the finest cavalry in the world. Napoleon good-humoredly disputed the assertion, and interrupted the son of Iran more than once; but the ambassador constantly returned with his pet cavalry to the charge, and getting warmer by degrees, pronounced his judgment with ever more and more decision. "There could be no doubt of it, the foot soldiers of Europe were excellent—but the Persian horse!"—Napoleon laughed outright as the interpreter rendered the sentences in French; and carelessly addressing Jaubert in reply, said, "Tell him that tomorrow we'll show him a little cavalry here." The Persian made his salaam and quitted the palace. The long-contested chess game was not even then finished. While pondering over the subsequent moves, the emperor found time to issue certain brief orders upon slips of paper, centralizing upon Paris the instant march of various bodies of horse soldiers from their cantonments in the vicinity. Like the knights on the chessboard, he had them all in his hand. The subject was not again alluded to; the game was played out; but the next morning saw forty thousand French cavalry defile before Napoleon and the Persian envoy, in all the glittering pomp of military decoration. Paris beheld that cavalry almost for the last time. Moscow awaited them.

Chess and Chessplayers.

SIR WALTER SCOTT ON CHESS
By H. R. H.

Scott made at least one sour remark about chess, but judging from his numerous allusions to the game, he must have been quite fond of it.

The frequent references to chess in the Waverly novels prove beyond doubt that the great novelist had more than a casual knowledge of the game. In the general preface to the Abbotsford Edition, the following passage occurs:

"I was plunged into the great ocean of reading without compass or pilot; and unless when someone had the charity to play at chess with me, I was allowed to do nothing, save read from morning to night."

In *The Antiquary,* a weak chessplayer is shadowed forth in the passage, "Francie was therefore foiled in his assaults upon the fidelity of the mendicant, and, like an indifferent chessplayer, became at every unsuccessful movement more liable to the counter checks of his opponents."

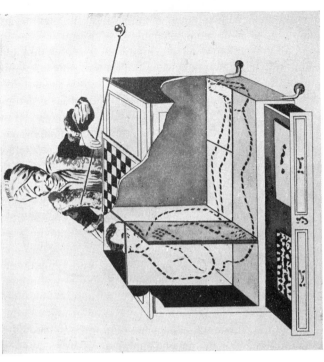

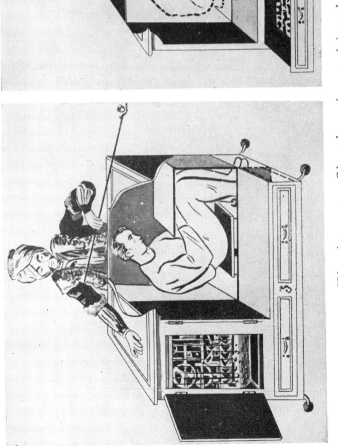

The Automaton Chessplayer (see 17 (1) and (2), page 306).

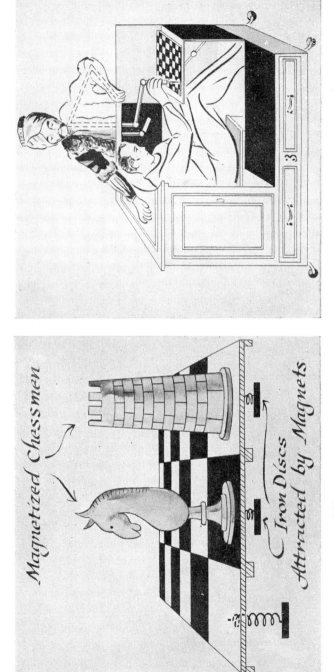

The Automaton Chessplayer (see 17 (3) and (4), page 306).

In *The Bride of Lammermoor,* in the following passage, Bucklaw addresses the Master of Ravenswood: "Oh, confusion to your state tricks! Your cold calculating maneuvers, which old gentlemen in wrought nightcaps and furred gowns execute like so many games at chess, and displace a treasurer or lord commissioner as they would take a rook or pawn."

A singular game of chess is described in *The Black Dwarf*—one which is not described in any work on chess to which I have had access:

"'I hope,' said Lucy, 'we have outlived the time of bloody feud, when a quarrel was carried down between two families from father to son, like a Spanish game at chess; and a murder or two committed in every generation, just to keep the matter from going to sleep.'" It might be thought that the tendency of the modern school rather leaned towards slow play, when opponents scarce dare venture on an attack, but patiently act on the defensive, in anxious expectation that the adversary may make a false move, and when time limits are so extended, that genius is borne down by painstaking analysis; but the Spanish game must have seemed tedious even to a modern player.

If we are to believe historians, Queen Elizabeth was a chessplayer, and we can imagine the imperious virgin paying scant courtesy to her bishops. In *Kenilworth,* Scott describes the Queen presenting Sir Walter Raleigh with a jewel of gold *in the form of a chessman;* we may imagine such a jewel being formed after the pattern of a knight, for in those days the Spanish form of a knight, a horse's head, was probably usual in England.

An expression occurs in *The Heart of Midlothian,* which forcibly recalls to mind the well-known ejaculation of Horwitz, "Brandy can't save it!" It is when the fussy amateur lawyer, Bartoline Saddletree, discussing the chances of poor Effie Deans escaping the hangman, asserts, "Brandy cannot save her."

There are many other references to chess in Scott's works: thus in *Guy Mannering,* Julia Mannering sets Hazlewood and Lucy Bertram down to a "pensive game of chess," and in the Abbotsford Edition there is an illustration drawn by Gilbert of the lovers apparently intent on mating each other. In *The Legend of Montrose,* the Highland gentlemen are described as amusing themselves with chess, backgammon, and other games. In *Woodstock,* the Cavalier, Roger Wildrake, devotes himself to Sir Henry Lee by playing chess with him in his old age.

Doubtless attentive readers of the works of the Wizard of the North will come across other references to chess and chessplayers. Whether Scott was a strong or a weak player, there can be but little doubt that he had an intelligent appreciation of the game.

British Chess Magazine, 1891.

POE'S FALLACY
By B. H. Wood

Several generations of chessplayers have been annoyed by Poe's flip dismissal of chess as inferior to checkers. The following well-reasoned discussion of Poe's superficial thesis suggests a plausible motivation for his viewpoint.

Edgar Allan Poe died a hundred years ago. How frequently it is said, "To have written such stuff, he must have had a diseased mind!" Granted that his tendency towards the macabre was so pronounced as to be almost monotonous, and sometimes even intruded so as to mar a picture good without it ... the very power and success of his writing speaks rather of a delicate, detached craftsmanship which intelligently utilized every literary device to bring about his effects.

In his *Murders in the Rue Morgue,* Poe made a few remarks about chess:

"To calculate is not to analyze. A chessplayer, for example, does the one, without effort at the other. It follows that the game of chess, in its effects upon mental character, is greatly misunderstood....

"The higher powers of the reflective intellect are more, and more usefully, tasked by the unostentatious game of draughts than by all the elaborate frivolity of chess. In the latter, where the pieces have different and bizarre actions, with various and variable values, what is only complex is mistaken (a not unnatural error) for what is profound.

"The attention is here called powerfully into play. If it flag for an instant, an oversight is committed, resulting in injury or defeat. The possible moves being not only manifold but involute, the changes of such oversights are multiplied; and in nine cases out of ten, it is the more concentrative rather than the more acute player who conquers."

Any keen chessplayer knows that these opinions just don't make sense—it is safe to say that they have puzzled more than rankled.

I must have read the words ten or twenty times before the truth came to me in a flash of insight—the sort that occurs rarely but when it does, fills you with a delicious certainty. Poe was a beginner at chess whose whole attention was engrossed in avoiding mistakes. He still had to concentrate on remembering the moves of the men.

Like a schoolgirl at the piano, anguishedly engaged in not playing the wrong note.

Or, to take a literary analogy, he was not even the youth who likes a penny dreadful but balks at Poe's own *Eulalie. He was still learning his letters,* laboriously telling an "a" from a "b," a "b" from a "c."

To appreciate this fully, please read the whole passage again carefully. Don't you agree?

We could only *prove* this by a process for which no layman could spare the time; by examining every biographical relic of Poe's life for mention of chess. I confidently predict that no evidence would be forthcoming that, when he penned these lines, he had played ten serious games of chess in his life.

Birmingham Post, 1949.

JOHN RUSKIN AND CHESS
By B. Goulding Brown

Ruskin was a man of volatile and passionate prejudices, and his views on chess were no exception. He was strictly a devotee of the bang-bang school, and even Morphy's games lacked liveliness to his way of thinking. At a time when Morphy was idolized, Ruskin dashed off marginal notes like: "Thoroughly dull till last move," "Entirely stupid from end to end," "A consummately stupid game," "The most tiresome game I ever saw."

...His whole life long Ruskin was a great lover of chess. At the age of twelve he writes his father of his Saturday night games of chess with his cousin, William Richardson, whom he calls "the best chessplayer I have ever known." As an undergraduate of eighteen he has chess parties. At 39 he is sending moral remarks on the game to the lady who was afterwards Mrs. Severn....

In 1874 he writes to C. E. Norton: "I shall play some games of chess with the automaton chessplayer. I get quite fond of him, and he gives me the most lovely lessons in chess. I say I shall play him some games, for I never keep him waiting for moves and he crushes me down steadily." In 1875-76 he and Severn are playing chess on a portable chessboard on their drive—which he found wearisome—over the Yorkshire moors. In 1878 his secretary, Lawrence Hilliard, beats him for the first time. In 1882 we hear of a chess tea party: "Mr. and Mrs. West at tea last night, quite delightful. Mr. West beat *me* at chess, and Artie beat Mrs. West, and I never saw four people together fonder of a game."

In 1885 it is correspondence chess. He writes to Kate Greenaway: "Resumed chess game by correspondence. Sent enemy a move. Don't think she's much chance left." (He seems to have spent half an hour over it, however.) Sending the Ruskin Prize to James Mortimer on July 11, 1885, he says: "I enjoy chess as I do drawing within my limits; and if, indeed, some time you condescended to beat me a game by correspondence, it would be a great delight."

His most frequent opponent by correspondence, when absence from Oxford interfered with their contest over the board, seems to have been Alexander MacDonald, drawing master under Ruskin as Slade Professor. I have read somewhere that when the games grew exciting Ruskin used to have recourse to the telegraph. Certainly he was an impatient player. "To keep a chessplayer waiting for a move," he wrote in 1880, "is like keeping St. Lawrence unturned." He was provoked by an opponent who moved slowly, as indeed was not unnatural on a board of red and green!

Apart from letters, Ruskin's formal works contain many references to chess. However, I must quote no more.... The upshot of it all is that Ruskin loved chess as a game and an art, but hated it as a science.

British Chess Magazine, 1923.

BUCKLE AS A CHESSPLAYER
By Charles Tomlinson

Chessplayers are astounded to learn of Buckle's eminence as a historian, and students of history are astounded to learn of Buckle's eminence as a chessplayer. R. N. Coles* has written interestingly about him:

"A new young player had recently begun to visit the Divan, and his play though logical was so full of imagination and his combinations so flawless that his table was invariably surrounded by spectators two and three deep. He was to be seen quietly smoking a cigar, and developing at times a nervous hiccup, which he endeavored to suppress by humming an air. This was Henry Thomas Buckle [1821-1862] who, in spite of missing almost all his normal schooling through ill health, had so mastered these early difficulties that at the age of thirty he spoke seven and read twelve languages. His life he devoted to history —the first part of his History of Civilization *appeared in 1857—and it was said of him that after Macaulay he possessed the most tenacious memory and amply-stored mind of any man. Chess he feared both because of the exhaustion a hard game induced in him and because of the fascination it exerted on him, yet he frequently missed an appointment through becoming engrossed in a game....He died in Damascus of typhoid fever, with the cry 'My book, my book! I shall never finish my book.'"*

We are not informed as to how or when Buckle learned chess. His proficiency in that difficult game, and indeed in all games requiring

---

* *British Chess Magazine, 1948.* Quoted in my *Treasury of British Chess Masterpieces* in connection with a beautiful win by Buckle against Kieseritzky.—F. R.

mental skill in contrast to physical exertion, was the result of that singular brain power which enabled him to master a difficult subject easily and pleasantly. He seems to have grasped the principle of the game much in the same way as it is said Deschapelles acquired draughts and chess; that is, by merely watching the players at the café. It does not appear that Buckle, any more than Deschapelles, Labourdonnais, Boncourt, McDonnell, and other great players, ever opened a book on chess, or even cared to record the games that they played. Hence we have but few published games of Philidor, or the early masters; and even in the best days of the Westminster Club, it was thought an innovation when Mr. Lewis published *Fifty Games* as specimens of modern play, but withholding the names of the players and adding no notes. So also in Mr. Cazenove's collection, published about the same time, the names of the players are not given. The same remark applies to the earlier collection by Greco. To have given the games would have been a breach of etiquette. The custom is even now partly followed when a professional player gives his own name, but not that of his amateur opponent, or gives only one or two letters of the name.

The publication of names, if not introduced was greatly promoted by Mr. George Walker, who was also the first to make chess books cheap. Buckle shared in the carelessness of the olden time. Many of his best games are lost, and the large number that are preserved fail, I think, for the most part, adequately to represent his skill. He seems to have known little or nothing of the book openings. He generally adopted the safe Giuoco Piano, and when second player he usually preferred an irregular defense....

Captain Kennedy thus refers to his play: "These contests of his at odds were always full of interest and entertainment to lookers-on in the Strand Divan, where it was his custom in the afternoon to recreate himself with his favorite game. I have occasionally heard roars of laughter elicited from the spectators by the crestfallen aspect of some poor discomfited rook player, who, with much care and solicitude, having obtained as he fondly believed, an impregnable position, had suddenly found his defenses scattered like chaff, and himself accommodated with a mate, after the sacrifice by his keen-witted opponent of two or three pieces in succession."

Buckle's strong play led him into some curious adventures on the Continent. For example at Dresden, after watching some chessplayers in a café, one of them challenged him. The German played carelessly at first, but soon acquiring a taste of Buckle's quality, bestowed more attention on his game. After receiving checkmate, he got up and made a profound bow, saying "Whoever you are, you should play only with the best players." Buckle did so, and soon got a reputation in the place, but one man spread a report that he had refused to play with so inferior a man as Buckle, whereupon Buckle posted up a large placard challenging the man to play a single game for five hundred dollars. It is scarcely necessary to add that the challenge was not accepted.

On another occasion, at Rome, while watching a game, he was invited to play for a scudo. Buckle assented. "Or perhaps a couple of scudi!" the man added. Buckle agreed. "Well, perhaps it would make a better game if we were to play for five scudi!" Buckle retorted, "I'll play you for a hundred scudi, if you like." But the man declined, probably suspecting that he had a strong player before him. When at Dublin, the owner of a bookseller's shop told him of the fame of the Dublin Chess Club, that their chessplayers were superior to the Saxons, and could easily beat Staunton, Buckle consented to visit the club in company with the bookseller, and it is needless to add that he beat their best players even, and then gave odds with a similar result.

British Chess Magazine, 1891.

MRS. CARLYLE PLAYS AT CHESS
By Jane Welsh Carlyle

...Our life is the most quiet and regular heart could desire—the drive, and the game at chess are the *excitements* of the day, the last indeed is becoming rather *too* exciting. It is long since I laid aside my chessplaying honors—and that anybody has been welcome to beat me. I was sure that I could never play well again because I had lost all interest in the game, and could not conceive myself recovering the interest—but one night soon after I came, Mr. Buller having beaten me with his usual facility, said in the most provokingly slighting tone: "I *do* wish you could improve a little!" And at this all my past triumphs stood up before me, and somehow I felt myself injured—he should see I was determined that I *could* play if I liked—and so I *beat* him the next game and the next—and he has had sore thrashing of his brains for any game he has won from me since. His astonishment is very amusing, but such laborious play is not a good preparation for sleep....

Chess, 1950.

DE MUSSET SEEKS CONSOLATION
AT THE CHESSBOARD
By Philibert Audebrand

J. H. Bennett, who translated and submitted this excerpt to Chess, *commented: "The de Musset here described is not the dandy of 1830, the 'spoiled darling' of French romanticism but the declining disappointed man of 20 years later, seeking in drink and chess some relief for his amorous disappointments."*

Musset has just arrived at the Café de la Régence—already somewhat tipsy. He waxes loquacious for a few minutes and then calls for board and men. They are brought and he and his opponent sit down. Musset says: "The English as you must know, old fellow, never begin a battle until the grog merchants have been ordered to refresh the troops. If you've no objections, we'll do the same. No need to have a British drink. I don't like gin or whiskey or the other rotgut concoctions they make in the British Isles. I've got my own habits though: I must have absinthe."

The absinthe is brought with iced water, and having satisfied himself Musset continues: "Now that the grog merchants have done their duty, let us fight and fight well."

... The astonishing thing was that this toper who only a moment ago had been pouring forth a never-ending stream of senseless chatter like some chaffinch, without being the least concerned about the meaning of his words, now stopped short and assumed the reflective, serious air of an army commander, keeping his mouth as tightly shut as any statue. You know what a game of chess is: a duel of strategy, an antagonism which must be practiced in icy composure, especially when the two adversaries are of equal strength. From time to time, every five minutes or so, de Musset would make a short pause to consult his glass; but apart from this one movement he was completely absorbed in the play, pushing king, rooks, and bishop like a consummate artist. But since I have never been able to understand the first thing about this Homeric game I speedily tired of such a monotonous sight and after nodding to the poet and making a gesture of farewell to his partner, I tiptoed out.

Petits Memoires du XIX Siecle.

CHARLES DICKENS AS A CHESSPLAYER

An interesting story of an old-time friend of Charles Dickens was published in the Baltimore *Sunday News* recently which mentioned the characteristics of the great novelist as a chessplayer. Miss Tregear, the lady mentioned, met Dickens when she was a child and later when she was about sixteen. The story goes on to say:

Miss Victoria Tregear often played whist there with Dickens. She also remembers a set of chessmen with which she frequently played chess with him. "She was very fond of chess, and had made a study of the gambits and variations. She was also fond of problems—'chestnuts,' as Dickens used to call them." She thinks that she and Dickens played a pretty even game. He was always annoyed when she beat him, and invariably wanted to play another game. Once, at midnight, a game between her and Dickens was drawn. "Well," he said, somewhat resignedly, "why not? Man and woman represent an equation after all. Discriminate as you will in favor of either, they are, when their mutual traits come to be considered, equals. Yes," he continued, "the woman who grows up with the idea that she is simply to be an amiable animal, to be caressed and coaxed, is invariably a bitterly disappointed woman. A game of chess will cure such a conceit forever. The woman that knows the most, thinks the most, feels the most, is the most. Intellectual affection is the only lasting love. Love that has a game of chess in it can checkmate any man and solve the problem of life."

Dickens moved very deliberately and only after careful thought. There was one peculiarity about him as a chessplayer. He always wanted Miss Tregear to play first. He followed all her play and accepted all her variations. "It was just so," she said, "in his novels. He lets a character lead, and then simply follows it, studies it, exhausts it. He never created a character."

Lasker's Chess Magazine, 1905.

LINCOLN FINDS THE RIGHT MOVE

By Walter Pulitzer

A really skillful devotee was Abraham Lincoln. Some years before he became President he used to play with Judge S. H. Treat, then Chief Justice of Illinois Supreme Court.

You may have heard how once the beloved "Tad" interfered in a game between these two important personages. Tad informed the great emancipator that ma wanted him, and was met with the abstracted reply, "I'll be there in a minute." The boy withdrew, but doubtless knowing what a chess minute meant, he returned presently and renewed the charge—"I say, ma wants you," he cried impatiently, but still the father sat motionless. Suddenly, without another word, Tad lifted his foot and kicked the board and chessmen over, which made Treat simply furious with rage—but produced no other effect upon the serene statesman than to make him remark calmly, "Well, Judge, I guess that's Tad's game."

American Chess Magazine, 1898.

SANTAYANA LOOKS AT CHESS
By George Santayana

...I am tempted to put a question that touches what I call the Realm of Essence, and the appeal it can make to the mind. Chess is a contest: but suppose we remove the motive of vanity or love of winning; you might satisfy that by seeing who can drink the other man under the table, rather than who can checkmate him upon it. And suppose we eliminate also any gambling or partisan interest in having one side win rather than the other, even if you are a mere onlooker.

Now my question is this: How much of the fascination of chess comes from the excitement of carrying out a purpose under opposition; a suggestion or after-image of difficulties *in living?* And how much comes from the interest in *formal relations,* as in mathematics or stained glass or arabesques? This latter interest is what I call interest in essences; of course, the interest itself, which we may feel, will be a form of life in us; but the *object* in which we are interested need not be living; and the point that touches my philosophy is whether the living interest in nonliving things is normal in man, or is a mere eccentricity or illusion, in that nothing can really concern us except our own life.

If this is unintelligible, don't bother about it; or submit it to some other chessplayer, who likes speculation.

Chess Review, 1937.

SINCLAIR LEWIS TRIES TO BEAT
A CHESSPLAYING CRONY
By I. A. Horowitz

"My name is Sinclair Lewis and I would like to take some chess lessons," he said, quickly coming to the point of his visit.

I must confess I was momentarily flabbergasted and I spoke

brusquely. "I'm sorry, I'm too busy." With rapid-transit reflection, however, I changed my mind. After all, he was Sinclair Lewis and deference was his due. "I'll teach you chess," I amended, "but my fee is steep—twenty-five dollars a lesson."

"And what is a lesson?" was his canny retort.

I explained that I would see him on a Saturday evening and discuss chess, until one of us got bored. The terms were suitable and the negotiations concluded. This was my introduction to the great Sinclair Lewis.

I am an old hand at teaching chess and, if I must say so myself, a good one. I know the various approaches—the scientific and the psychological—and I can teach a kid of six or sixty. I know when someone wants to learn and when someone thinks he wants to learn. What was the angle here? Lewis at sixty certainly had no aspirations of becoming a chessmaster.

Our first meeting cleared up everything. Lewis was more or less of a dilettante at the royal game. He had a smattering of all phases of chess, but he lacked the connoisseur's grasp of the fine points. In short, he was a woodshifter. Why should he try to become adept at his age? A few leading questions elicited the information that his chessboard crony, Ridder, had been administering some sound drubbings to him. And he wished to remedy this situation.

No formula can substitute for talent or time. It was almost too late to add some wrinkle to Lewis' game. So I came up with my pet version of the Giuoco Piano, which I sometimes refer to as the Giuoco Pianola —the game that plays itself.

Upon hearing "Giuoco Piano," Lewis immediately consulted an English-Italian dictionary for meaning and proper pronunciation. This episode was typical of Lewis throughout our meetings. It was not until he was satisfied on any such point that we could get down to the business at hand. In all, I had about half a dozen meetings with the famous writer. If I am not mistaken, he was at work on *Cass Timberlane* at the time, and some of his newly acquired chess lore went into that book. And doubtless for the same reason he paid occasional visits to the Manhattan Chess Club during this period.

In Caissa's Valhalla, where Morphy and Steinitz and Pillsbury and Lasker and Capablanca and Marshall are having their *parties,* accompanied by the banter peculiar to chess, I can picture Sinclair Lewis adding to his vocabulary and wondering why he had never come across such babble on land or sea.

Of Chess and Chessplayers

One of Blackburne's opponents in a simultaneous display ordered himself a pick-me-up. The next time Blackburne arrived at that board, he drained the glass at a draught, made his move and passed on. Asked afterwards how he had managed to beat that man so quickly, he explained: "My opponent left a glass of whiskey *en prise* and I took it *en passant*. That little mistake wrecked his game."

B. H. WOOD, *Illustrated London News*, 1950.

At an auction of Lord Cunliffe's library of 500 books, all printed before 1640, *The Game and Playe of the Chesse,* printed by William Caxton in 1474, one of the earliest books to be printed in the English language, was sold at a high price; the bidding reached the sum of £1900. In 1813 the book was sold for £54 12s. The only other copy sold this century fetched £1800 in 1914.

British Chess Magazine, 1946.

I got in a position where only a desperate maneuver could save me. Tarrasch had outplayed me in the opening, but he lacked the passion that whips the blood when great stakes can be gained by resolute and self-confident daring. [From a newspaper interview after the second game of the 1908 World Championship Match.]

EMANUEL LASKER, *American Chess Bulletin*, 1908.

The people under the great Mogul's Government delight much in chess, as do likewise the Persians. In the houses at Ispahan, where the people meet to drink tea, they commonly play at chess, at which they are excellent, and go beyond the Muscovites, who are the best gamesters at chess of any in Europe. The Persians call this game "Sedrants," that is "hundred-cares," because those who play at it are to apply all their thoughts thereto.

Travels Into Persia (1634).

An amusing match between the bald-headed and full-haired members has taken place at the Manhattan Club, New York. There were 26 participants, and with the score at 12 all, Mr. Lipschütz * (full-haired) had yet to finish his game with a venerable antagonist, who had gaily promised the club a basket of champagne if he succeeded in beating his renowned opponent. Mr. Lipschütz had swept off nearly all the bald man's pieces, and the latter had offered to resign. Mr. L., however, did not accept this, but with a view to a further exhibition of his own skill, continued the game till he forced the ancient one to mate him with his last pawn. The baldheads immediately set up a claim to the victory, which had to be allowed. It is not stated whether the champagne was opened, but in the next match Mr. Lipschütz is condemned to be shaved, and made to play on the other side.

British Chess Magazine, 1891.

Scandal has already smeared baseball, football, and basketball. The only sports we can still trust are chess contests and marble tournaments.

New York *Daily News*, 1951.

Here are some of the questions and answers to an examination paper in chess that was given some time ago by Dr. Tarrasch. Some of the answers to the questions, though flippant, contain a grain of truth and are, besides, interesting.

Q. What is the object of playing a gambit opening?

* Then one of America's best players.—F. R.

A. To acquire a reputation of being a dashing player at the cost of losing a game.

Q. Account briefly for the popularity of the Queen Pawn Opening in matches of a serious nature.

A. Laziness.

Q. What is the duty of an umpire where a player wilfully upsets the board?

A. Remove the bottle.

Q. What exceptional circumstances will justify the stopping of clocks during a tournament game?

A. Strangling a photographer.

Chess Review, 1935.

The passed pawn is a criminal, who should be kept under lock and key. Mild measures, such as police surveillance, are not sufficient.

ARON NIMZOVICH, *My System.*

...A memory of Hastings twenty years ago. Rubinstein is due to play G. M. Norman, but half an hour after the time of commencement, no sign of him. Another half hour passes with his clock ticking merrily against him, when one of the officials looks in at Rubinstein's nearby hotel. The grandmaster is found peacefully asleep, having forgotten all about his game. Unceremoniously awakened, Rubinstein finds he has only 30 minutes in which to make 40 moves. Result: his *opponent* overstepped the time limit!

M. E. GOLDSTEIN, *Chess World,* 1946.

It strikes one as remarkable that Lasker, the onetime world chess champion, had no disciples. Steinitz had founded a school. Nearly all modern masters have learned from Tarrasch. One perceives quite clearly the mind of young Rubinstein in the chess praxis of later years. Only Lasker is inimitable. Why is it? We ask: Can he be said to have given us nothing lasting towards the progress of our game?

RICHARD RETI, *Modern Ideas in Chess.*

The pin is mightier than the sword.

FRED REINFELD.

Of my fifty-seven years I have applied at least thirty to forgetting most of what I had learned or read, and since I succeeded in this I have acquired a certain ease and cheer which I should never again like to be without. If need be, I can increase my skill in chess, if need be I can do that of which I have no idea at present. I have stored little in my memory, but I can apply that little, and it is of good use in many and varied emergencies. I keep it in order, but resist every attempt to increase its dead weight.

EMANUEL LASKER, *Manual of Chess.*

[*International Team Tournament, Warsaw, 1935*] One incident caused a lot of bother. Pleci of Argentina claims his game against Najdorf (Poland) on the time limit. He says that Najdorf's second hour petered out before he had made his 36th move. Najdorf retorts: "I made my move, just in the nick of time, but before I could press the button, Pleci picked up the clock and ran away with it!" The tournament director observes that Najdorf's 36th move has been made on the board. "I couldn't forcibly stop him making his move and writing down his score!" wails Pleci. The tournament director observes that the clock has passed the hour. "I couldn't force him to put the clock back on the table," cries Najdorf. All the judges are called up, two lawyers and two honest men, Alekhine, Oskam, Sir George Thomas, and Professor Vidmar, under the presidency of the tournament director, Przepiorka.

The rules of the F.I.D.E. state that the infringement of the time limit only counts *"tant qu'il est manifeste"*; and that accidents which have nothing to do with the game should not be allowed to count. Alekhine to Sir George: "How would a case like this be decided in England?" Sir George, coldly: "The question would not arise in England."

The silent witness, the clock, decided the issue, Poland receiving a nought. And now Najdorf became noble. "I should not have liked another verdict, playing, as we are, in Poland," he said.

GEORGE KOLTANOWSKI, *Chess*, 1935.

Did you think it fantastic to suggest that a chess machine might play in a tournament? It happened. In 1878, the entry of the automaton, "Mephisto," was accepted for the English Counties' Chess Association handicap, in which leading English players participated. The Rev. G. A. MacDonnell refused to play unless told the identity of the player in the machine. As this could not be revealed, MacDonnell withdrew. "Mephisto" won first prize. The player at that time was the master, Isidor Gunsberg. Don't confuse the Rev. G. A. with the great Alexander McDonnell [the opponent of Labourdonnais].

C. J. S. PURDY, *Chess World*, 1951.

Behind many games of chess lie things beyond the loser's philosophy, or even the critics'. Tarrasch, after losing two world championship matches to Lasker, filled books with proofs that he should have won. Bogolyubov against Alekhine was so nonplused at some of his own lapses that he could only hazard the theory that his great adversary must have been hypnotizing him. How often has a tournament winner been called lucky, because of his opponents' demonstrable oversights? You read of games which were "unworthy of the tournament in which they were played, both sides committing gross blunders." More discriminating investigation might reveal that the ultimate winner had managed at all costs and even some risks to force the game, into just the sort of position his opponent hated. To make him paint railway engines when he wanted to paint horses! Which is enough to spoil the most academical style.

B. H. WOOD, *Illustrated London News*, 1949.

In the course of a game at the Argentine Chess Club, Buenos Aires, a well-known player made a queen's move of decisive character. His opponent studied the position some little time, and then said: "That threatens mate."

"Yes, señor, in three moves."

"Then why did you not announce it?"

"Because I didn't see it!"

British Chess Magazine, 1920.

Habitués of the Old Crosby Hall at luncheon, or later of the Ship and Turtle, will not easily forget his happy smile as a particularly fine trap secured a win in an apparently lost situation. On one occasion, against a player very intent on his attack on one side of the board, he queened a pawn on the other, to lose it to a rook. A spectator silently handed it back to him under the table. The pawn was again queened, and yet a third time, the unsuspecting opponent blandly taking it off each time, far too intent on his attack to detect the deception, which caused much laughter among the onlookers.

British Chess Magazine, 1920.

A rival to young Capablanca has been found in Mr. T. Winter-Wood, who it is stated "is 86 years of age and has played chess for more than 80 years, and is still an extremely tough customer to deal with."

Lasker's Chess Magazine, 1905.

A combination composed of a sacrifice has a more immediate effect upon the person playing over the game in which it occurs than another combination, because the apparent senselessness of the sacrifice is a convincing proof of the design of the player offering it. Hence it comes that the risk of material, and the victory of the weaker material over the stronger material, gives the impression of a symbol of the mastery of mind over matter.

Now we see wherein lies the pleasure to be derived from a chess combination. It lies in the feeling that a human mind is behind the game dominating the inanimate pieces with which the game is carried on, and giving them the breath of life. We may regard it as an intellectual delight, equal to that afforded us by the knowledge that behind so many apparently disconnected and seemingly chance happenings in the physical world lies the one great ruling spirit—the law of Nature.

RICHARD RETI, *Modern Ideas in Chess.*

The most usual of all [combinative] motifs is the weakness of a piece of little or no mobility.... To name this motif, let us emphasize the two ideas underlying it: the idea of superior force at a given point, and that of immobility. What is immobile must suffer violence. The light-winged bird will easily escape the huge dragon, but the firmly rooted big tree must remain where it is and may have to give up its leaves, fruit, perhaps its life.

EMANUEL LASKER, *Manual of Chess.*

During a Paris tournament once, Baratz asked me if I would pose while he sculptured my head. Feeling greatly flattered, I consented. When I left, he promised to send the result on to Antwerp for me. Next year I met him and asked what had become of it. "Oh, I sold it to a friend of mine," he answered. "Oh, how nice," I replied, mollified at once; "who was it wanted a bust of me?" "They didn't want a bust of you," he replied, "they wanted one of Alekhine."

GEORGE KOLTANOWSKI, *Chess,* 1935.

When we play over Capablanca's games, we are irresistibly reminded of Morphy. Both had Spanish blood, both learned the moves at an early age, both were child prodigies, both journeyed from the New World to the Old in search of glory.

A first-rate Capablanca game gives us the feeling that chess is a very easy game indeed: his finest victories seem lucid, simple, inevitable. It is a delusion, but a delicious one. Champions, like other mortals, yearn for the secret of eternal youth; and before every champion there stands the specter of eventual decline and dethronement.

FRED REINFELD, *Relax With Chess.*

I remember what a young Dutch journalist told me: "We all love Señor Capablanca more than any other player in the world because there is no greater gentleman in chess. No one can lose as graciously as he does, or win in a more detached manner. How different with the other!"—and he named another great master.

OLGA CAPABLANCA, *Chess World,* 1945.

Chess is 99% tactics.

RICHARD TEICHMANN.

Dr. Tartakover tells the following amusing anecdote:

During the course of the London (1922) tournament, he and some of the other participants paid a visit to the London Zoo. They were particularly interested in the sea lions, who drowsed dreamily in the sun. Finally their keepers came to feed them and threw herrings into the cage. Despite their somnolence the animals jumped up with extraordinary agility and snapped up the herrings in mid-air. "You see," said Bogolyubov to Tartakover, "that is just the way *you* play chess. You maneuver and stall endlessly, until your opponent finally comes along with a herring (a mistake). Then you leap like lightning on your miserable victim and gobble him up."

FRED REINFELD AND IRVING CHERNEV, *Chess Strategy and Tactics.*

When Labourdonnais was requested by a French publisher to prepare an elementary work on chess, the author wrote with a shovel instead of a pen; that is, he carted into his book large extracts from Philidor and George Walker. Indeed, the book fell stillborn from the press. I cannot imagine Labourdonnais as a teacher. He was too fiery and impatient. His place was at the chessboard, playing games at various odds by the score, and marking the number by pegging the holes which he had ordered to be made in the frame of the board. After playing a match game from which McDonnell would retire exhausted, the more vigorous antagonist would sit up for hours, accomplishing the above feat, and drinking *bière à la portère.*

CHARLES TOMLINSON, *British Chess Magazine,* 1891.

When I first met Alekhine, at Pasadena in 1932, I began to understand the secret of his genius. He was showing a game with Euwe played at Berne a few months earlier, and his eyes and bearing had a strange intensity which I had never seen before. The man loved chess, it was the breath of life to him. At the bridge table he would suddenly start talking about an obscure variation in the Scotch; on the train to Mexico he assiduously devoted four hours a day to the analysis of new lines; any game, played by anybody anywhere, was good enough to sit him down and evolve new ideas for hours on end; on off days and periods he amused himself by playing rapid transit. He lived for chess, and chess alone.

REUBEN FINE, *The World's a Chessboard.*

At Baden-Baden [*1870*], beneath the castle on the hill, Paulsen was dissatisfied with his lodgings and made an excursion to find something better. He went up the hill and wandered about and at length found what he wanted. The next step was to find a porter to remove his belongings, and both were amazed to find that nothing more was required than to carry the boxes downstairs from one flat to another immediately below it!

FRED REINFELD AND IRVING CHERNEV, *Chess Strategy and Tactics.*

A particular point of attraction for Anderssen proved to be a certain cellar, situated in the heart of Berlin, and the particular magnet there. was the youthful and very pretty daughter of the keeper, whose duty it was to serve the sparkling draught to her father's guests. Annie, as was the name of the charming girl, was also a chessplayer, and not averse to having now and then a game with our professor. The latter was, of course, too chivalrous to win many games, and managed generally to let his lovely adversary get the better of him, although she was, of course, no match for him. But on one occasion she had the temerity to gain two games in succession, which feat elated her to such an extent that she ran excitedly around the room, telling everybody of her remarkable luck. This angered Anderssen. The lion within him had been roused. Annie was checkmated five times in rapid succession, which defeat made her so low-spirited that she sulkily retreated from our table, and for a long time after refused to show herself in the barroom.

ERNST FALKBEER, *Memoirs.*

International master Boris Kostich has a prodigious memory.

During his first visit to America, I played an exhibition game with him at the Manhattan Chess Club, then located at Carnegie Hall. Kostich erred in the middle game and a pawn sacrifice put him in *Zugzwang.* Shortly afterwards he resigned.

About eight years later, I had my ego considerably deflated. I had not seen Kostich in all this time and at our first meeting he inquired if I remembered the exhibition game. Immediately, he rattled off the game, move for move, and then asked me what I would have done if he had made another move. Then he proceeded to show an amazing wealth of intricate variations—all ending in his favor.

Unfortunately, he was correct. But, as over the-board play differs from analysis, I am still proud of my victory.

L. B. MEYER.

Reti studies mathematics although he is not a dry mathematician; represents Vienna without being Viennese; was born in old Hungary yet he does not know Hungarian; speaks uncommonly rapidly only in order to act all the more maturely and deliberately; and will yet become the best chessplayer without, however, becoming world champion.

SAVIELLY TARTAKOVER, *Die Hypermoderne Schachpartie.*

In Life we are all duffers.

EMANUEL LASKER, *Manual of Chess.*

Methodical thinking is of more use in chess than inspiration.

C. J. S. PURDY.

I can find no weak spot in Schlechter.

EMANUEL LASKER, *British Chess Magazine,* 1949.

Najdorf drew the number 13 in the table at the Bled tournament and was easily first there. He again drew this number at the opening ceremony at the Amsterdam tournament and again was first—and yet this is supposed to be an unlucky number.

H. GOLOMBEK, *British Chess Magazine,* 1951.

Donner is a new recruit to the race of giants among Dutch masters. Prins and Dr. Euwe are 6 ft. 4 and 6 ft. 3 respectively. Donner is even taller.

J. DU MONT, *Manchester Guardian,* 1951.

There lived a chess fiend in Thermopylae
Whose pride suffered many a topple; he
Seemed marked down by fate
To achieve a stalemate
Every time that he tried to mate properly.

Australasian Chess Review, 1936.

Another of my clients at Purssell's was a wealthy City merchant, Mr. Pizzi, an Italian by birth, but naturalized in England. His English was worse than mine, and when a third party interfered in his game, making remarks on a certain move, Mr. Pizzi would say, very indignantly: "Sir, you must not talk into the chess."

...I was not long at Simpson's, when one day Mason confided to me, in an undertone: "Steinitz has invented chess altogether, and Zukertort has invented 1 P-K4."

O. C. MULLER, *British Chess Magazine,* 1932.

Once upon a time, during one of the Hungarian championships, Balla was playing Breyer. Both players were hunched over the board. Suddenly Balla looked up excitedly: "Mate in two!" he crowed. The spectators all stared at Breyer. He looked rather bored, but otherwise showed no reaction. Astonished, Balla stared at the position again, and to his horror, he found that the mate in two didn't exist!

However, after further study, he found the solution. "Mate in three!" he shouted, more excited than ever. But Breyer still looked bored. Crestfallen, Balla turned back to the position, grew pale...there was no mate in three either!! What to do? He studied and studied and studied. Suddenly he came to a conclusion...the spectators hung on his words..."I resign," he whispered.

Rubber check-mate!

I. A. HOROWITZ, *Chess Review,* 1946.

I believe in Magic....There is Magic in the creative faculty such as great poets and philosophers conspicuously possess, and equally in the creative chessmaster.

EMANUEL LASKER, *Book of the World Championship Match,* 1934.

Chess is a matter of vanity.

ALEXANDER ALEKHINE, *Chess Review,* 1934.

Decent prizes are necessary and proper incentives to good chess and good tournaments. Before I am deluged with protests by well-meaning amateurs that one should play chess for the love of the game let me say that I love the game just as much and perhaps more than most of them do. But the exercise of skill and the playing of hard and strenuous games should meet with a due reward. Such incentives result in that high seriousness which pertains to great chess as well as to great poetry.

H. GOLOMBEK, *British Chess Magazine*, 1946.

Fifteen days before his death, I was called on the telephone and heard Dr. Alekhine ask me sadly whether I wanted to work with him on "Comments on the Best Games of the Hastings Tournament," adding: "I am completely out of money and I have to make some to buy my cigarettes."

FRANCISCO LUPI, *Chess World*, 1946.

It is said that, as his circumstances would not allow him to buy the German *Handbuch*, he borrowed it from a schoolfellow and copied it out by hand!

P. W. SERGEANT, *Charousek's Games of Chess*.

NOTES ON THE ILLUSTRATIONS

1. This Delhi chess set, of typical Indian workmanship, was made for the British East India Company in the 1790s. The White Pawns evidently represent native troops, while the Black Pawns (not shown) apparently are native sepoys. (*From the collection of Alex Hammond, London.*)

2. Left to right: early nineteenth-century Siamese ivory; eleventh-century Egyptian bone; Rhages Persian pottery, conventionalized, throne type, fourteenth century; 1400 A.D. Persian ivory, ridged and painted; German boxwood, 1650, effigy of Henry IV of France; late nineteenth-century German boxwood; eight-century Burmese ivory; eighteenth-century French filigree gold. (*Courtesy of John F. Harbeson.*)

3. Ancient chess kings (first three shaped like a King's throne): (left to right) eleventh-century crystal King, now in the Behague collection; ninth-century ivory King, now in the Metropolitan Museum, excavated at Nishapur, Persia; twelfth-century Nordic ivory King, now in Cluny Museum; fifteenth-century King, made of crystal with gold mountings, formerly belonging to the French royal house, now also in the Cluny Museum; Byzantine King, Treasury Museum, Istanbul, Turkey, fifteenth-century crystal with gold bands and inset precious stones. (*Courtesy of the Metropolitan Museum and John F. Harbeson.*)

4. A late eighteenth-century Chinese set, all the pieces being in the form of rats! Both White and Black are in white ivory, with ruby eyes for the White pieces and amber eyes for the Black pieces. (*From the collection of Alex Hammond, London.*)

5. Left to right: eighteenth-century French King, Lyons type, turned boxwood with ivory mountings; nineteenth-century Russian, Byzantine type of ivory; French Sèvres porcelain, 1925; Hungarian, circa 1885, made of fruitwood; twentieth-century Nigerian, made of wood with cotton robe. (*Courtesy of the Metropolitan Museum.*)

6. Left to right: two Polynesian Kings of painted wood, circa 1880; Indian King of polychromed ivory, 1780; Chinese ivory representation of Louis XVI, 1780; nineteenth-century Spanish bone; contemporary Brazilian-made King; modern Staunton type, made of vegetable-ivory. (*Courtesy of John F. Harbeson.*)

7. Many of the greatest players of the day were either participants or spectators in the first international tournament held at London in 1851. Howard Staunton, a notable teacher and authority on the game, had an unfortunate tendency to be pompous and arrogant. Samuel Boden, one of the finest players of his time, resisted the doubtful blandishments of a professional chess career. Jakob Loewenthal is chiefly remembered today for his collection of the great Paul Morphy's games. Adolf Anderssen won the London tournament in very superior style. Saint-Amant, Staunton's worthy rival in "the great match between England and France" in 1843, had retired from serious play by 1851. Daniel Harrwitz, as arrogant as Staunton but not so pompous, was a famous player of the day and one of the pioneer popularizers of blindfold exhibitions.

8. Paul Morphy (see page 98) is still regarded by most chess fans as the greatest chessmaster of all time. Experts may question this verdict, but the fascination of his games and personality is undeniable.

9. It was in the great tournament at St. Petersburg in 1914 that the twenty-two-year-old Alekhine (standing third from left) gained recognition as a Grandmaster. Seated in the front row, left to right, are Gunsberg, Blackburne, Lasker, Tarrasch, Burn, Gebhardt, Rubinstein, Bernstein, Capablanca, and Janowski. Alekhine is flanked by Marshall (left) and Nimzovich (right).

10. Adolf Anderssen, one of the most brilliant masters of the game, proved himself the strongest master of his day by winning the London tournament of 1851. His loss to Morphy in 1858 deprived him of his preeminent position; but Morphy's early retirement again left Anderssen on top.

Wilhelm Steinitz, one of the most striking figures in the world of chess, reigned as world champion for twenty-eight years after dethroning Anderssen in 1866. Known as the father of the modern positional style of chess,

Steinitz fought a continual battle with his contemporaries, at the chessboard and away from it.

José Raoul Capablanca learned to play at the age of four, won the Cuban championship at twelve and the world title at thirty-two (1921). His dizzy rise to fame enthralled his admirers as did the elegance, simplicity, and rapidity of his play. In later years, the seamy side of such a style became deplorably apparent.

11. Alexander Alekhine, in the editor's opinion was the greatest player in the history of chess. Alekhine had an all-round mastery of the game which has been equaled by no other player. This is seen in his unsurpassable brilliancies, his authoritative knowledge of the openings, his masterly understanding of position play, and his fine technical abilities in the domain of the endgame.

Alekhine was an extremely interesting subject for photography. The early picture was taken in 1912 (when he was 20) at Stockholm, the scene of his first great triumph in a strong international tournament. The picture at top right shows him in the palmy days of his maturity, about the time he won the world championship from Capablanca in 1927. The bottom picture shows a weary, time-ravaged Alekhine, shorn of his title, playing in the first round of the great Nottingham tournament of 1936.

12. On a board of 400 square meters at the Blanche Theatre, Stockholm, Sweden, an actual clock game (foreground) is enacted by living pieces, with moves broadcast on loud-speaker by chess fan, radio announcer, and sports correspondent B. Ahlborn.

19 Tdl:d4—Rook captures actress Siv Ruwd, Black Queen, exacting revenge for the black deed.

13. Dr. Max Euwe, a schoolteacher by profession, achieved the impossible by beating Alekhine in their world championship match in 1935. In their return match in 1937, Alekhine redeemed himself by regaining the title. Both matches are remarkable for the delightfully enterprising spirit displayed by these great masters.

Frank Marshall, who held the American title for some 30 years before he relinquished it in 1936, was famous for the imaginative genius of his combinative play, which made his games a joy to all spectators and students. No risk was too great, no hazard too wild, for Marshall.

Harry Nelson Pillsbury, Marshall's predecessor as American champion, died in 1906 at the age of 35. A potential world champion and a phenomenal blindfold player, Pillsbury did not live long enough to fulfill the promise of his early years.

14. Highspot of the 1942 Championship: Sammy Reshevsky receives Horowitz's congratulations on achieving a legendary draw in a "hopeless" position. The precious half-point enabled Sammy to tie for the title.

15. The Automaton Chessplayer. The right-hand compartment had two doors, but only one is shown. In this section are a cushion and lettered tablet, the latter used to spell out answers to questions. In the drawer are chessmen and a box of six miniature chess sets with endings played by the Turk. At the right is the mysterious casket, supposed to hold the secret of the Automaton's power.

16. The Automaton Chessplayer. In 1821, Robert Willis analyzed correctly the positions of the hidden player during the inspection of the cabinet's interior. At top: front and side views of player in his first position when door A was opened. Lower left: second position, when all front doors were open. Lower right, supposed fourth position, but this was incorrect. Illustrations are from an article by Willis.

17. The Automaton Chessplayer. (1) When the show began, the operator was in the large compartment, seated on a sliding stool in a trough behind the telescopic drawer. The hinged floor was raised up by his knees. The left-hand compartment was shown to the audience. (2) Second position, when the doors of the large compartment were opened. The player was completely hidden. Machinery (not shown) concealed the dividing partition in the small compartment. Both compartments were lined with dark cloth. (3) The opponents' moves were communicated to the hidden player by magnetism. When a piece was lifted from a square, the iron disk underneath dropped down. When moved to a new square, the disk under that square swung upward. (4) The player followed the game on a peg-in set, made the Turk's moves by a pantograph lever. When the pointer was inserted in a hole of the peg-in set, the Turk's arm moved to the corresponding square on the board above.

A CATALOGUE OF SELECTED DOVER BOOKS
IN ALL FIELDS OF INTEREST

A CATALOGUE OF SELECTED DOVER BOOKS
IN ALL FIELDS OF INTEREST

AMERICA'S OLD MASTERS, James T. Flexner. Four men emerged unexpectedly from provincial 18th century America to leadership in European art: Benjamin West, J. S. Copley, C. R. Peale, Gilbert Stuart. Brilliant coverage of lives and contributions. Revised, 1967 edition. 69 plates. 365pp. of text.

21806-6 Paperbound $3.00

FIRST FLOWERS OF OUR WILDERNESS: AMERICAN PAINTING, THE COLONIAL PERIOD, James T. Flexner. Painters, and regional painting traditions from earliest Colonial times up to the emergence of Copley, West and Peale Sr., Foster, Gustavus Hesselius, Feke, John Smibert and many anonymous painters in the primitive manner. Engaging presentation, with 162 illustrations. xxii + 368pp.

22180-6 Paperbound $3.50

THE LIGHT OF DISTANT SKIES: AMERICAN PAINTING, 1760-1835, James T. Flexner. The great generation of early American painters goes to Europe to learn and to teach: West, Copley, Gilbert Stuart and others. Allston, Trumbull, Morse; also contemporary American painters—primitives, derivatives, academics—who remained in America. 102 illustrations. xiii + 306pp. 22179-2 Paperbound $3.00

A HISTORY OF THE RISE AND PROGRESS OF THE ARTS OF DESIGN IN THE UNITED STATES, William Dunlap. Much the richest mine of information on early American painters, sculptors, architects, engravers, miniaturists, etc. The only source of information for scores of artists, the major primary source for many others. Unabridged reprint of rare original 1834 edition, with new introduction by James T. Flexner, and 394 new illustrations. Edited by Rita Weiss. 6⅝ x 9⅝.

21695-0, 21696-9, 21697-7 Three volumes, Paperbound $13.50

EPOCHS OF CHINESE AND JAPANESE ART, Ernest F. Fenollosa. From primitive Chinese art to the 20th century, thorough history, explanation of every important art period and form, including Japanese woodcuts; main stress on China and Japan, but Tibet, Korea also included. Still unexcelled for its detailed, rich coverage of cultural background, aesthetic elements, diffusion studies, particularly of the historical period. 2nd, 1913 edition. 242 illustrations. lii + 439pp. of text.

20364-6, 20365-4 Two volumes, Paperbound $6.00

THE GENTLE ART OF MAKING ENEMIES, James A. M. Whistler. Greatest wit of his day deflates Oscar Wilde, Ruskin, Swinburne; strikes back at inane critics, exhibitions, art journalism; aesthetics of impressionist revolution in most striking form. Highly readable classic by great painter. Reproduction of edition designed by Whistler. Introduction by Alfred Werner. xxxvi + 334pp.

21875-9 Paperbound $2.50

Two Little Savages; Being the Adventures of Two Boys Who Lived as Indians and What They Learned, Ernest Thompson Seton. Great classic of nature and boyhood provides a vast range of woodlore in most palatable form, a genuinely entertaining story. Two farm boys build a teepee in woods and live in it for a month, working out Indian solutions to living problems, star lore, birds and animals, plants, etc. 293 illustrations. vii + 286pp.

20985-7 Paperbound $1.95

Peter Piper's Practical Principles of Plain & Perfect Pronunciation. Alliterative jingles and tongue-twisters of surprising charm, that made their first appearance in America about 1830. Republished in full with the spirited woodcut illustrations from this earliest American edition. 32pp. $4\frac{1}{2}$ x $6\frac{3}{8}$.

22560-7 Paperbound $1.00

Science Experiments and Amusements for Children, Charles Vivian. 73 easy experiments, requiring only materials found at home or easily available, such as candles, coins, steel wool, etc.; illustrate basic phenomena like vacuum, simple chemical reaction, etc. All safe. Modern, well-planned. Formerly *Science Games for Children*. 102 photos, numerous drawings. 96pp. $6\frac{1}{8}$ x $9\frac{1}{4}$.

21856-2 Paperbound $1.25

An Introduction to Chess Moves and Tactics Simply Explained, Leonard Barden. Informal intermediate introduction, quite strong in explaining reasons for moves. Covers basic material, tactics, important openings, traps, positional play in middle game, end game. Attempts to isolate patterns and recurrent configurations. Formerly *Chess*. 58 figures. 102pp.   (USO) 21210-6 Paperbound $1.25

Lasker's Manual of Chess, Dr. Emanuel Lasker. Lasker was not only one of the five great World Champions, he was also one of the ablest expositors, theorists, and analysts. In many ways, his Manual, permeated with his philosophy of battle, filled with keen insights, is one of the greatest works ever written on chess. Filled with analyzed games by the great players. A single-volume library that will profit almost any chess player, beginner or master. 308 diagrams. xli x 349pp.

20640-8 Paperbound $2.50

The Master Book of Mathematical Recreations, Fred Schuh. In opinion of many the finest work ever prepared on mathematical puzzles, stunts, recreations; exhaustively thorough explanations of mathematics involved, analysis of effects, citation of puzzles and games. Mathematics involved is elementary. Translated by F. Göbel. 194 figures. xxiv + 430pp.   22134-2 Paperbound $3.00

Mathematics, Magic and Mystery, Martin Gardner. Puzzle editor for Scientific American explains mathematics behind various mystifying tricks: card tricks, stage "mind reading," coin and match tricks, counting out games, geometric dissections, etc. Probability sets, theory of numbers clearly explained. Also provides more than 400 tricks, guaranteed to work, that you can do. 135 illustrations. xii + 176pp.

20338-2 Paperbound $1.50

ALPHABETS AND ORNAMENTS, Ernst Lehner. Well-known pictorial source for decorative alphabets, script examples, cartouches, frames, decorative title pages, calligraphic initials, borders, similar material. 14th to 19th century, mostly European. Useful in almost any graphic arts designing, varied styles. 750 illustrations. 256pp. 7 x 10.   21905-4 Paperbound $4.00

PAINTING: A CREATIVE APPROACH, Norman Colquhoun. For the beginner simple guide provides an instructive approach to painting: major stumbling blocks for beginner; overcoming them, technical points; paints and pigments; oil painting; watercolor and other media and color. New section on "plastic" paints. Glossary. Formerly *Paint Your Own Pictures*. 221pp.   22000-1 Paperbound $1.75

THE ENJOYMENT AND USE OF COLOR, Walter Sargent. Explanation of the relations between colors themselves and between colors in nature and art, including hundreds of little-known facts about color values, intensities, effects of high and low illumination, complementary colors. Many practical hints for painters, references to great masters. 7 color plates, 29 illustrations. x + 274pp.
20944-X Paperbound $2.50

THE NOTEBOOKS OF LEONARDO DA VINCI, compiled and edited by Jean Paul Richter. 1566 extracts from original manuscripts reveal the full range of Leonardo's versatile genius: all his writings on painting, sculpture, architecture, anatomy, astronomy, geography, topography, physiology, mining, music, etc., in both Italian and English, with 186 plates of manuscript pages and more than 500 additional drawings. Includes studies for the Last Supper, the lost Sforza monument, and other works. Total of xlvii + 866pp. 7⅞ x 10¾.
22572-0, 22573-9 Two volumes, Paperbound $10.00

MONTGOMERY WARD CATALOGUE OF 1895. Tea gowns, yards of flannel and pillow-case lace, stereoscopes, books of gospel hymns, the New Improved Singer Sewing Machine, side saddles, milk skimmers, straight-edged razors, high-button shoes, spittoons, and on and on . . . listing some 25,000 items, practically all illustrated. Essential to the shoppers of the 1890's, it is our truest record of the spirit of the period. Unaltered reprint of Issue No. 57, Spring and Summer 1895. Introduction by Boris Emmet. Innumerable illustrations. xiii + 624pp. 8½ x 11⅝.
22377-9 Paperbound $6.95

THE CRYSTAL PALACE EXHIBITION ILLUSTRATED CATALOGUE (LONDON, 1851). One of the wonders of the modern world—the Crystal Palace Exhibition in which all the nations of the civilized world exhibited their achievements in the arts and sciences—presented in an equally important illustrated catalogue. More than 1700 items pictured with accompanying text—ceramics, textiles, cast-iron work, carpets, pianos, sleds, razors, wall-papers, billiard tables, beehives, silverware and hundreds of other artifacts—represent the focal point of Victorian culture in the Western World. Probably the largest collection of Victorian decorative art ever assembled—indispensable for antiquarians and designers. Unabridged republication of the Art-Journal Catalogue of the Great Exhibition of 1851, with all terminal essays. New introduction by John Gloag, F.S.A. xxxiv + 426pp. 9 x 12.
22503-8 Paperbound $4.50

THE RED FAIRY BOOK, Andrew Lang. Lang's color fairy books have long been children's favorites. This volume includes Rapunzel, Jack and the Bean-stalk and 35 other stories, familiar and unfamiliar. 4 plates, 93 illustrations x + 367pp.
21673-X Paperbound $1.95

THE BLUE FAIRY BOOK, Andrew Lang. Lang's tales come from all countries and all times. Here are 37 tales from Grimm, the Arabian Nights, Greek Mythology, and other fascinating sources. 8 plates, 130 illustrations. xi + 390pp.
21437-0 Paperbound $1.95

HOUSEHOLD STORIES BY THE BROTHERS GRIMM. Classic English-language edition of the well-known tales — Rumpelstiltskin, Snow White, Hansel and Gretel, The Twelve Brothers, Faithful John, Rapunzel, Tom Thumb (52 stories in all). Translated into simple, straightforward English by Lucy Crane. Ornamented with headpieces, vignettes, elaborate decorative initials and a dozen full-page illustrations by Walter Crane. x + 269pp.
21080-4 Paperbound $1.75

THE MERRY ADVENTURES OF ROBIN HOOD, Howard Pyle. The finest modern versions of the traditional ballads and tales about the great English outlaw. Howard Pyle's complete prose version, with every word, every illustration of the first edition. Do not confuse this facsimile of the original (1883) with modern editions that change text or illustrations. 23 plates plus many page decorations. xxii + 296pp.
22043-5 Paperbound $2.00

THE STORY OF KING ARTHUR AND HIS KNIGHTS, Howard Pyle. The finest children's version of the life of King Arthur; brilliantly retold by Pyle, with 48 of his most imaginative illustrations. xviii + 313pp. 6⅛ x 9¼.
21445-1 Paperbound $2.00

THE WONDERFUL WIZARD OF OZ, L. Frank Baum. America's finest children's book in facsimile of first edition with all Denslow illustrations in full color. The edition a child should have. Introduction by Martin Gardner. 23 color plates, scores of drawings. iv + 267pp.
20691-2 Paperbound $1.95

THE MARVELOUS LAND OF OZ, L. Frank Baum. The second Oz book, every bit as imaginative as the Wizard. The hero is a boy named Tip, but the Scarecrow and the Tin Woodman are back, as is the Oz magic. 16 color plates, 120 drawings by John R. Neill. 287pp.
20692-0 Paperbound $1.75

THE MAGICAL MONARCH OF MO, L. Frank Baum. Remarkable adventures in a land even stranger than Oz. The best of Baum's books not in the Oz series. 15 color plates and dozens of drawings by Frank Verbeck. xviii + 237pp.
21892-9 Paperbound $2.00

THE BAD CHILD'S BOOK OF BEASTS, MORE BEASTS FOR WORSE CHILDREN, A MORAL ALPHABET, Hilaire Belloc. Three complete humor classics in one volume. Be kind to the frog, and do not call him names . . . and 28 other whimsical animals. Familiar favorites and some not so well known. Illustrated by Basil Blackwell. 156pp.
(USO) 20749-8 Paperbound $1.25

LAST AND FIRST MEN AND STAR MAKER, TWO SCIENCE FICTION NOVELS, Olaf Stapledon. Greatest future histories in science fiction. In the first, human intelligence is the "hero," through strange paths of evolution, interplanetary invasions, incredible technologies, near extinctions and reemergences. Star Maker describes the quest of a band of star rovers for intelligence itself, through time and space: weird inhuman civilizations, crustacean minds, symbiotic worlds, etc. Complete, unabridged. v + 438pp. 21962-3 Paperbound $2.00

THREE PROPHETIC NOVELS, H. G. WELLS. Stages of a consistently planned future for mankind. *When the Sleeper Wakes,* and *A Story of the Days to Come,* anticipate *Brave New World* and *1984,* in the 21st Century; *The Time Machine,* only complete version in print, shows farther future and the end of mankind. All show Wells's greatest gifts as storyteller and novelist. Edited by E. F. Bleiler. x + 335pp. (USO) 20605-X Paperbound $2.00

THE DEVIL'S DICTIONARY, Ambrose Bierce. America's own Oscar Wilde— Ambrose Bierce—offers his barbed iconoclastic wisdom in over 1,000 definitions hailed by H. L. Mencken as "some of the most gorgeous witticisms in the English language." 145pp. 20487-1 Paperbound $1.25

MAX AND MORITZ, Wilhelm Busch. Great children's classic, father of comic strip, of two bad boys, Max and Moritz. Also Ker and Plunk (Plisch und Plumm), Cat and Mouse, Deceitful Henry, Ice-Peter, The Boy and the Pipe, and five other pieces. Original German, with English translation. Edited by H. Arthur Klein; translations by various hands and H. Arthur Klein. vi + 216pp.
20181-3 Paperbound $1.50

PIGS IS PIGS AND OTHER FAVORITES, Ellis Parker Butler. The title story is one of the best humor short stories, as Mike Flannery obfuscates biology and English. Also included, That Pup of Murchison's, The Great American Pie Company, and Perkins of Portland. 14 illustrations. v + 109pp. 21532-6 Paperbound $1.00

THE PETERKIN PAPERS, Lucretia P. Hale. It takes genius to be as stupidly mad as the Peterkins, as they decide to become wise, celebrate the "Fourth," keep a cow, and otherwise strain the resources of the Lady from Philadelphia. Basic book of American humor. 153 illustrations. 219pp. 20794-3 Paperbound $1.25

PERRAULT'S FAIRY TALES, translated by A. E. Johnson and S. R. Littlewood, with 34 full-page illustrations by Gustave Doré. All the original Perrault stories— Cinderella, Sleeping Beauty, Bluebeard, Little Red Riding Hood, Puss in Boots, Tom Thumb, etc.—with their witty verse morals and the magnificent illustrations of Doré. One of the five or six great books of European fairy tales. viii + 117pp. 8⅛ x 11. 22311-6 Paperbound $2.00

OLD HUNGARIAN FAIRY TALES, Baroness Orczy. Favorites translated and adapted by author of the *Scarlet Pimpernel.* Eight fairy tales include "The Suitors of Princess Fire-Fly," "The Twin Hunchbacks," "Mr. Cuttlefish's Love Story," and "The Enchanted Cat." This little volume of magic and adventure will captivate children as it has for generations. 90 drawings by Montagu Barstow. 96pp.
(USO) 22293-4 Paperbound $1.95

THE ARCHITECTURE OF COUNTRY HOUSES, Andrew J. Downing. Together with Vaux's *Villas and Cottages* this is the basic book for Hudson River Gothic architecture of the middle Victorian period. Full, sound discussions of general aspects of housing, architecture, style, decoration, furnishing, together with scores of detailed house plans, illustrations of specific buildings, accompanied by full text. Perhaps the most influential single American architectural book. 1850 edition. Introduction by J. Stewart Johnson. 321 figures, 34 architectural designs. xvi + 560pp.

22003-6 Paperbound $4.00

LOST EXAMPLES OF COLONIAL ARCHITECTURE, John Mead Howells. Full-page photographs of buildings that have disappeared or been so altered as to be denatured, including many designed by major early American architects. 245 plates. xvii + 248pp. 7⅞ x 10¾.

21143-6 Paperbound $3.00

DOMESTIC ARCHITECTURE OF THE AMERICAN COLONIES AND OF THE EARLY REPUBLIC, Fiske Kimball. Foremost architect and restorer of Williamsburg and Monticello covers nearly 200 homes between 1620-1825. Architectural details, construction, style features, special fixtures, floor plans, etc. Generally considered finest work in its area. 219 illustrations of houses, doorways, windows, capital mantels. xx + 314pp. 7⅞ x 10¾.

21743-4 Paperbound $3.50

EARLY AMERICAN ROOMS: 1650-1858, edited by Russell Hawes Kettell. Tour of 12 rooms, each representative of a different era in American history and each furnished, decorated, designed and occupied in the style of the era. 72 plans and elevations, 8-page color section, etc., show fabrics, wall papers, arrangements, etc. Full descriptive text. xvii + 200pp. of text. 8⅜ x 11¼.

21633-0 Paperbound $5.00

THE FITZWILLIAM VIRGINAL BOOK, edited by J. Fuller Maitland and W. B. Squire. Full modern printing of famous early 17th-century ms. volume of 300 works by Morley, Byrd, Bull, Gibbons, etc. For piano or other modern keyboard instrument; easy to read format. xxxvi + 938pp. 8⅜ x 11.

21068-5, 21069-3 Two volumes, Paperbound $8.00

HARPSICHORD MUSIC, Johann Sebastian Bach. Bach Gesellschaft edition. A rich selection of Bach's masterpieces for the harpsichord: the six English Suites, six French Suites, the six Partitas (Clavierübung part I), the Goldberg Variations (Clavierübung part IV), the fifteen Two-Part Inventions and the fifteen Three-Part Sinfonias. Clearly reproduced on large sheets with ample margins; eminently playable. vi + 312pp. 8⅛ x 11.

22360-4 Paperbound $5.00

THE MUSIC OF BACH: AN INTRODUCTION, Charles Sanford Terry. A fine, nontechnical introduction to Bach's music, both instrumental and vocal. Covers organ music, chamber music, passion music, other types. Analyzes themes, developments, innovations. x + 114pp.

21075-8 Paperbound $1.25

BEETHOVEN AND HIS NINE SYMPHONIES, Sir George Grove. Noted British musicologist provides best history, analysis, commentary on symphonies. Very thorough, rigorously accurate; necessary to both advanced student and amateur music lover. 436 musical passages. vii + 407 pp.

20334-4 Paperbound $2.25

AGAINST THE GRAIN (A REBOURS), Joris K. Huysmans. Filled with weird images, evidences of a bizarre imagination, exotic experiments with hallucinatory drugs, rich tastes and smells and the diversions of its sybarite hero Duc Jean des Esseintes, this classic novel pushed 19th-century literary decadence to its limits. Full unabridged edition. Do not confuse this with abridged editions generally sold. Introduction by Havelock Ellis. xlix + 206pp. 22190-3 Paperbound $2.00

VARIORUM SHAKESPEARE: HAMLET. Edited by Horace H. Furness; a landmark of American scholarship. Exhaustive footnotes and appendices treat all doubtful words and phrases, as well as suggested critical emendations throughout the play's history. First volume contains editor's own text, collated with all Quartos and Folios. Second volume contains full first Quarto, translations of Shakespeare's sources (Belleforest, and Saxo Grammaticus), Der Bestrafte Brudermord, and many essays on critical and historical points of interest by major authorities of past and present. Includes details of staging and costuming over the years. By far the best edition available for serious students of Shakespeare. Total of xx + 905pp.
21004-9, 21005-7, 2 volumes, Paperbound $5.25

A LIFE OF WILLIAM SHAKESPEARE, Sir Sidney Lee. This is the standard life of Shakespeare, summarizing everything known about Shakespeare and his plays. Incredibly rich in material, broad in coverage, clear and judicious, it has served thousands as the best introduction to Shakespeare. 1931 edition. 9 plates. xxix + 792pp. (USO) 21967-4 Paperbound $3.75

MASTERS OF THE DRAMA, John Gassner. Most comprehensive history of the drama in print, covering every tradition from Greeks to modern Europe and America, including India, Far East, etc. Covers more than 800 dramatists, 2000 plays, with biographical material, plot summaries, theatre history, criticism, etc. "Best of its kind in English," *New Republic*. 77 illustrations. xxii + 890pp.
20100-7 Clothbound $7.50

THE EVOLUTION OF THE ENGLISH LANGUAGE, George McKnight. The growth of English, from the 14th century to the present. Unusual, non-technical account presents basic information in very interesting form: sound shifts, change in grammar and syntax, vocabulary growth, similar topics. Abundantly illustrated with quotations. Formerly *Modern English in the Making*. xii + 590pp.
21932-1 Paperbound $3.50

AN ETYMOLOGICAL DICTIONARY OF MODERN ENGLISH, Ernest Weekley. Fullest, richest work of its sort, by foremost British lexicographer. Detailed word histories, including many colloquial and archaic words; extensive quotations. Do not confuse this with the Concise Etymological Dictionary, which is much abridged. Total of xxvii + 830pp. 6½ x 9¼.
21873-2, 21874-0 Two volumes, Paperbound $5.50

FLATLAND: A ROMANCE OF MANY DIMENSIONS, E. A. Abbott. Classic of science-fiction explores ramifications of life in a two-dimensional world, and what happens when a three-dimensional being intrudes. Amusing reading, but also useful as introduction to thought about hyperspace. Introduction by Banesh Hoffmann. 16 illustrations. xx + 103pp. 20001-9 Paperbound $1.00

JOHANN SEBASTIAN BACH, Philipp Spitta. One of the great classics of musicology, this definitive analysis of Bach's music (and life) has never been surpassed. Lucid, nontechnical analyses of hundreds of pieces (30 pages devoted to St. Matthew Passion, 26 to B Minor Mass). Also includes major analysis of 18th-century music. 450 musical examples. 40-page musical supplement. Total of xx + 1799pp.
(EUK) 22278-0, 22279-9 Two volumes, Clothbound $15.00

MOZART AND HIS PIANO CONCERTOS, Cuthbert Girdlestone. The only full-length study of an important area of Mozart's creativity. Provides detailed analyses of all 23 concertos, traces inspirational sources. 417 musical examples. Second edition. 509pp. (USO) 21271-8 Paperbound $3.50

THE PERFECT WAGNERITE: A COMMENTARY ON THE NIBLUNG'S RING, George Bernard Shaw. Brilliant and still relevant criticism in remarkable essays on Wagner's Ring cycle, Shaw's ideas on political and social ideology behind the plots, role of Leitmotifs, vocal requisites, etc. Prefaces. xxi + 136pp.
21707-8 Paperbound $1.50

DON GIOVANNI, W. A. Mozart. Complete libretto, modern English translation; biographies of composer and librettist; accounts of early performances and critical reaction. Lavishly illustrated. All the material you need to understand and appreciate this great work. Dover Opera Guide and Libretto Series; translated and introduced by Ellen Bleiler. 92 illustrations. 209pp.
21134-7 Paperbound $1.50

HIGH FIDELITY SYSTEMS: A LAYMAN'S GUIDE, Roy F. Allison. All the basic information you need for setting up your own audio system: high fidelity and stereo record players, tape records, F.M. Connections, adjusting tone arm, cartridge, checking needle alignment, positioning speakers, phasing speakers, adjusting hums, trouble-shooting, maintenance, and similar topics. Enlarged 1965 edition. More than 50 charts, diagrams, photos. iv + 91pp. 21514-8 Paperbound $1.25

REPRODUCTION OF SOUND, Edgar Villchur. Thorough coverage for laymen of high fidelity systems, reproducing systems in general, needles, amplifiers, preamps, loudspeakers, feedback, explaining physical background. "A rare talent for making technicalities vividly comprehensible," R. Darrell, *High Fidelity.* 69 figures. iv + 92pp. 21515-6 Paperbound $1.00

HEAR ME TALKIN' TO YA: THE STORY OF JAZZ AS TOLD BY THE MEN WHO MADE IT, Nat Shapiro and Nat Hentoff. Louis Armstrong, Fats Waller, Jo Jones, Clarence Williams, Billy Holiday, Duke Ellington, Jelly Roll Morton and dozens of other jazz greats tell how it was in Chicago's South Side, New Orleans, depression Harlem and the modern West Coast as jazz was born and grew. xvi + 429pp.
21726-4 Paperbound $2.50

FABLES OF AESOP, translated by Sir Roger L'Estrange. A reproduction of the very rare 1931 Paris edition; a selection of the most interesting fables, together with 50 imaginative drawings by Alexander Calder. v + 128pp. 6½x9¼.
21780-9 Paperbound $1.25

POEMS OF ANNE BRADSTREET, edited with an introduction by Robert Hutchinson. A new selection of poems by America's first poet and perhaps the first significant woman poet in the English language. 48 poems display her development in works of considerable variety—love poems, domestic poems, religious meditations, formal elegies, "quaternions," etc. Notes, bibliography. viii + 222pp.

22160-1 Paperbound $2.00

THREE GOTHIC NOVELS: THE CASTLE OF OTRANTO BY HORACE WALPOLE; VATHEK BY WILLIAM BECKFORD; THE VAMPYRE BY JOHN POLIDORI, WITH FRAGMENT OF A NOVEL BY LORD BYRON, edited by E. F. Bleiler. The first Gothic novel, by Walpole; the finest Oriental tale in English, by Beckford; powerful Romantic supernatural story in versions by Polidori and Byron. All extremely important in history of literature; all still exciting, packed with supernatural thrills, ghosts, haunted castles, magic, etc. xl + 291pp.

21232-7 Paperbound $2.00

THE BEST TALES OF HOFFMANN, E. T. A. Hoffmann. 10 of Hoffmann's most important stories, in modern re-editings of standard translations: Nutcracker and the King of Mice, Signor Formica, Automata, The Sandman, Rath Krespel, The Golden Flowerpot, Master Martin the Cooper, The Mines of Falun, The King's Betrothed, A New Year's Eve Adventure. 7 illustrations by Hoffmann. Edited by E. F. Bleiler. xxxix + 419pp.

21793-0 Paperbound $2.50

GHOST AND HORROR STORIES OF AMBROSE BIERCE, Ambrose Bierce. 23 strikingly modern stories of the horrors latent in the human mind: The Eyes of the Panther, The Damned Thing, An Occurrence at Owl Creek Bridge, An Inhabitant of Carcosa, etc., plus the dream-essay, Visions of the Night. Edited by E. F. Bleiler. xxii + 199pp.

20767-6 Paperbound $1.50

BEST GHOST STORIES OF J. S. LEFANU, J. Sheridan LeFanu. Finest stories by Victorian master often considered greatest supernatural writer of all. Carmilla, Green Tea, The Haunted Baronet, The Familiar, and 12 others. Most never before available in the U. S. A. Edited by E. F. Bleiler. 8 illustrations from Victorian publications. xvii + 467pp.

20415-4 Paperbound $2.50

THE TIME STREAM, THE GREATEST ADVENTURE, AND THE PURPLE SAPPHIRE— THREE SCIENCE FICTION NOVELS, John Taine (Eric Temple Bell). Great American mathematician was also foremost science fiction novelist of the 1920's. *The Time Stream,* one of all-time classics, uses concepts of circular time; *The Greatest Adventure,* incredibly ancient biological experiments from Antarctica threaten to escape; The *Purple Sapphire,* superscience, lost races in Central Tibet, survivors of the Great Race. 4 illustrations by Frank R. Paul. v + 532pp.

21180-0 Paperbound $3.00

SEVEN SCIENCE FICTION NOVELS, H. G. Wells. The standard collection of the great novels. Complete, unabridged. *First Men in the Moon, Island of Dr. Moreau, War of the Worlds, Food of the Gods, Invisible Man, Time Machine, In the Days of the Comet.* Not only science fiction fans, but every educated person owes it to himself to read these novels. 1015pp.

20264-X Clothbound $5.00

A HISTORY OF COSTUME, Carl Köhler. Definitive history, based on surviving pieces of clothing primarily, and paintings, statues, etc. secondarily. Highly readable text, supplemented by 594 illustrations of costumes of the ancient Mediterranean peoples, Greece and Rome, the Teutonic prehistoric period; costumes of the Middle Ages, Renaissance, Baroque, 18th and 19th centuries. Clear, measured patterns are provided for many clothing articles. Approach is practical throughout. Enlarged by Emma von Sichart. 464pp. 21030-8 Paperbound $3.00

ORIENTAL RUGS, ANTIQUE AND MODERN, Walter A. Hawley. A complete and authoritative treatise on the Oriental rug—where they are made, by whom and how, designs and symbols, characteristics in detail of the six major groups, how to distinguish them and how to buy them. Detailed technical data is provided on periods, weaves, warps, wefts, textures, sides, ends and knots, although no technical background is required for an understanding. 11 color plates, 80 halftones, 4 maps. vi + 320pp. 6⅛ x 9⅛. 22366-3 Paperbound $5.00

TEN BOOKS ON ARCHITECTURE, Vitruvius. By any standards the most important book on architecture ever written. Early Roman discussion of aesthetics of building, construction methods, orders, sites, and every other aspect of architecture has inspired, instructed architecture for about 2,000 years. Stands behind Palladio, Michelangelo, Bramante, Wren, countless others. Definitive Morris H. Morgan translation. 68 illustrations. xii + 331pp. 20645-9 Paperbound $2.50

THE FOUR BOOKS OF ARCHITECTURE, Andrea Palladio. Translated into every major Western European language in the two centuries following its publication in 1570, this has been one of the most influential books in the history of architecture. Complete reprint of the 1738 Isaac Ware edition. New introduction by Adolf Placzek, Columbia Univ. 216 plates. xxii + 110pp. of text. 9½ x 12¾.
21308-0 Clothbound $10.00

STICKS AND STONES: A STUDY OF AMERICAN ARCHITECTURE AND CIVILIZATION, Lewis Mumford.One of the great classics of American cultural history. American architecture from the medieval-inspired earliest forms to the early 20th century; evolution of structure and style, and reciprocal influences on environment. 21 photographic illustrations. 238pp. 20202-X Paperbound $2.00

THE AMERICAN BUILDER'S COMPANION, Asher Benjamin. The most widely used early 19th century architectural style and source book, for colonial up into Greek Revival periods. Extensive development of geometry of carpentering, construction of sashes, frames, doors, stairs; plans and elevations of domestic and other buildings. Hundreds of thousands of houses were built according to this book, now invaluable to historians, architects, restorers, etc. 1827 edition. 59 plates. 114pp. 7⅞ x 10¾.
22236-5 Paperbound $3.00

DUTCH HOUSES IN THE HUDSON VALLEY BEFORE 1776, Helen Wilkinson Reynolds. The standard survey of the Dutch colonial house and outbuildings, with constructional features, decoration, and local history associated with individual homesteads. Introduction by Franklin D. Roosevelt. Map. 150 illustrations. 469pp. 6⅝ x 9¼. 21469-9 Paperbound $3.50

EAST O' THE SUN AND WEST O' THE MOON, George W. Dasent. Considered the best of all translations of these Norwegian folk tales, this collection has been enjoyed by generations of children (and folklorists too). Includes True and Untrue, Why the Sea is Salt, East O' the Sun and West O' the Moon, Why the Bear is Stumpy-Tailed, Boots and the Troll, The Cock and the Hen, Rich Peter the Pedlar, and 52 more. The only edition with all 59 tales. 77 illustrations by Erik Werenskiold and Theodor Kittelsen. xv + 418pp. 22521-6 Paperbound $3.00

GOOPS AND HOW TO BE THEM, Gelett Burgess. Classic of tongue-in-cheek humor, masquerading as etiquette book. 87 verses, twice as many cartoons, show mischievous Goops as they demonstrate to children virtues of table manners, neatness, courtesy, etc. Favorite for generations. viii + 88pp. 6½ x 9¼.
22233-0 Paperbound $1.25

ALICE'S ADVENTURES UNDER GROUND, Lewis Carroll. The first version, quite different from the final *Alice in Wonderland,* printed out by Carroll himself with his own illustrations. Complete facsimile of the "million dollar" manuscript Carroll gave to Alice Liddell in 1864. Introduction by Martin Gardner. viii + 96pp. Title and dedication pages in color. 21482-6 Paperbound $1.00

THE BROWNIES, THEIR BOOK, Palmer Cox. Small as mice, cunning as foxes, exuberant and full of mischief, the Brownies go to the zoo, toy shop, seashore, circus, etc., in 24 verse adventures and 266 illustrations. Long a favorite, since their first appearance in St. Nicholas Magazine. xi + 144pp. 6⅝ x 9¼.
21265-3 Paperbound $1.50

SONGS OF CHILDHOOD, Walter De La Mare. Published (under the pseudonym Walter Ramal) when De La Mare was only 29, this charming collection has long been a favorite children's book. A facsimile of the first edition in paper, the 47 poems capture the simplicity of the nursery rhyme and the ballad, including such lyrics as I Met Eve, Tartary, The Silver Penny. vii + 106pp. 21972-0 Paperbound $1.25

THE COMPLETE NONSENSE OF EDWARD LEAR, Edward Lear. The finest 19th-century humorist-cartoonist in full: all nonsense limericks, zany alphabets, Owl and Pussycat, songs, nonsense botany, and more than 500 illustrations by Lear himself. Edited by Holbrook Jackson. xxix + 287pp. (USO) 20167-8 Paperbound $1.75

BILLY WHISKERS: THE AUTOBIOGRAPHY OF A GOAT, Frances Trego Montgomery. A favorite of children since the early 20th century, here are the escapades of that rambunctious, irresistible and mischievous goat—Billy Whiskers. Much in the spirit of *Peck's Bad Boy,* this is a book that children never tire of reading or hearing. All the original familiar illustrations by W. H. Fry are included: 6 color plates, 18 black and white drawings. 159pp. 22345-0 Paperbound $2.00

MOTHER GOOSE MELODIES. Faithful republication of the fabulously rare Munroe and Francis "copyright 1833" Boston edition—the most important Mother Goose collection, usually referred to as the "original." Familiar rhymes plus many rare ones, with wonderful old woodcut illustrations. Edited by E. F. Bleiler. 128pp. 4½ x 6⅜. 22577-1 Paperbound $1.25

DESIGN BY ACCIDENT; A BOOK OF "ACCIDENTAL EFFECTS" FOR ARTISTS AND DESIGNERS, James F. O'Brien. Create your own unique, striking, imaginative effects by "controlled accident" interaction of materials: paints and lacquers, oil and water based paints, splatter, crackling materials, shatter, similar items. Everything you do will be different; first book on this limitless art, so useful to both fine artist and commercial artist. Full instructions. 192 plates showing "accidents," 8 in color. viii + 215pp. 8⅜ x 11¼. 21942-9 Paperbound $3.50

THE BOOK OF SIGNS, Rudolf Koch. Famed German type designer draws 493 beautiful symbols: religious, mystical, alchemical, imperial, property marks, ɩ nes, etc. Remarkable fusion of traditional and modern. Good for suggestions of timelessness, smartness, modernity. Text. vi + 104pp. 6⅛ x 9¼. 20162-7 Paperbound $1.25

HISTORY OF INDIAN AND INDONESIAN ART, Ananda K. Coomaraswamy. An unabridged republication of one of the finest books by a great scholar in Eastern art. Rich in descriptive material, history, social backgrounds; Sunga reliefs, Rajput paintings, Gupta temples, Burmese frescoes, textiles, jewelry, sculpture, etc. 400 photos. viii + 423pp. 6⅜ x 9¾. 21436-2 Paperbound $3.50

PRIMITIVE ART, Franz Boas. America's foremost anthropologist surveys textiles, ceramics, woodcarving, basketry, metalwork, etc.; patterns, technology, creation of symbols, style origins. All areas of world, but very full on Northwest Coast Indians. More than 350 illustrations of baskets, boxes, totem poles, weapons, etc. 378 pp. 20025-6 Paperbound $2.50

THE GENTLEMAN AND CABINET MAKER'S DIRECTOR, Thomas Chippendale. Full reprint (third edition, 1762) of most influential furniture book of all time, by master cabinetmaker. 200 plates, illustrating chairs, sofas, mirrors, tables, cabinets, plus 24 photographs of surviving pieces. Biographical introduction by N. Bienenstock. vi + 249pp. 9⅞ x 12¾. 21601-2 Paperbound $3.50

AMERICAN ANTIQUE FURNITURE, Edgar G. Miller, Jr. The basic coverage of all American furniture before 1840. Individual chapters cover type of furniture— clocks, tables, sideboards, etc.—chronologically, with inexhaustible wealth of data. More than 2100 photographs, all identified, commented on. Essential to all early American collectors. Introduction by H. E. Keyes. vi + 1106pp. 7⅞ x 10¾. 21599-7, 21600-4 Two volumes, Paperbound $7.50

PENNSYLVANIA DUTCH AMERICAN FOLK ART, Henry J. Kauffman. 279 photos, 28 drawings of tulipware, Fraktur script, painted tinware, toys, flowered furniture, quilts, samplers, hex signs, house interiors, etc. Full descriptive text. Excellent for tourist, rewarding for designer, collector. Map. 146pp. 7⅞ x 10¾. 21205-X Paperbound $2.00

EARLY NEW ENGLAND GRAVESTONE RUBBINGS, Edmund V. Gillon, Jr. 43 photographs, 226 carefully reproduced rubbings show heavily symbolic, sometimes macabre early gravestones, up to early 19th century. Remarkable early American primitive art, occasionally strikingly beautiful; always powerful. Text. xxvi + 207pp. 8⅜ x 11¼. 21380-3 Paperbound $3.00

PLANETS, STARS AND GALAXIES: DESCRIPTIVE ASTRONOMY FOR BEGINNERS, A. E. Fanning. Comprehensive introductory survey of astronomy: the sun, solar system, stars, galaxies, universe, cosmology; up-to-date, including quasars, radio stars, etc. Preface by Prof. Donald Menzel. 24pp. of photographs. 189pp. 5¼ x 8¼.
21680-2 Paperbound $1.50

TEACH YOURSELF CALCULUS, P. Abbott. With a good background in algebra and trig, you can teach yourself calculus with this book. Simple, straightforward introduction to functions of all kinds, integration, differentiation, series, etc. "Students who are beginning to study calculus method will derive great help from this book." Faraday House Journal. 308pp. 20683-1 Clothbound $2.00

TEACH YOURSELF TRIGONOMETRY, P. Abbott. Geometrical foundations, indices and logarithms, ratios, angles, circular measure, etc. are presented in this sound, easy-to-use text. Excellent for the beginner or as a brush up, this text carries the student through the solution of triangles. 204pp. 20682-3 Clothbound $2.00

TEACH YOURSELF ANATOMY, David LeVay. Accurate, inclusive, profusely illustrated account of structure, skeleton, abdomen, muscles, nervous system, glands, brain, reproductive organs, evolution. "Quite the best and most readable account,' *Medical Officer.* 12 color plates. 164 figures. 311pp. 4¾ x 7.
21651-9 Clothbound $2.50

TEACH YOURSELF PHYSIOLOGY, David LeVay. Anatomical, biochemical bases; digestive, nervous, endocrine systems; metabolism; respiration; muscle; excretion; temperature control; reproduction. "Good elementary exposition," *The Lancet.* 6 color plates. 44 illustrations. 208pp. 4¼ x 7. 21658-6 Clothbound $2.50

THE FRIENDLY STARS, Martha Evans Martin. Classic has taught naked-eye observation of stars, planets to hundreds of thousands, still not surpassed for charm, lucidity, adequacy. Completely updated by Professor Donald H. Menzel, Harvard Observatory. 25 illustrations. 16 x 30 chart. x + 147pp. 21099-5 Paperbound $1.25

MUSIC OF THE SPHERES: THE MATERIAL UNIVERSE FROM ATOM TO QUASAR, SIMPLY EXPLAINED, Guy Murchie. Extremely broad, brilliantly written popular account begins with the solar system and reaches to dividing line between matter and nonmatter; latest understandings presented with exceptional clarity. Volume One: Planets, stars, galaxies, cosmology, geology, celestial mechanics, latest astronomical discoveries; Volume Two: Matter, atoms, waves, radiation, relativity, chemical action, heat, nuclear energy, quantum theory, music, light, color, probability, antimatter, antigravity, and similar topics. 319 figures. 1967 (second) edition. Total of xx + 644pp. 21809-0, 21810-4 Two volumes, Paperbound $4.00

OLD-TIME SCHOOLS AND SCHOOL BOOKS, Clifton Johnson. Illustrations and rhymes from early primers, abundant quotations from early textbooks, many anecdotes of school life enliven this study of elementary schools from Puritans to middle 19th century. Introduction by Carl Withers. 234 illustrations. xxxiii + 381pp.
21031-6 Paperbound $2.50

MATHEMATICAL PUZZLES FOR BEGINNERS AND ENTHUSIASTS, Geoffrey Mott-Smith. 189 puzzles from easy to difficult—involving arithmetic, logic, algebra, properties of digits, probability, etc.—for enjoyment and mental stimulus. Explanation of mathematical principles behind the puzzles. 135 illustrations. viii + 248pp.
20198-8 Paperbound $1.25

PAPER FOLDING FOR BEGINNERS, William D. Murray and Francis J. Rigney. Easiest book on the market, clearest instructions on making interesting, beautiful origami. Sail boats, cups, roosters, frogs that move legs, bonbon boxes, standing birds, etc. 40 projects; more than 275 diagrams and photographs. 94pp.
20713-7 Paperbound $1.00

TRICKS AND GAMES ON THE POOL TABLE, Fred Herrmann. 79 tricks and games— some solitaires, some for two or more players, some competitive games—to entertain you between formal games. Mystifying shots and throws, unusual caroms, tricks involving such props as cork, coins, a hat, etc. Formerly *Fun on the Pool Table*. 77 figures. 95pp.
21814-7 Paperbound $1.00

HAND SHADOWS TO BE THROWN UPON THE WALL: A SERIES OF NOVEL AND AMUSING FIGURES FORMED BY THE HAND, Henry Bursill. Delightful picturebook from great-grandfather's day shows how to make 18 different hand shadows: a bird that flies, duck that quacks, dog that wags his tail, camel, goose, deer, boy, turtle, etc. Only book of its sort. vi + 33pp. 6½ x 9¼.
21779-5 Paperbound $1.00

WHITTLING AND WOODCARVING, E. J. Tangerman. 18th printing of best book on market. "If you can cut a potato you can carve" toys and puzzles, chains, chessmen, caricatures, masks, frames, woodcut blocks, surface patterns, much more. Information on tools, woods, techniques. Also goes into serious wood sculpture from Middle Ages to present, East and West. 464 photos, figures. x + 293pp.
20965-2 Paperbound $2.00

HISTORY OF PHILOSOPHY, Julián Marias. Possibly the clearest, most easily followed, best planned, most useful one-volume history of philosophy on the market; neither skimpy nor overfull. Full details on system of every major philosopher and dozens of less important thinkers from pre-Socratics up to Existentialism and later. Strong on many European figures usually omitted. Has gone through dozens of editions in Europe. 1966 edition, translated by Stanley Appelbaum and Clarence Strowbridge. xviii + 505pp.
21739-6 Paperbound $3.00

YOGA: A SCIENTIFIC EVALUATION, Kovoor T. Behanan. Scientific but non-technical study of physiological results of yoga exercises; done under auspices of Yale U. Relations to Indian thought, to psychoanalysis, etc. 16 photos. xxiii + 270pp.
20505-3 Paperbound $2.50

Prices subject to change without notice.
Available at your book dealer or write for free catalogue to Dept. GI, Dover Publications, Inc., 180 Varick St., N. Y., N. Y. 10014. Dover publishes more than 150 books each year on science, elementary and advanced mathematics, biology, music, art, literary history, social sciences and other areas.

/